Alfred Schaufelberger

Blacks and the Trial by Jury

The black man's experience in the courts

| KF 8975 S3 | Schaufelberger, Alfred |
|---|---|
| | Blacks and the trial by jury |

# European University Papers

*Europäische Hochschulschriften*
*Publications Universitaires Européennes*

Series III
**History, paleography and numismatics**

Reihe III    Série III
Geschichte und ihre Hilfswissenschaften
Sciences historiques et sciences auxiliaires de l'histoire

**Vol./Bd. 27**

Alfred Schaufelberger

Blacks and the Trial by Jury
The black man's experience in the courts

Herbert Lang Bern
Peter Lang Frankfurt/M.
1973

Alfred Schaufelberger

# Blacks and the Trial by Jury
The black man's experience in the courts

Herbert Lang Bern
Peter Lang Frankfurt/M.
1973

ISBN 3 261 01068 1

© Herbert Lang & Co. Ltd., Bern (Switzerland)
Peter Lang Ltd., Frankfurt/M. (West-Germany)
1973. All rights reserved.

Reprint or reproduction even partially and in all forms as microfilm, xerography, microfiche, microcard, offset strictly prohibited.

Printed by Lang Druck Ltd., Liebefeld/Berne (Switzerland)

# TABLE OF CONTENTS

INTRODUCTION 9

    Problem - 9
    Literature - 10
    Working Hypothesis - 15

CHAPTER I: Blacks in Midwestern Society: a Statistical Analysis     17

    Introduction - 17
    Demography - 18
    Politics - 26
    Economy and Society - 31
    Conclusion - 41

CHAPTER II: History and Development of Trial by Jury     43

    Introduction - 43
    History of trial by jury from the Carolingian Royal
        Inquisition to Blackstone - 44
    The Formulators - 51
    Trial by jury in America until the adoption of the
        Federal Constitution - 57
    The Legal process today: Arrest, indictment, trial,
        and appeal - 64
    Conclusion - 75

CHAPTER III: Judicial Reasoning on Trial by Jury     79

    Introduction - 79
    Common law and statute law: Historical argumentation - 81
    Definition of trial by jury, right to trial by jury, and
        the duties of judge and jury - 88
    Prejudice, the presumption of innocence, and the
        presumption of guilt - 97
    Jury selection - 106
    Challenges, vicinage, change of venue, and mixed
        juries - 118
    Conclusion - 127

CONCLUSION 129

BIBLIOGRAPHY 135

FOOTNOTES 157

## ACKNOWLEDGEMENT

I gratefully acknowledge the generous help of the following individuals and institutions, without whose assistance this book could not have been written:

Prof. Dr. Max Silberschmidt encouraged me from the very beginning in my academic work and guided me through all its stages;

Prof. Dr. Leo Schelbert and his family twice opened their home in Evanston to me so that I could research in a stimulating environment and free from the care for food and shelter;

The Swiss American Society for Cultural Relations and the Swiss American Exchange Alumni Association contributed to the costs of traveling and researching on two continents;

Almost ten years ago, Mr. and Mrs. Donald H. Wilson of Towson, Md., initiated me into the American civilization so charmingly and thoughtfully that I have never ceased to study this fascinating subject;

My parents always actively supported my academic pursuits with a great deal of understanding and personal interest;

My wife has not only been a most loving and patient partner, she has also contributed her talents as a very competent research assistant.

My father did not live to see this book in print. To his memory it is dedicated.

A. S.

Equal Justice Under Law

Inscription on the frieze of
the Supreme Court building
in Washington, D. C.

INTRODUCTION

The primary aim of historical scholarship must be the study of man; at the beginning of The Historian's Craft, Marc Bloch defined the good historian as resembling the ogre of the fairy-tales:

> "Là où il flaire la chair humaine, il sait que là est son gibier." (1)

This study is concerned with the black man, and woman, in the United States, and the fundamental question asked is: Was there a basic pervasive pattern that underlied, or governed, the black man's experience in America?

It is immediately obvious that at this stage of our knowledge of black American history no one researcher can answer this question in one publication. A unified theory of Afro-American history is not yet possible. But it is hoped that this dissertation will contribute to the development of such a theory.

It is implied in the fundamental question that it is not the intellectual or economic or social activities and achievements of blacks that will be studied in this book. Until very recently black experience was determined only marginally by what blacks did themselves. They lived (and live) in a white world and white, Western values shaped their experience. This study will therefore concentrate, not on black people, but on white institutions.

One can only do justice to a society if one regards it as represented by its best members - "best" in its own value judgment - because these, not its deviant products, formulate best its values, hopes, and anxieties and show most clearly its possibilities and limitations.

On these premises it would probably seem most advisable to study outstanding American poets and philosophers (which often is the same), a very difficult and subtle task. For various practical and theoretical reasons the subject of this dissertation is not the thinking of poets and philosophers but of judges - many of whom are, or think they are, poets and philosophers, too. The original, general question has thus been narrowed down and specified. It now reads: Was there a basic pervasive pattern of j u d i c i a l  r e a s o n i n g  that underlied, or governed, the black man's experience in America?

But this question is still too general, quite apart from the fact that very recently an answer to it has been attempted with convincing results. (2) Again relying on the judicious views of Marc Bloch it can be argued that a further narrowing down of the field of investigation can only be advantageous:

> Aussi bien, pour demeurer fidèle à la vie dans le constant entre-croisement de ses actions et réactions, il n'est nullement nécessaire de prétendre l'embrasser tout entière, par une [sic] effort ordinairement trop vaste pour les possibilités d'un seul savant. Rien de plus légitime, rien souvent de plus salutaire que de centrer l'étude d'une société sur un de ses aspects particuliers, ou, mieux encore, sur un

des problèmes précis que soulève tel ou tel de ses aspects: croyances, économie, structure de classes ou de groupes, crises politiques ... Par ce choix raisonné, les problèmes ne seront pas seulement, à l'ordinaire, plus fermement posés: il n'est pas jusqu'aux faits de contact et d'échange qui ne ressortiront avec plus de clarté. A condition, simplement, de vouloir les découvrir. (3)

One will therefore be best advised to analyze judicial reasoning on one of the fundamental problems confronting blacks in America, today and in the past, on that of inequality.

The question, therefore, is finally: Was there a basic pervasive pattern of judicial reasoning on the equality of races which underlied, or governed, the black man's experience in America?

Among the best sources of our knowledge of judicial reasoning are the opinions written by judges in support of or against decisions in cases that came before the courts. There is a class of cases where judges time and again have been called upon to consider questions of equality and inequality, namely those concerning a defendant's right to be tried by a jury of his equals and the black citizen's right to sit on juries. One of the primary functions of the government is to resolve conflicts within the population, (4) and the courts are the institutions where these conflicts are resolved peacefully. The jury is the focus where the democratic ideal of the American political constitution and social philosophy is carried into the courts. The answer to the question of judicial reasoning on the equality of races will therefore be an analysis of cases involving the jury system, because it is there that it has been most prominently asked.

It would seem unreasonable to analyze all cases from all jurisdictions; the result would hardly justify the effort, the corpus would be too large. The cases studied in connection with this dissertation were decided in the United States Supreme Court and in the Illinois Supreme Court. About half of the Illinois cases date from 1890-1940 because the massive in-migration of blacks into the big industrial centers of the North during that time created acute problems of inequality and made judicial answers to related questions mandatory. The results of this analysis must therefore be qualified, of course, by these limits of time and geography. This will be done in the conclusion. (5)

The sifting of the literature on a subject not only builds a solid foundation for further investigation, but also often modifies the original question somewhat in that it shows that certain approaches have already been tried, successfully or unsuccessfully.

The literature dealing directly with the problem of blacks and the trial by jury is surprisingly small and consists mainly of a handful of scattered articles and chapters of more comprehensive books that describe general aspects of either race or legal procedure. They are, in chronological order:

Stephenson, Gilbert T., <u>Race Distinctions in American Law</u>, London: Appleton, 1910.
    Describing the legal status of blacks around 1910 in the North and in the South and showing the almost universal exclusion of blacks from jury service in the South. See especially pp. 247-272.

Hale v. Kentucky, 303 U.S. 614 (1938), Annotation in 82 L. Ed., 1053-1082. The
    legal view of the rights of the defendant and the violation of these
    rights. Title: "Violation of the constitutional rights of defendant in
    criminal case by unfair practices in selection of grand or petit jury."
Mangum, Charles S., The Legal Status of the Negro, Chapel Hill: University of
    North Carolina Press, 1940. A statement of the law on blacks and
    the trial by jury as interpreted by the courts, pp. 308-342.
Myrdal, Gunnar, An American Dilemma: The Negro Problem and Modern De-
    mocracy, New York: Harper, 1944. The jury system receives at-
    tention in Part VI, "Justice," and the great extent of exclusion of
    blacks from juries is stressed.
Brown, G. Gordon, Law Administration and Negro-White Relations in Philadelphia,
    Philadelphia, Bureau of Municipal Research, 1947. An insight into the
    problem on the local level. Opinions of informants on blacks and the
    legal process (pp. 136-152).
U.S. Commission on Civil Rights, Report 5: Justice, Washington: Government
    Printing Office, 1961. Chapter 7 is on jury exclusion and notes its
    persistence (p. 103).
The Supreme Court on Racial Discrimination, ed. Joseph Tussman, Excerpts from
    seven opinions on discrimination and the jury. No background in-
    formation or analysis by the editor.
Discrimination and the Law, ed. Vern Countryman, Chicago: University of Chicago
    Press, 1965, mentions the jury system only briefly in the introduction
    by the editor.
Finkelstein, Michael O., "The Application of Statistical Decision Theory to Jury
    Discrimination Cases," in Harvard Law Review, vol. 80, nr. 2 (Dec.,
    1966), pp. 338-376. Shows the extreme improbability that nondis-
    criminatory selection occurred where courts have decided that it did.
Kalven, Harry, Jr., and Hans Zeisel, The American Jury, Boston: Little, Brown,
    1966. Most interesting is a table (nr. 65 on p. 211) showing a "sympa-
    thy index" of defendants by sex, age, and race. This index is the per-
    centage of sympathetic defendants minus the percentage of unattractive
    defendants in each group. 13% of the black defendants were found to
    be attractive, 20% unattractive; the index is therefore -7. For whites
    the figures are 22%, 16%, and + 6 for the index. The other indexes:
    males, + 1; females, + 11; age below 21, + 17; age 21-55, 0; age
    over 55, + 8. The total index for all cases analyzed (3576) was + 2.
    The most unattractive defendant, statistically, is black, male, age
    21-55. His indexes add up to -6. The most attractive defendant is a
    white girl under 21. Her indexes add up to + 34. A very significant
    result in view of the many rape cases in which the defendant is black
    and the victim white.
Miller, Loren, The Petitioners: The Story of the Supreme Court of the United
    States and the Negro, New York: Pantheon, 1966. Details on several
    famous trials in which jury exclusion was an issue.
Miller, Charles A., "Constitutional History and the Rhetoric of Race," in Law in
    American History, ed. Fleming and Bailyn, Cambridge, Mass.:

Charles Warren Center for American History, 1971 (= vol. 5 of Perspectives in American History), pp. 147-200. Although Miller is not specifically concerned with blacks and the trial by jury, this study is very helpful in the interpretation of the evidence on this problem. It shows that American courts have developed numerous rhetorical devices in order to evade or hide the issues of race and the law. These devices are: "not deciding at all, deciding but on non-racial grounds, and deciding through unique application of legalistic reasoning" (fiction), p. 162.

Trial by jury without special reference to racial questions has been more extensively treated. There exists a solid basic literature on the development of this institution from the earliest times to the present. It is cited in chapter 2 of this dissertation and the respective bibliography (pp. 43/4 and 148/9, below). On the jury system itself there are in addition to those mentioned above:

Johnson, Julia E., Jury System, vol. 5, nr. 6 of The Reference Shelf, New York: Wilson, 1928, summarizing the advantages and the disadvantages of the jury system and presenting opinions in favor of and against it. A bibliography is included (pp. 23-42); and

Zeisel, Hans, "Dr. Spock and the Case of the Vanishing Women Jurors," in The University of Chicago Law Review, vol 37, nr. 1 (Fall, 1969) pp. 139-156. The defense of Dr. Spock challenged the array of the jurors in the famous 1967 trial of the doctor, because only nine of 100 jurors drawn were women. Professor Zeisel wrote this article in aid of the defense and showed "the mystery of the vanishing women." (p. 139)

The jury system of Illinois and Cook County (Chicago and suburbs) has been described and criticised in two articles in the Illinois Law Review:

Ross, Carl A., "The Jury System of Cook County, Illinois," in vol. 5, nr. 5 (Dec., 1910), pp. 283-299, and

Harker, Oliver A., "The Illinois Juror in the Trial of Criminal Cases," in vol. 5, nr. 6 (1911), pp. 468-475.

Ross illustrated well the discrepancy between the law and its administration, while Harker believed that the Illinois juror in criminal cases was vested with too much power because he could decide not only the facts but also the law applicable.

Blacks and the law, without special reference to trial by jury, has also been the subject of many books. Some recent publications are:

Greenberg, Jack, Race Relations and the American Law, New York: Columbia University Press, 1959.

Abraham, Henry J., Freedom and the Court: Civil Rights and Liberties in the United States, New York: Oxford University Press, 1967. The civil rights of the individual and those of the community. For race relations,

see. pp. 245-312.
Tresolini, Rocco, These Liberties: Case Studies in Civil Rights, Philadelphia: Lipincott, 1968. Civil rights cases and their background.
Motley, Constance Baker, "The Legal Status of the Negro in the United States," in The American Negro Reference Book, ed. John P. Davis, Englewood Cliffs: Prentice Hall, 1966, pp. 484-521.

Judicial reasoning, the focus of this dissertation, has received increasing attention during the past fifty years. The path of investigation of judicial decision making is shown by the following books:

Haines, Charles G., "General Observations on the Effects of Personal, Political, and Economic Influences in the Decisions of Judges," in Illinois Law Review, vol 17 (1923), pp. 96-116. Haines exposed the shortcomings of the theory of mechanical jurisprudence, according to which judges mete out some pre-existing higher law and are themselves not subject to influences from outside the courtroom.
Fuller, Lon L., Legal Fictions, Stanford: Stanford UP, 1967. Fiction as one of the main tools of judicial reasoning, and the motives behind it.
Hamilton, Walton H., "Judicial Process," in Encylcopedia of the Social Sciences, vol. 8 (1932), pp. 450-457. "The intellectual procedure by which judges decide cases." (p. 450).
Frankfurter, Felix, "Supreme Court, United States," Ibid., vol. 14 (1934), pp. 474-482. The renowned author's own experience on the bench from 1939 to 1962 adds interest to this study.
Vaihinger, Hans, Die Philosophie des Als Ob, Berlin: Reuther und Reichard, 1911. English: London: Kegan Paul, 1924. On the theory and the uses of fiction.
Rosenblum, Victor G., Law as a Political Instrument, Garden City, N.J.: Doubleday, 1955.
Schubert, Glendon, "Judicial Behavior," in International Encyclopedia of the Social Sciences, vol. 8 (1968), pp. 307-315. Valuable synopsis of research on judicial behavior, 1920 to 1965, and bibliography.

On the complex questions surrounding judicial reasoning there is therefore literature from social scientists and jurists, but little from competent historians, with some notable exceptions:

Commager, Henry S., "Constitutional History and the Higher Law," in Pennsylvania Magazine of History and Biography, vol. 62, nr. 1 (Jan., 1938), pp. 20-40.
"The fact is that a certain divinity has hedged the court and its cabalistic oracles, until it has come to seem almost blasphemous for historians to suggest that the court is a political institution or that jurisprudence is sociological, though deans of law schools may, apparently, make these observations with impunity. ...
We must realize that the law, like other faiths, lives by symbols, and

that the two symbols most passionately cherished are those of Reason (a brood omniscience in the sky, Holmes called it) and of consistency.
....
It is indeed a common observation that certainty in law is more important than justice." (pp. 32, 34/5)

Horowitz, Morton J., "The Instrumental Conception of American Law, 1780-1820," in Law in American History (see above, pp. 11/12, Miller Charles A.), pp. 267-326. Law as an instrument for attaining definite ends.

Two further books are important from a methodological point of view:

Friedman, Lawrence N., "Some Problems and Possibilities of American Legal History," in The State of American History, ed. Herbert J. Bass, Chicago: Quadrangle, 1970, pp. 3-21. Research in American legal history is mainly about the Supreme Court and this institution has therefore been overemphasized.

Hurst, James W., "Legal Elements in United States History," in Law in American History (see above, pp. 11/12, Miller, Charles A.) pp. 3-92. The practical side of research in American legal history. Because of their arcane language and technicalities, legal sources have so far largely been neglected by historians.

Asking, then, what has been done, one can summarize: little on the specific question of blacks and the jury. Most books and articles are either narrative, giving examples of exclusion and inclusion of blacks on jury panels, or simply reporting, i.e. quoting from Supreme Court opinions. Finkelstein, Kalven and Zeisel, and Charles A. Miller go beyond this and offer valuable interpretations and analyses, but only Finkelstein is primarily concerned with blacks and the jury. The jury system itself has been extensively studied in its development, and books and articles treating the actual state of this institution were mainly written by reformers who perceived some shortcomings in it and wanted to expose them. Blacks and the law has been the subject of numerous books and monographs on civil rights, but most of them, too, are written on an activist level and do little beyond scratching the surface.

This is a historical, not a legal, dissertation. Its aim must therefore be to convert "scattered, difficult primary sources into a coherent, intellegible secondary source."(6) In the first half it will concentrate on the following background:

Fig. 1   The migration of the jury system and of the black people who are tried by it into America and Illinois

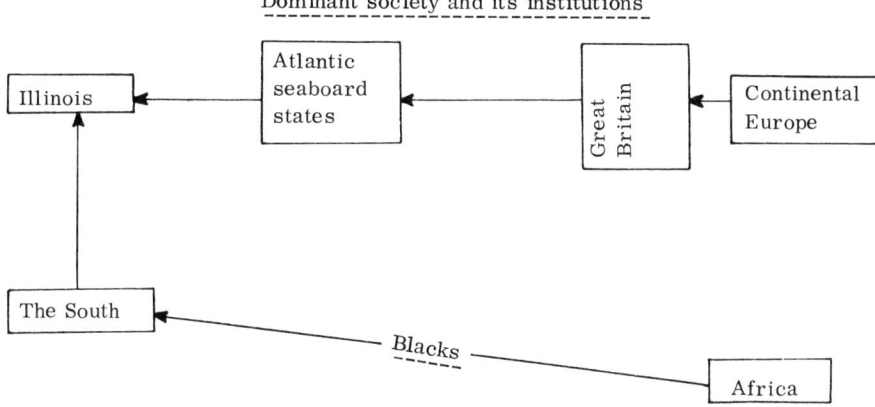

The first chapter will analyze the situation of the black community in the Midwest and particularly in Illinois, seen as a result of the migration of Southern blacks into the industrial North. Four central fields of experience will be looked at: demography, politics, economy, and society (in a narrow sense). The sources for this will be published statistics.

The second chapter will trace the history and development of trial by jury from its earliest beginnings in medieval Europe to England and her colonies on the seaboard of America, and its reception into the American legal system. A survey of criminal procedure in Illinois will show the result of this development, the actual operation of the instrument, and will prepare the reader for chapter three, by explaining the basic technicalities of trial by jury. Sources for this chapter will be the secondary literature on English and American legal history and the charters, constitutions, laws, and statutes of Great Britain and America.

Chapter three will ask how judges interpreted and used the instruments described in chapter two in cases involving the population whose situation was analyzed in chapter one. This should show how judges reasoned. Sources are the published opinions of the Supreme Court of the United States and of the Illinois Supreme Court.

CHAPTER I

BLACKS IN MIDWESTERN SOCIETY: A STATISTICAL ANALYSIS

INTRODUCTION

Where did blacks living in the Midwest from 1890 to 1930 come from? What were the differences in life style between the states of origin and the states of residence of these blacks? What were the difficulties they had to overcome and how big were these difficulties?

Valuable bibliographies on the problems of black migration can be found in Gilbert Osofsky's Harlem: The Making of a Ghetto (1966; nr. 89), pp. 191-2: "Negro Migration and Settlement," and in Allan Spear's Black Chicago: The Making of a Negro Ghetto, 1890-1920 (1967; nr. 91), pp. 234-5: "Negro Migration." These two books are mainly concerned with migration and urbanization. They are case studies; the first of New York, the second of Chicago.

More direct sources can be found in Emmett J. Scott's "Letters of Negro Migrants of 1916-1918," in the Journal of Negro History, nr. 4 (July/October 1919), pp. 290-340 and 412-275. Some of the letters edited here by Scott are reproduced in a book by the same author, Negro Migration During the War (1920; nr. 90).

Analyses of this migration abound. Besides Spear and Osofsky, Carter G. Woodson's A Century of Negro Migration (Washington: Woodson, 1918) which traces black migration back to 1815 and also contains bibliography (pp. 193-211) is very informative. Myrdal has a chapter on the problem (nr. 15, chapter 8, pp. 182-201). The most authoritative modern researchers in the field are Karl E. and Alma F. Taeuber of Chicago: "The Negro Population in the United States" (1966, nr. 93) and Negroes in Cities: Residential Segregation and Neighborhood Change (1965; nr. 92). Irene C. Taeuber contributed "Migration, Mobility and the Assimilation of the Negro," in American Negro at Mid-Century, Population Bulletin, Nov., 1958.

The main sources are three government publications on blacks, which cover the years 1790-1932 (nrs. 95, 96, 97), the volumes of the Population Censuses, the three volumes edited by Simon Kuznets and Dorothy Swaine Thomas (1957-1964; nr. 84), and chapters A and C of the Historical Statistics.

For black experience in general twenty-eight books are cited in section 4 of the bibliography below (pp. 186-188). Experience in the Midwest is described in the works of Carl Sandburg, Sinclair Lewis, Sherwood Anderson, Ringgold W. Lardner, James T. Farrell and Robert Herrick. See John T. Flanagan, America is West: An Anthology of Middlewestern Life and Literature, Minneapolis: The

University of Minnesota Press, 1945 and Spiller's Literary History of the United States, vol. III (1948), pp. 318-319 and vol. IV (1959), p. 63, particularly on Illinois.

It seems that four fields of experience were central for blacks who migrated from the South into the industrial North: Migration itself (demography), the different political climate in the new environment (politics), the work they found and the pay they got (economy), and their individual and social integration in the North (health and crime). An analysis of the statistical material existing on these four fields will yield information that will enable us to see underlying patterns:

> Statistical measurement is the only means of extracting a coherent pattern from the chaos of personal behaviour and of discovering which is a typical specimen and which a sport. Failure to apply such controls has led to much wild and implausible generalization about social phenomena, based upon a handful of striking and well-documented examples. (1)

It is not necessary that the figures be exact in a strict mathematical sense. Even the best statistics are notoriously unreliable and no attempt has been made to improve the value of the printed sources (census statistics, Kuznets, Historical Statistics). The figures and ratios in this chapter are to be understood as indicators only; they show certain trends and greater exactitude is not required.

> We must not look for equal exactness in all departments of study, but only such as belongs to the subject matter of each, and in such a degree as is appropriate to the particular line of enquiry. (2)

## MIGRATION AND URBANIZATION

During the fifty years from 1890 to 1940 the population of the United States more than doubled, from 63 million to 132 million inhabitants. (3) During the same period the percentage of blacks in proportion to the total population decreased from twelve to ten percent. The East North Central Region's share of the total population of the United States remained constant at slightly over twenty percent. 75 to 90 percent of all blacks still lived in the South (comprising the South Atlantic, East South Central, and West South Central divisions). (4) The percentage of blacks in the North East Central division was during the whole time well below the national average. It almost tripled, however, from 1.5 percent in 1890 to 4 percent in 1940, or from 207'000 to 1'070'000 persons. This development is well illustrated by the figures for the State of Illinois. In the following graph the curves for the increase of the black and of the white populations are plotted in a semi-logarithmic coordinate system, in order to show the relative importance of the increases, not of the absolute census figures. The curves for Cook County and for its center, Chicago, are added to indicate in a first approximation the degree of urbanization of the two populations.

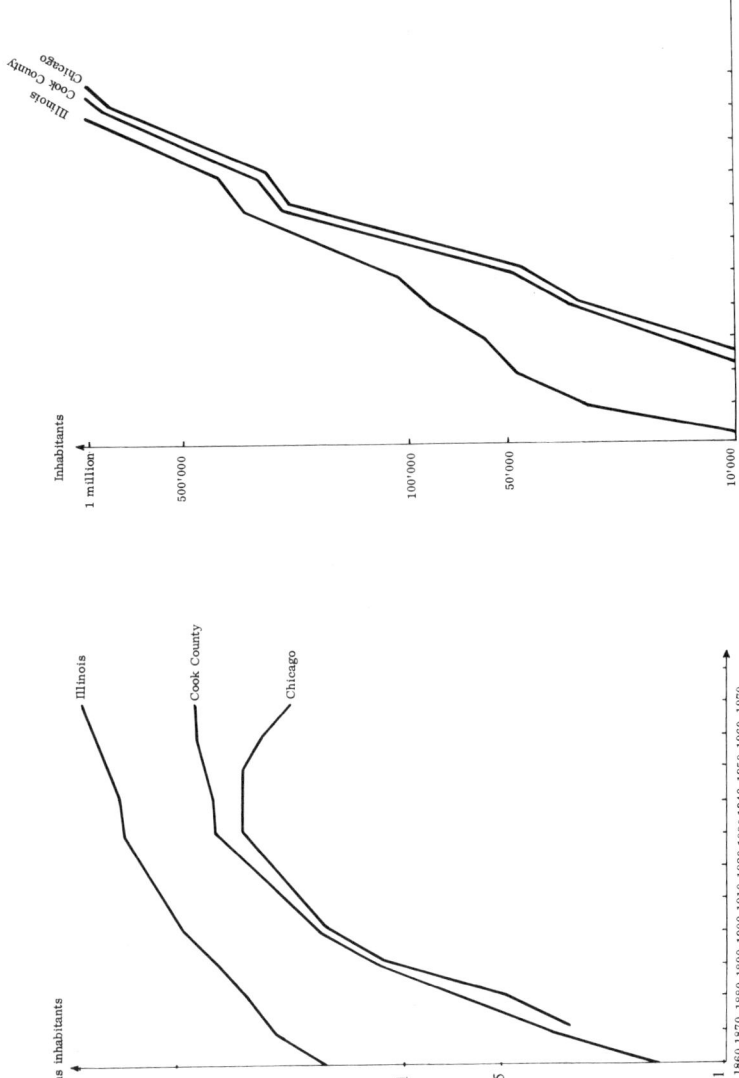

Fig. 2  Development of the white population, 1860–1970

Development of the black population, 1860–1970

Source: U. S. censuses

Where did the black population come from? The most likely answer is that they must have come mainly from the South and a detailed analysis of the population censuses bears this out.

Migration rates varied greatly, in respect to both time and place. Michigan, for example, had during the period of 1880 to 1890 a net rate of 68 blacks per 1'000 resident black population l e a v i n g its territory. The same state had for the decade from 1910 to 1920 a net in-migration rate of 1'126 blacks, computed on the same basis. Ohio's figures steadily rose from 1880 to 1920 (from +71 to + 538), and then fell again until 1940 (when the ratio was more or less what it had been sixty years before). Indiana's ratios fell from 1880 until 1910, rose until 1920, and fell again down to the level of 1910. The figures for Illinois show the same tendency as those for Ohio, but they never went below + 160. (5)

Nevertheless, a certain trend can be observed from the statistics, especially from the weighed figures for the whole region. A significant increase of in-migration in the 1890s and another such increase in the second decade of this century are followed by a sharp falling-off during the depression years of the thirties. Graphically, the curve looks like this:

Fig. 3       Net migration rates for the Midwest, 1880s to 1930s

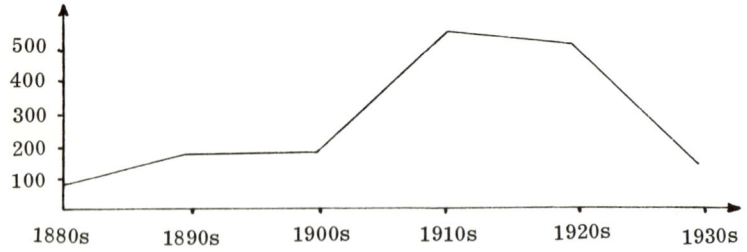

Between thirty and sixty percent of the total nonwhite population of the East North Central division were born there. 84 to 92 percent of the remainder were born in one of the three Southern divisions. 50 to 60 percent of the East North Central nonwhites came from the East South Central division, 20 to 30 percent from the Atlantic seaboard states south of Maryland, and the rest came from the West South Central division.

Turning to the major contributing states, the largest share of the black population, about one third, came from Kentucky, reflecting this state's border position between the South and the Middle West. Mississippi, Tennessee, and Georgia contributed about a fifth each, Alabama a tenth, and Virginia about half as many. The Carolinas and Florida were relatively insignificant in this connection. The maps below give a visual impression of the importance of the source states of migration. Missouri contributed to conterminous Illinois, and so did Minnesota to adjacent Wisconsin. (6)

Fig. 4    The origin of black migrants who settled in the Midwest, for the various states and for the whole region.

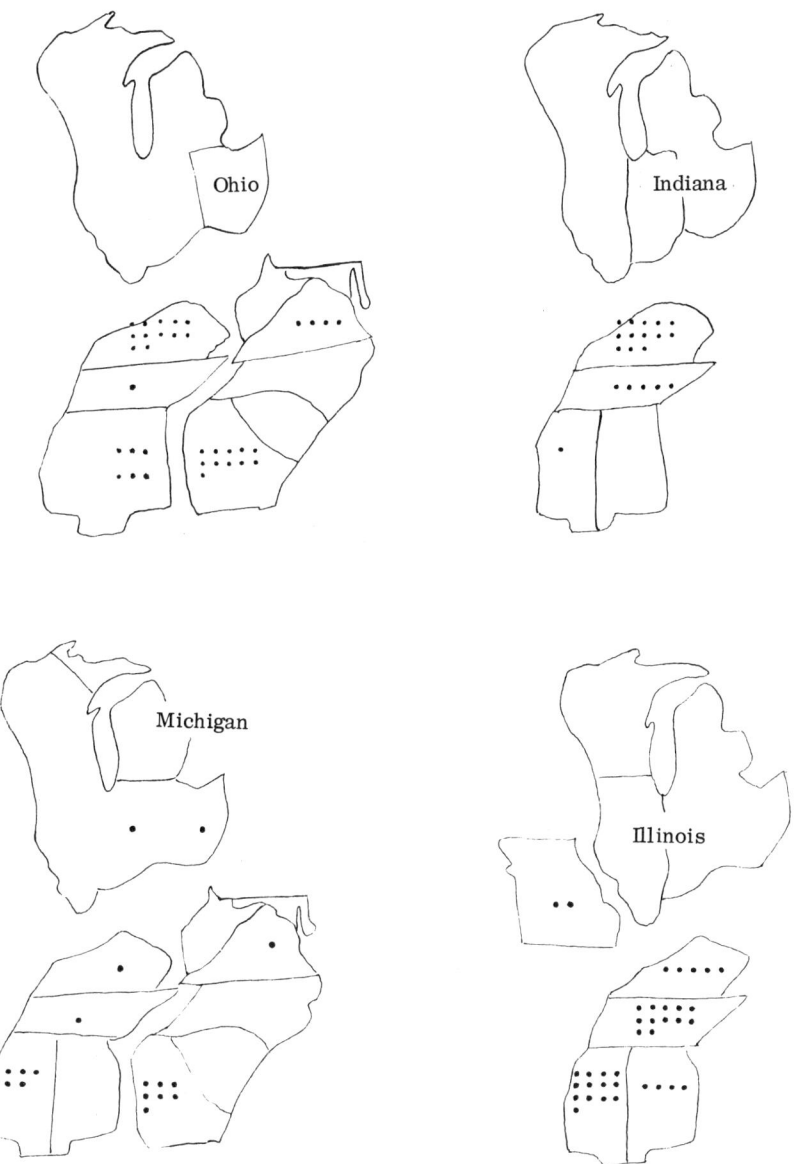

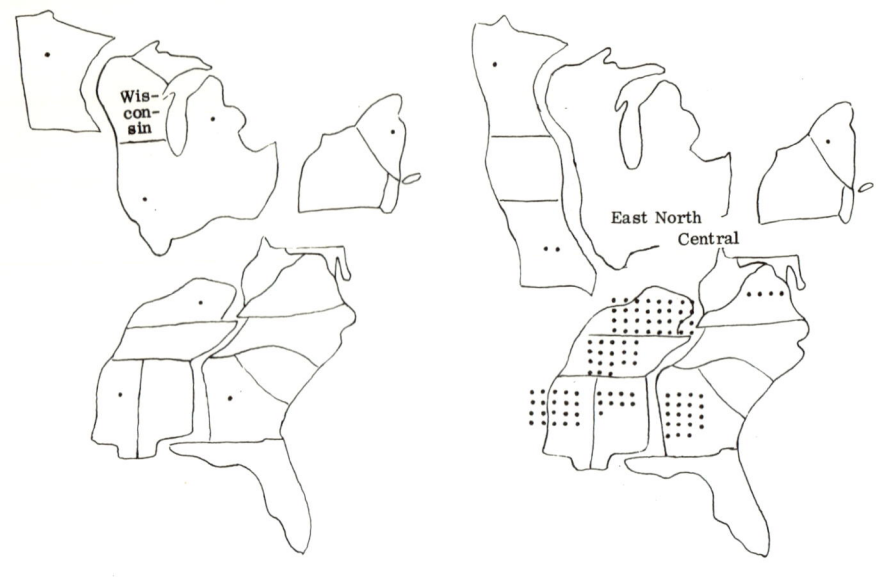

The following population distribution synopsis reveals some interesting further details. (7) In 1890, 11.8 percent of the total United States population were black. This figure decreased steadily to 9.65 in 1930 and then turned upward again. One important development in this connection was the concentration of black people in urban centers outside the South. The United States was at that time already a highly urbanized country, with between 35 and 55 percent of the population living in urban centers. The figures for the East North Central division were during the whole period even higher: between 38 and 65 percent of the population were urban. This contrasts significantly with the degree of urbanization in the East South Central division, where the corresponding figures were only one third to one half of the national average.

Illinois was more highly urbanized than the East North Central division as a whole. Sixty to ninety percent of its black population lived in urban centers - mainly in and around Chicago - while only an eighth to a third of the East South Central black population lived in cities. Although the urbanization of blacks progressed more rapidly in the South than in the North, the percentage for the latter region was consistently three to five times as high as that for the former. Probability theory, if nothing else, permits the conclusion that migration by blacks from the South to the North was accompanied by considerable urbanization. The problems involved in this process have been treated extensively in the literature on this subject. (8)

Table 1    Population distribution synopsis.

|  | 1890 | 1900 | 1910 | 1920 | 1930 | 1940 |
|---|---|---|---|---|---|---|
| Population US (mio.) | 63,056 | 76,094 | 92,407 | 106,466 | 123,077 | 131,954 |
| Blacks (mio.) | 7,489 | 8,834 | 9,828 | 10,463 | 11,891 | 12,865 |
| Blacks % of US | 11.8 | 11.6 | 10.6 | 9.8 | 9.65 | 9.75 |
| ENC (000) | 13,478 | 15,986 | 18,251 | 21,476 | 25,297 | 26,626 |
| ENC % of US | 21.3 | 21.0 | 19.8 | 20.1 | 20.5 | 20.3 |
| ENC blacks (000) | 207 | 258 | 301 | 515 | 931 | 1,070 |
| Blacks % of ENC | 1.5 | 1.6 | 1.7 | 2.4 | 3.7 | 4.0 |
| % urban for US | 35.1 | 39.7 | 45.7 | 51.2 | 56.2 | 56.5 |
| % urban for ENC | 38.0 | 45.2 | 52.8 | 60.8 | 66.5 | 65.5 |
| ENC % urban blacks | 60.1 | 69.8 | 76.6 | 87.3 | 91.1 | 91.5 |
| % urban for ESC | 12.7 | 15.0 | 18.7 | 22.4 | 28.1 | 29.5 |
| ESC % urban blacks | 12.9 | 15.5 | 19.2 | 22.7 | 28.6 | 32.1 |
| Ill. pop. (000) | 3,826 | 4,822 | 5,639 | 6,485 | 7,631 | 7,897 |
| Ill. blacks (000) | 57 | 85 | 109 | 182 | 329 | 387 |
| Blacks % of Ill. | 1.5 | 1.8 | 1.9 | 2.8 | 4.3 | 4.9 |
| % urban for Ill. | 44.9 | 54.2 | 61.8 | 68.2 | 73.8 | 73.7 |
| Ill. % urban blacks | 60.3 | 71.6 | 78.6 | 88.5 | 92.4 | 92.3 |

Source: see footnote (3) of this chapter

One aspect of this population movement not usually treated shall here be dealt with in some detail. Migration from the South involved distances of hundreds of miles. Consideration must therefore also be given to the means of transportation available to migrants.

By 1865 the frontier was a line running up from eastern Texas through Oklahoma, Kansas, Nebraska, Iowa, and Wisconsin. (9) The Homestead Act of 1861 favored expansion into the prairie. After the Civil War many veterans settled there. Heberle mentioned the increased demand for agricultural products from the West as one of the underlying factors of this development. (10) Accompanying it was a rapid expansion of the railway system (11), which not only carried a great majority of Southern blacks into the North, but also offered jobs in the big industrial centers of this region:

| | |
|---|---|
| 1865 | 35,000 miles of track in US |
| 1874 | 70,000 |
| 1887 | 157,000 |
| 1900 | 200,000 |

This development deeply influenced not only the iron and steel industries and internal migration, but it also created new forms of business enterprise and of trade and commerce.

Complaints about the dominance of the railroads in so many walks of life were argued in the courts. The control of the grain elevators and the Union Stockyards of Chicago by the railroads enraged Middle Western farmers, and the Illinois Constitution of 1870 provided for the State legislature to intervene in cases of monopolistic price "fixing" by the railroads and later enacted laws checking such abuses and creating a Railway and Warehouse Commission "to regulate roads, grain elevators, and warehouses." (12) This again led to litigation in the courts. (13) The governing mentality was still one of laissez faire. Not Henry George, whose Progress and Poverty (1873) "takes high rank by reason of its content, style and influence" (14), represented the general body of thought but E. L. Godkin and his disciple, William James, with their emphasis on social Darwinism. "The ideas of William James, especially some of his social opinions, betrayed the limitations of his personal experience as a member of the advantaged class." (15)

In spite of this unfavorable socio-economic climate, the improved transportation system had one immediate advantage for Southern blacks: It shortened the distance to what they regarded as the "promised land", (16) the North. This must have been one of the primary incentives for black migration out of the South.

In 1868 a trip from New Orleans to Chicago would look like this: From New Orleans to Canton, Mississippi, one could take a train of the "New Orleans Jackson and Great Northern Railroad Company". It left New Orleans at 7.00 a.m. and arrived in Canton at 6.25 p.m. "Mississippi Central" would then take one from there to Jackson, Tennessee, leaving at 6.30. It arrived in Jackson at 7.00 a.m. Jackson was connected with Cairo, Illinois, by "Mobile & Ohio." This company's trains left Jackson at 7.10 a.m. "Illinois Central" finally took one from Cairo to Chicago, leaving at 2.40 p.m. and arriving seventeen and a half hours later. Total traveling time was 48.5 hours on the trains. (17)

Twenty-three years later, in 1891, the route went from New Orleans to Jackson, Mississippi, and from there via Grand Junction, Tennessee, Cairo, Centralia, and Champaign to Chicago. The whole trip took 28 hours 44 minutes and 29 hours in the opposite direction and there were three trains daily in both directions. (18)

By 1905 this time was not considerably shorter, but there were four daily trains now in each direction over the 912 mile stretch. (19) By 1915 there were five daily trains from Chicago to New Orleans (a fast one taking 13 hours 35 minutes for the trip) and four in the opposite direction. (20) An alternative route via St. Louis, Memphis, and Grenada registered four trains every day in each direction. (21) Since then, service has not been measurably enlarged. (22) Fifty years later, a 1965 schedule looked like this (23):

| | | |
|---|---|---|
| Chicago | 7.45 am | 11.40 pm |
| Cairo | 2.03 pm | 5.11 pm |
| Memphis | 5.15 pm | 2.00 pm |
| Jackson | 9.10 pm | 10.10 am |
| N.O. | 12.25 am | 7.10 pm |

Fig. 5    Routes of the Chicago - New Orleans railroad connections

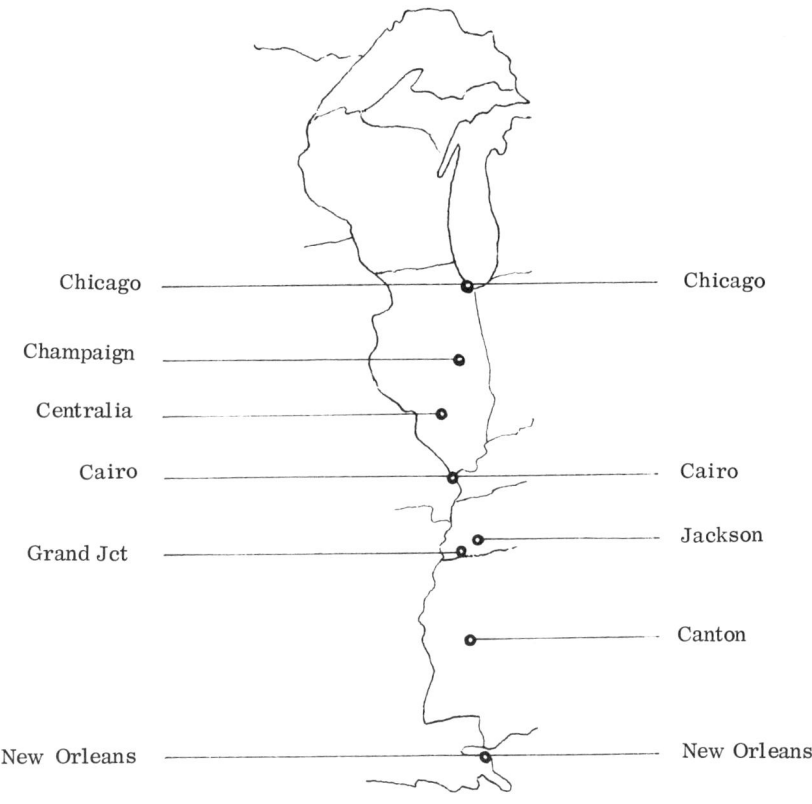

25

As the country grew together because of faster and better transportation facilities, people experienced the differences of life-styles and standards of living in the various regions more acutely. A comparison of several statistical indicators in the next section shall enable the reader to estimate somewhat the extent of these differences.

## POLITICS

For a rough approximation of the political climate one can rely on the results of the Presidential elections. (24) The underlying assumption is that in a region where each major party gets about an equal share of the votes political life will be more dynamic than in a region where one party holds almost absolute sway. In the first case minorities will be wooed and activated because they might tip the balance; in the second case minority participation will not be desired. The party in power will even have reason to fear it. The opposition party might hurt its own interests irreparably by such a "radical" move and, besides, it might not even have the opportunity to register minority voters because all key posts are held by the dominating party. (25)

The distribution of votes in Presidential elections is tabulated below for the years 1892 to 1936. At first glance it is evident that in two-party contests in the North roughly fifty percent voted for either party, the results being often, but not always, in favor of the Republicans. The Deep South voted solidly Democratic, with such extreme results as that of Mississippi in 1936, when 97.5 percent of the voters cast their ballot for Roosevelt. Kentucky and Tennessee stand between the North and the South, in that they do not show the extreme percentages of the Deep South but always voted in favor of the Democratic party, too.

To get a better hold of these relationships one can devise indexes that show the tendency of a state towards one-party rule. The highest and the lowest percentages achieved in any election, for example, are added for each party. For Illinois these figures are: Democrats, 56.5 and 33.7, adding up to 90.2; Republicans, 66.3 and 33.3, equals 99.6. Subtracting the Republican from the Democratic result one gets - 9.4. In a state where one party received all the votes every time, the index would be plus or minus 200, depending on which party this was. This would then be the index for a one-party state. Taking the three southern states of the East North Central division (Illinois, Indiana, and Ohio) and the four states of the East South Central division (Kentucky, Tennessee, Alabama, and Mississippi) the indexes are very clear:

Table 2        Tendency towards one-party rule in seven states.

| Ill.  | Ohio  | Ind. | Ky.  | Tenn. | Ala. | Miss. |
|-------|-------|------|------|-------|------|-------|
| - 9.4 | - 8.7 | 10.8 | 20.0 | 36.1  | 86.1 | 157.2 |

The sources for table 2 are the exact percentage figures for each of these states, as summed up in the following table.

Table 2a    Percentage distribution of votes in Presidential elections, 1892-1936.

|      |   | Ill. | Ind. | Ohio | Ky. | Tenn. | Ala. | Miss. |
|------|---|------|------|------|-----|-------|------|-------|
| 1892 | R | 47.1 | 47.1 | 49.1 | 40.6 | 38.7 | 3.9 | 1.9 |
|      | D | 50.3 | 48.8 | 49.1 | 52.2 | 52.1 | 59.5 | 78.8 |
|      | P | 2.6  | 4.1  | 1.8  | 7.2  | 9.2  | 36.6 | 19.2 |
| 1896 | R | 56.7 | 51.4 | 52.4 | 50.0 | 47.6 | 30.1 | 7.4 |
|      | D | 43.3 | 48.6 | 47.6 | 50.0 | 52.4 | 69.9 | 92.6 |
| 1900 | R | 54.8 | 51.9 | 53.4 | 49.1 | 45.9 | 36.6 | 10.5 |
|      | D | 45.2 | 48.1 | 46.6 | 50.9 | 54.1 | 63.4 | 89.5 |
| 1904 | R | 55.8 | 57.4 | 63.5 | 48.6 | 44.3 | 21.6 | 5.4 |
|      | D | 44.2 | 42.6 | 36.5 | 51.4 | 55.7 | 78.4 | 94.6 |
| 1908 | R | 53.2 | 50.8 | 53.2 | 49.1 | 46.5 | 26.0 | 6.3 |
|      | D | 46.8 | 49.2 | 46.8 | 50.9 | 53.5 | 74.0 | 93.8 |
| 1912 | R | 33.3 | 25.4 | 29.8 | 26.5 | 24.2 | 8.7 | 3.2 |
|      | D | 47.9 | 47.4 | 45.6 | 50.1 | 53.6 | 71.3 | 90.5 |
|      | P | 18.8 | 27.2 | 24.7 | 23.3 | 22.2 | 20.0 | 6.3 |
| 1916 | R | 51.0 | 50.5 | 46.0 | 47.3 | 43.3 | 22.7 | 4.8 |
|      | D | 49.0 | 49.5 | 54.0 | 52.7 | 56.7 | 77.3 | 95.2 |
| 1920 | R | 57.0 | 57.7 | 60.2 | 49.8 | 51.4 | 32.5 | 14.8 |
|      | D | 43.0 | 42.3 | 39.8 | 50.2 | 48.6 | 67.5 | 85.2 |
| 1924 | R | 57.8 | 55.5 | 58.4 | 49.0 | 43.5 | 26.2 | 7.2 |
|      | D | 36.7 | 38.8 | 23.8 | 46.4 | 52.8 | 68.9 | 90.1 |
|      | P | 5.6  | 5.7  | 17.8 | 4.7  | 3.7  | 4.9  | 2.7 |
| 1928 | R | 66.3 | 60.1 | 65.3 | 59.4 | 55.4 | 48.6 | 17.2 |
|      | D | 33.7 | 39.9 | 34.7 | 40.6 | 44.6 | 51.4 | 82.8 |
| 1932 | R | 51.4 | 44.0 | 48.5 | 40.5 | 32.9 | 14.6 | 3.4 |
|      | D | 48.6 | 56.0 | 51.5 | 59.5 | 67.1 | 85.4 | 96.6 |
| 1936 | R | 43.5 | 42.5 | 39.2 | 40.7 | 30.9 | 12.8 | 2.5 |
|      | D | 56.5 | 57.5 | 60.8 | 59.3 | 69.1 | 87.2 | 97.5 |

R    Votes for the Republican Party

D     Votes for the Democratic Party
P     Votes for the Populist Party / People's Party

Source:   Historical Statistics, Series Y 80-128

One gets similar results by a somewhat more sophisticated method. Plotting the results of the Presidential elections in a coordinate system, one can draw curves which show how many people voted for which party in a given circumscription. For the whole United States, for example, the curve for the Republican party looks like this:

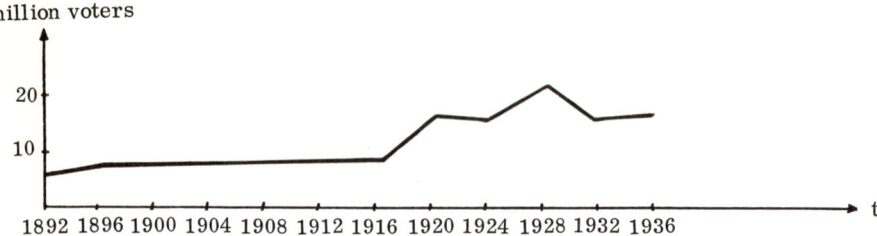

The same curve for Illinois:

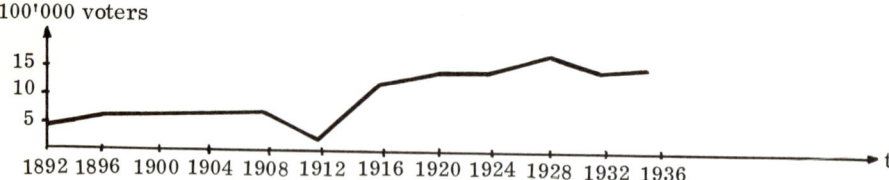

And for South Carolina:

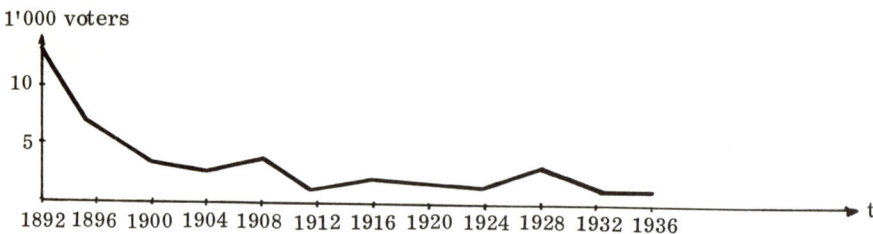

Source: Historical Statistics, Series Y 80-128

It is obvious that the curve for Illinois is much closer to that of the United States than the curve for South Carolina. This "closeness" can be expressed by the correlation coefficient. A correlation coefficient of + 1 indicates that two curves are exactly congruent, one of - 1 that they are exactly inverse, i.e. that whenever there was a nationwide increase of Republican votes, the Democratic votes in the state under consideration decreased, and vice versa. If the national curve is the norm, a correlation coefficient of + 1 indicates complete conformity, and one of - 1 complete abnormity. Since these curves are drawn on the basis of absolute numbers of votes one has to allow for demographic changes, so that coefficients of + 1 would be a coincidence rather than a proof of complete conformity. In the following table the correlation coefficients for all coterminous states except Utah are presented by regions.

Table 3   Correlation coefficients for Presidential elections, 1892-1936 for Continental United States except Utah.

New England

| Connecticut | 0.97195 |
| Maine | 97032 |
| Massachusetts | 97126 |
| New Hampshire | 97456 |
| Rhode Island | 95379 |
| Vermont | 96623 |

Middle Atlantic

| Delaware | 0.98786 |
| Maryland | 94434 |
| New York | 98191 |
| New Jersey | 98799 |
| Pennsylvania | 97675 |

South Atlantic

| Florida | 0.89910 |
| Georgia | 35293 |
| North Carolina | 93033 |
| South Carolina | - 0.41895 |
| Virginia | 0.46271 |
| West Virginia | 98859 |

East South Central

| Alabama | 0.71168 |
| Kentucky | 98281 |
| Mississippi | 74698 |
| Tennessee | 76436 |

West South Central

| Arkansas | 0.40844 |
| Louisiana | 79953 |
| Oklahoma | 93895 |
| Texas | 66468 |

East North Central

| Illinois | 0.96664 |
| Indiana | 99410 |
| Michigan | 98160 |
| Ohio | 98409 |
| Wisconsin | 91115 |

West North Central

| Iowa | 0.94354 |
| Kansas | 97917 |
| Minnesota | 95988 |
| Missouri | 98704 |
| Nebraska | 97952 |

West

| Colorado | 0.92412 |
| Idaho | 87119 |
| Montana | 90324 |
| Nevada | 86664 |
| Wyoming | 96186 |

| North Dakota | 0.84971 | Arizona    | 0.97559 |
| South Dakota | 96127   | New Mexico | 99248   |

Pacific

| Washington | 0.94402 |
| Oregon     | 93652   |
| California | 97574   |

Source: Historical Statistics,
Series Y 80-128 (26)

All states with coefficients between 0.900000 and 1.000000 can be said to have voted, in the long run, in accordance with the general political climate of the nation. All states with results below 0.900000 did not follow the national trend. The geographic distribution of the latter states is revealing: there are none in the New England, Middle Atlantic, East North Central, and the Pacific divisions, and one each in the West North Central and the Western divisions, possibly for demographic rather than for political reasons. In the three Southern districts only Oklahoma, Kentucky, North Carolina, and West Virginia lie above 0.90000; the other ten states have smaller coefficients. The lowest result is reached by South Carolina. It is negative, and a glance at its curve, above, shows why: While the United States curve rises slightly from 1892 to 1916, the South Carolina curve basically falls during the same time, often quite sharply.

With respect to politics therefore the Deep South forms a distinct region, and blacks migrating from this area to the Northern states crossed the borders of this region.

Fig. 6    States with correlation coefficients of less than 0.90000 for Presidential elections, 1892-1936.

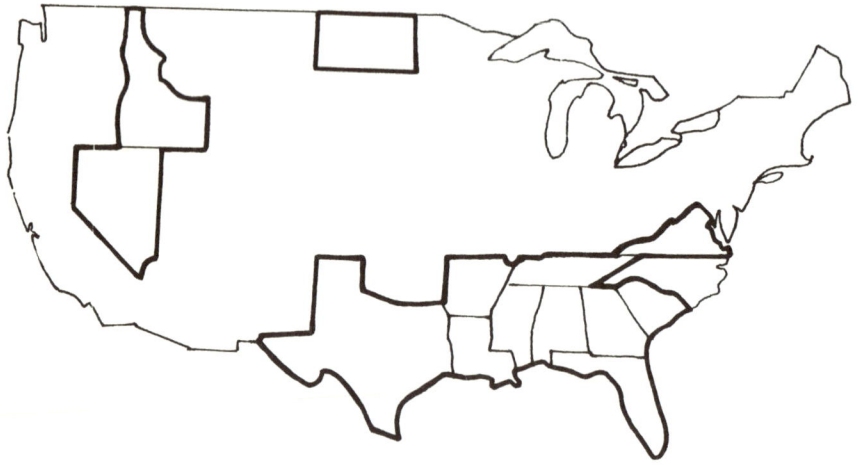

ECONOMY AND SOCIETY

In a democratic society, based primarily on private enterprise, the work that an individual does largely determines his income, his status and his way of life. (27)

In the 1890s the black labor force grew by some three percent annually; by 1915 this percentage had shrunk to some 0.5 percent. During the depression of the 1930s more blacks were laid off than hired, while the white labor force still grew at the rate of some six percent per year. Even if one takes into consideration the decrease of the proportion of blacks in the total population it is clear that at least since the turn of the century there was a tendency in the labor market to hire them last and dismiss them first.

Fig. 7    Percentage change in labor force

Source: Ginzberg/Hiestand in Davis (12), 207

At the same time blacks tended to be concentrated in the lowest occupational fields. This low status was determined mainly by lack of education and training, and by discrimination in the economy.

In 1910 the percentage figures for blacks and for whites employed in the manual and service sector were very close (46.6 and 48.2) but there was a great divergence in regard to white collar jobs, which were held by only three percent of the blacks but by 25 percent of the whites. Within the manual and service sector, 81 percent of the whites had skilled and semi-skilled jobs, while 83 percent of the blacks were confined to laborer and service jobs. Blacks were thus in the lowest positions of the occupational structure. Joseph H. Douglass even spoke of an "occupational ghetto." (28) More than half of the blacks worked in the nonfarm sector. This picture remained essentially constant during the following decade. (29)

There is an interdependence between the job opportunities available to blacks and their geographical distribution. Scott observed that prior to 1914 blacks were "forced to enter the field of domestic service in the North and farming in the South". (30) This changed somewhat with the arrival of World War I, when the new war industries offered jobs to blacks, although Northern industrialists complained that they were too slow and unwilling to work outdoors in winter. (31)

Not only the job opportunities but also the average service incomes (as opposed to property incomes) showed great geographical disparities during the entire period under consideration:

Table 4    Service income per worker, U.S = 100

|  | 1880 | 1900 | 1919-21 | 1949-51 |
|---|---|---|---|---|
| East North Central | 110 | 112 | 110 | 112 |
| East South Central | 55 | 52 | 60 | 68 |

Source: Kuznets (84) vol. 3, 352, 356-365

One can distinguish economic migrations (those to a region with a higher average income) and noneconomic migrations (to a region with a lower average income). (32) Migration from the East South Central division to the East North Central was at all times an economic move. Eldridge and Thomas (33) computed the economic and the noneconomic intercensal increase of native whites and of native nonwhites born out (living in) and born in (living out) each division, by relative divisional income per worker. The percentage for native nonwhites in the East South Central are listed as follows:

| 1880-1890 | 1900-1910 | 1919-1921 | 1949-1951 |
|---|---|---|---|
| 68.2 | 82.2 | 96.5 | 95.1 |

Between 70 and 95 percent, roughly, of the nonwhites living in the East North Central but born in another division or born in the East North Central but living in another division had therefore gained economically by not residing in their state of birth. One can further break down the numer of economic migrations into economic in-migrations into the East North Central and economic out-migrations out of this division for nonwhites:

|  | 1880-1890 | 1900-1910 | 1919-1921 | 1949-1951 |
|---|---|---|---|---|
| in-migrations | 58 | 278 | 3117 | 4445 |

|           | 1880-1890 | 1900-1910 | 1919-1921 | 1949-1951 |
|-----------|-----------|-----------|-----------|-----------|
| out-migrations | 17 | 26 | 71 | 97 (34) |

Thus vastly more nonwhites gained by migrating into East North Central than by migrating out of it. The ratios lie between 3.4 and 46.3.

A brief look at the Real Gross Domestic Product per man hour in the farm and the nonfarm sectors and the output per man hour in the steel and motor vehicle industries shows convincingly how much a person migrating from the rural South into the industrial North must have had to adapt to the pace of innovation in the new environment.

Fig. 8    Productivity per man hour in selected farm and nonfarm jobs, 1889-1939

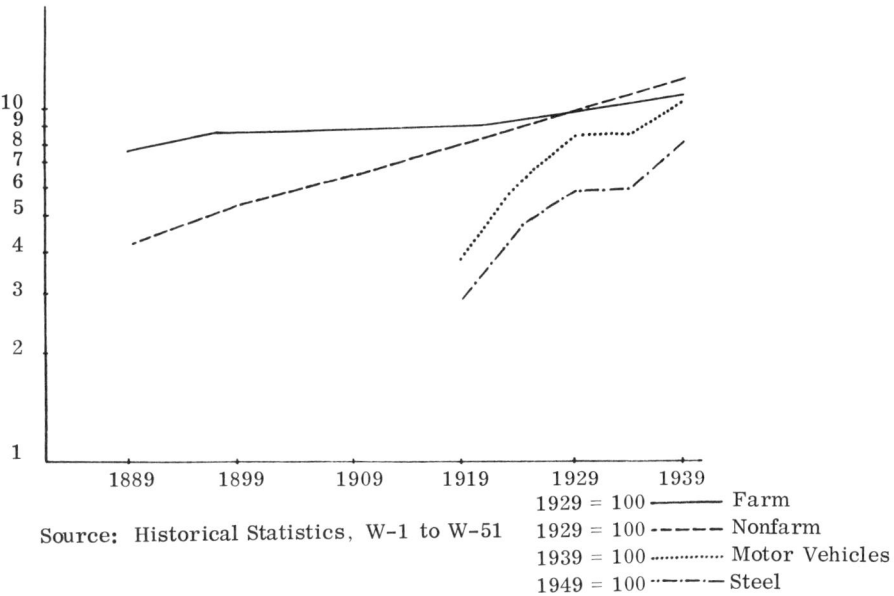

Source: Historical Statistics, W-1 to W-51

1929 = 100 ——— Farm
1929 = 100 - - - - - Nonfarm
1939 = 100 ············ Motor Vehicles
1949 = 100 —··—··— Steel

The low economic status of the nonwhite group is also one of the reasons for the great disparity in health between blacks and whites. This disparity is evident in both physical and mental health statistics. Stone, in a paper on Stirling's depressed communities, noted that

> Many studies in other places have shown a strong association of poor health with poverty . ... We find complaints suggesting a considerable prevalence of chronic diseases - high blood pressure, arthritis, peptic ulcer, and bronchitis - as well as chronic anxiety and depression. Not only is disease sometimes a by-product of poverty; it probably serves

to perpetuate poverty either by actual disablement or by a considerable reduction in energy level and physical endurance. (35)

Weinberg studied the interrelation between mental health and migration into Israel and arrived, among others, at the following conclusions:

> Migration may exert an unfavourable influence on mental health. ... Social psychiatric research points to the existence of an interrelation between mental health and adjustment of migrants. (36)

Taeuber and Taeuber have demonstrated that the expectation of life at birth for blacks was constantly below or equal (in the early 1930s) that for whites. (37) This is true for both sexes. A more detailed analysis of the cause of death for blacks and whites adds further insight into the health situation. Such an analysis for the period immediately prior to World War I leads to the following conclusions:
1. The general death rate for all causes was in 1910 1.7 times as high for blacks as that for whites (27.6 vs. 15.8 deaths per 1,000 population of all ages).
2. Tuberculosis, pneumonia, and organic diseases of the heart were the three principal causes of death for both races.
3. Among the black population, tuberculosis was almost twice as frequently the cause of death than among the white population. The same was true for violent deaths except suicide (12 white suicides for 1,000 deaths for all causes, compared to 3 black suicides on the same basis). Pneumonia and organic diseases of the heart occurred with almost the same frequency among both races.
4. Terminal cancer occurred twice as often among whites than among blacks.
5. The principal causes of death are in general the same for black men and for black women.
6. A comparison of urban and rural death rates is revealing:

|  |  | Urban | Rural |
|---|---|---|---|
| U.S. | Blacks | 27.1 | 19.5 |
|  | Whites | 15.6 | 13.3 |
| North and | Blacks | 24.4 | 20.4 |
| West | Whites | 15.5 | 13.4 |
| South | Blacks | 29.3 | 18.3 |
|  | Whites | 16.8 | 11.9 (38) |

If blacks migrated from a Southern rural area into a Northern urban environment, their mortality increased, although the same is not true if they migrated from a Southern town into a Northern one. It is significant that the lowest death rate for blacks anywhere (Southern rural) was higher than the highest death rate for whites anywhere (Southern urban), and that the ratios of the various death rates are about the same for blacks and for whites.

Similar statistics showing the percentage of the rural and the urban insane admitted to mental institutions lead to the conclusion that the figures were generally "higher for the urban than for the rural population among both Negroes and whites," and:

> These differences, however, probably largely represent more adequate provisions for the insane in urban communities as compared with rural, and can not be taken as indicating accurately the effect of urban conditions as factors conducing to insanity. (39)

This is of course a caveat one constantly has to bear in mind in this connection. Not only are the institutions for treatment vastly different in different parts of the country, but there are often inhibitions and ignorance among the less well educated about physical and, especially, mental diseases. On the other hand, many members of the well-to-do strata of society receive professional treatment for conditions that the other sub-group would not even recognize as being deviant.

Weinberg defined positive mental health as being characterized by free, undisturbed interpersonal and intrapersonal relations. (40) One wonders how anybody - segregationist or segregate - living under a system of discrimination and segregation can on this premise be mentally sane.

Underlying this argumentation is a theory of equilibrium and disequilibrium, according to which an individual is well balanced if his education, his occupation and income, his social status, his habitat, and other such vitally important matters are congruent and that he is in disequilibrium if these determinants are incongruent. The result of such a disequilibrium is anomie in its widest sense, a deviation from a state or behaviour which is accepted as "normal". Illness of body and of mind is such a deviation from the norm of health; it has been shown in the preceding section in what respect the black population exhibits characteristics which could be called "abnormal". In the following paragraph the result of a real or imaginary deviation from the judicial laws of the society will be analyzed. In this connection the number of arrests is a statistically well documented quantity that can easily be scrutinized.

The number of arrests can only be significantly appraised if it is compared to the number of the population at large. One can define as "arrest rate" the number of arrests per one hundred population. This percentage is often called "crime rate", but this is wrong mainly because "arrests" is in no way synonymous with "crimes": many people who have committed a crime are never arrested, and many people who are arrested have never committed a crime.

In 1880 Chicago had a white population of 496,495 persons. (41) Of these, 15,485 persons were arrested. (42) The arrest rate was therefore 15,485 divided by 4,965 = 3.1. The following table shows the development of this rate until 1930, the last year for which the Chicago Police Department reported arrest figures by race.

Table 5    Arrest rates for whites and for blacks in Chicago, 1880-1930.

|  | Population | Arrests | Arrest rate |
|---|---|---|---|
| a) Whites | | | |
| 1880 | 496,495 | 15,485 | 3.1 |
| 1890 | 1,084,998 | 33,955 | 3.1 |
| 1900 | 1,667,140 | 43,169 | 2.6 |
| 1916 | est. 2,400,000 | 63,299 | 2.6 |
| 1920 | 2,588,169 | 55,078 | 2.1 |
| 1930 | 3,376,438 | 104,713 | 3.4 |
| b) Blacks | | | |
| 1880 | 6,480 | 1,366 | 21.0 |
| 1890 | 14,271 | 5,527 | 38.6 |
| 1900 | 30,150 | 5,512 | 18.3 |
| 1916 | est. 75,000 | 8,502 | 11.3 |
| 1920 | 109,485 | 9,856 | 9.1 |
| 1930 | 233,903 | 46,487 | 19.1 (43) |

Note: The arrest figures for 1910 were not available for the compilation of this table. The closest ones were those for 1916. The population for this year has been estimated according to the formula for the average annual population increase rate:

$$100 \left( \sqrt[10]{\frac{\text{Pop. 1920}}{\text{Pop. 1910}}} - 1 \right)$$

One should see the reality behind these figures: In 1920, when the arrest rate for blacks was at its lowest, one out of every nine blacks was arrested, and in 1890, when it was at its highest, one out of every three was detained by police. At this rate every black man, women, and child in the city would have been arrested within three years.

A look at the growth rates can give more insight into these statistics. Did the general population grow faster or the arrests? The growth rate of the population, gp, is defined simply as

$$gp = \frac{\text{population 1}}{\text{population 0}} .$$

The growth rate of arrests, ga, is

$$ga = \frac{\text{arrests 1}}{\text{arrests 0}} .$$

For reasons of comparison one can create the index d

$$d = \frac{gp}{ga} \quad \frac{\text{population 1}}{\text{population 0}} \cdot \frac{\text{arrests 0}}{\text{arrests 1}} = \frac{\text{arrest rate 0}}{\text{arrest rate 1}}.$$

If d equals 1 (unit), population and arrests grow at the same rate. If d is bigger than 1, population grows faster than arrests, if it is smaller than 1, vice versa.

Computed on the basis of arrest rates, rather than absolute figures, the resulting table of d's looks like this:

Table 5a   Comparison between population growth and arrest growth, 1880-1930

|  | 1880-90 | 1890-1900 | 1900-1916 | 1916-1920 | 1920-1930 |
|---|---|---|---|---|---|
| black | 0.54 | 2.11 | 1.62 | 1.24 | 0.48 |
| white | 1.00 | 1.19 | 1.00 | 1.24 | 0.62 |

So far the arrest rate was computed by dividing the number of arrests by one percent of the total population. But the aggregate number of the total population is hardly a good basis, because the sub-groups which are unlikely to be arrested should be excluded. Police very rarely detain minors under the age of fifteen years or people over 65. (44) The arrest rate should therefore be computed on the basis of the population figures for those aged fifteen to sixty-five.

It is very important to realize this because of the different age structure of the black and the white populations. This is due to the demographic movements described above. Migration brought mostly working blacks over fifteen into the North, while the very young and the very old stayed behind, at least for a time. (45) This is well reflected by the population pyramids. In 1880, the pyramids for the entire black and for the entire white population of the United States had similar shapes. They were generally pyramidal with only minor irregularities.

Fig. 9   Population pyramids, 1880. United States

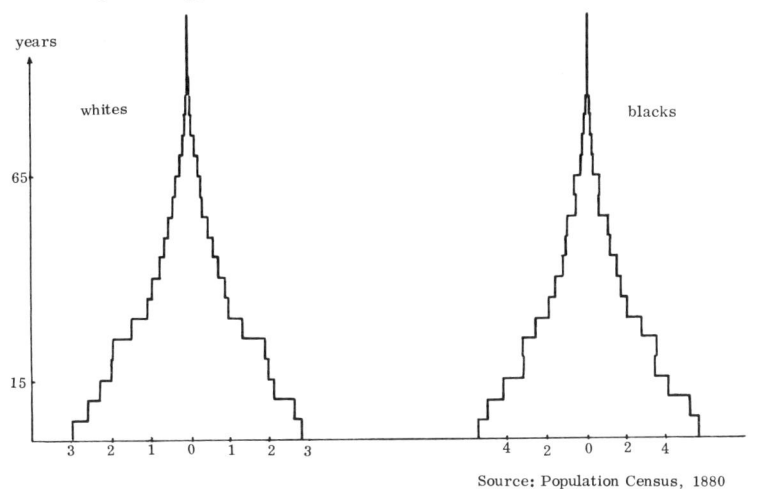

Source: Population Census, 1880

The pyramids for the same year for the State of Illinois already show marked irregularities, stemming very likely from the in-migration of blacks:

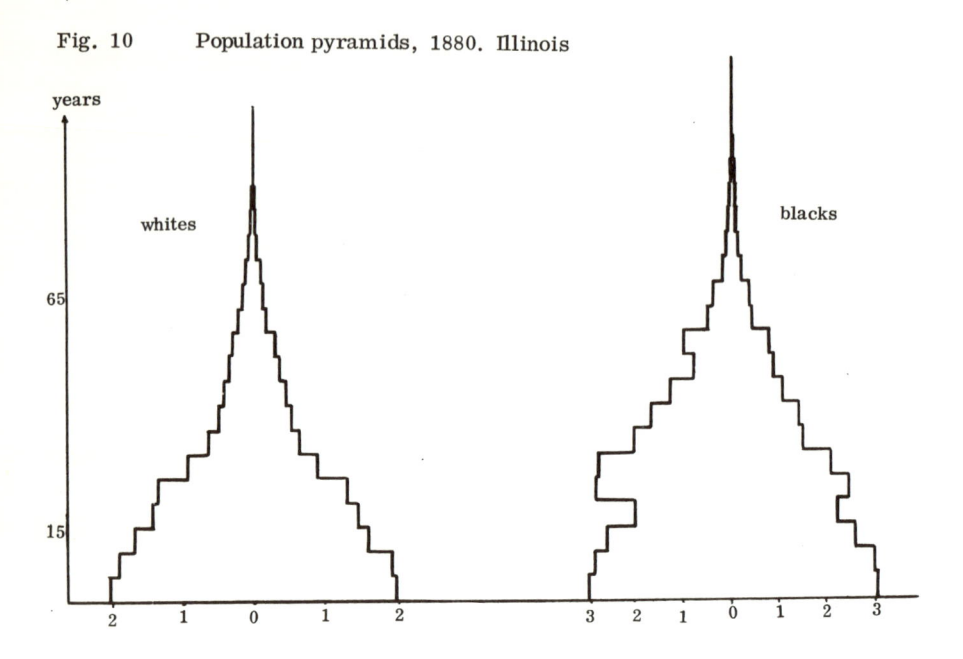

Fig. 10    Population pyramids, 1880. Illinois

Source: Population Census, 1880

By 1920 this had become even more obvious. The base of the pyramid of the black population had become very narrow and the overwhelming majority of the population was between twenty and fourty years old, i.e. in the age group most likely to be arrested.

Fig. 11    Population pyramids, 1920. Illinois

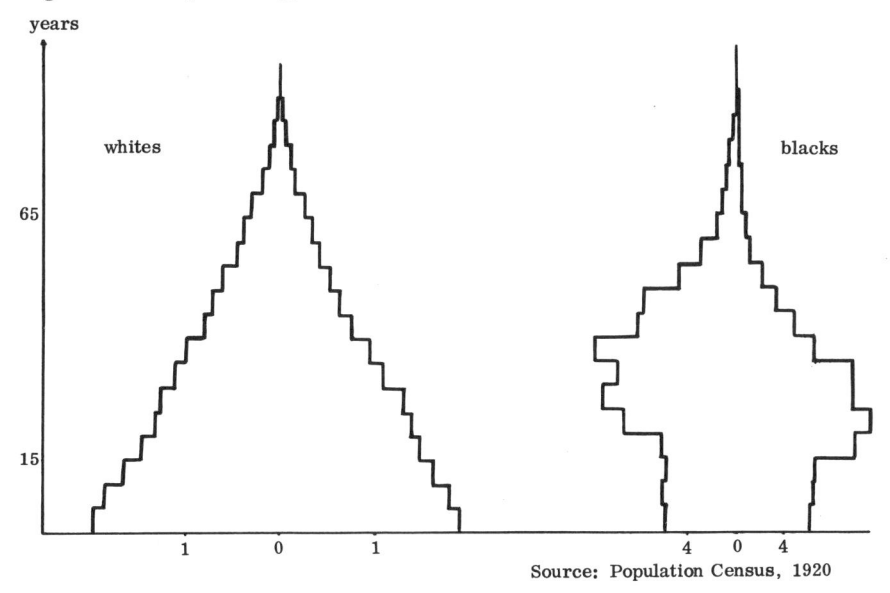

years

65

15

whites

blacks

1    0    1

4    0    4

Source: Population Census, 1920

The census statistics for Chicago do not report detailed data on the age of the population: only the aggregate numbers for the ages twenty through fourty-four and for fourty-five and above are listed. For an approximation one can assume that those aggregate figures were distributed evenly over the respective periods (which is of course not true) and draw pyramids on this assumption. They look like this:

39

Fig. 12    Population pyramids, 1920. Chicago

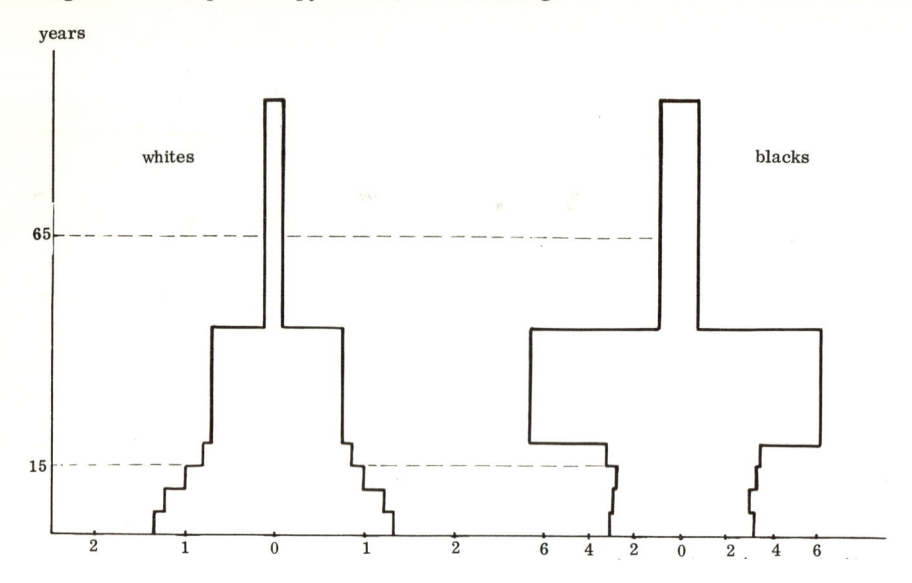

Source: Population Census, 1920

Here, too, it is evident that the bulk of the population was of the age group which was most likely to come into contact with law enforcement.

How much do the arrest rates change if one takes this into account?

In 1880 some fourty percent of the native white population of Chicago were under the age of fifteen, while the analogous figure for blacks was only seventeen percent. (46) The arrest rates therefore increase from 9.1 to 10.9 for blacks and from 2.1 for whites to 3.6. The ratio of the two (black over white) was reduced, too, from 4.3 : 1 to 3.0 : 1. For 1920 we can similarly compute an increase of from 9.1 to 11.4 for blacks and from 2.1 to 3.65 for whites. The ratio declines from 4.3 to 3.1. (47)

CONCLUSION

Where did the blacks who lived in the Midwest from 1890 to 1930 come from? Thirty to sixty percent of East North Central nonwhites were born there. Eighty-four to ninety-two percent of the rest came from the South, fifty to sixty percent from the South Central division. About a third came from Kentucky, a fifth each from Mississippi, Tennessee, and Georgia, a tenth from Alabama, and a twentieth from Virginia.

What were the differences in life-style between the states of origin and the states of residence of these blacks? How big were the differences they had to overcome?

While the South, and its black population, was still heavily rural, sixty to ninety percent of Midwestern blacks lived in cities. But migration and the concomitant urbanization did not solve the problems blacks had fled from, they only created new ones. The political difference between the South and the North can most impressively be shown by an analysis of Presidential election data, which shows that in the South there was a very strong tendency towards one-party rule, while in the North the forces were more balanced; this also reflects the complex problem of political participation. In the economic sector the statistics are equally conclusive: blacks were on the lowest rung of the occupational ladder (in the "occupational ghetto"); the service income in the South (where between seventy-five and ninety percent of the blacks still lived) was only about half that of the North; and even in the North blacks were mostly confined to the lowest paying jobs in the manual and service sector. Expectation of life at birth for blacks was below that for whites; the death rate for blacks was almost twice as high as that for whites; tuberculosis and violent death - except suicide - were twice as frequent as causes of death among the black population; urban death rates were higher than rural ones. Three times as many blacks as whites were arrested, on a proportional basis.

All statistical evidence presented in this chapter leads to the conclusion that blacks in the Middle West formed a class of citizens of its own: Their origin, their migration, and their political, economic, and social status set them off from native whites and immigrants. The differences between the rural South and the industrial North lead to the conclusion that for all practical purposes they could be considered strangers, even foreigners, to the urban environment where they had settled. Strangers, moreover, who bore the stigma of color.

Confronted with such a situation the student of legal history immediately asks if the legal system makes allowances for this peculiarity, if there is a mechanism to account for these special circumstances.

How the law deals with a minority is indeed a very old problem. Precedents show in what way it has been solved, or left unsolved, in the Ancient World (metoikoi in Greece, non-Italics in the Roman Empire) and in medieval times (foreign merchants in market towns). It can even be argued that the ideas of human rights and of international law originated to a large extent under the influence of the question of how to treat foreigners and other minorities under a local system of jurisdiction.

The American legal system does not have an unlimited range of possibilities to react to the special situation originally created by the importation of black laborers from Africa. The judicial process in America has a long heritage, reaching back into medieval Britain and even continental Europe. It is replete with notions and ideologies which cannot easily be displaced or substituted by new ones. The historian therefore must first turn to the long-range developments - the "macrohistory" - in order to find out to what extent the system was so conditioned as to be unable to respond to the exigencies of an unforeseen situation, and to learn what ideas have been incorporated into it during its long history and what the resulting present structure of it is.

CHAPTER II

HISTORY AND DEVELOPMENT OF TRIAL BY JURY

INTRODUCTION

What was the history and development of trial by jury? The answer shall help to understand the present structure and problems of this institution.

As will be seen in this chapter, the history and development of trial by jury has always been seen by jurists and the popular imagination as closely linked to the development of a democratic ideal of justice and, especially, to the influence of Magna Carta on the British understanding of law and legality.

Nobody can write today about Magna Carta without using Williams S. McKechnie's Magna Carta: A Commentary on the Great Charter of King John (1905; nr. 130.)* Although the work is almost seventy years old, it is still a standard authority on the subject. It marked a clear break with the old "Whig" view of Magna Carta, which was more romantic and to which even Stubbs succumbed. William Stubbs, Select Charters etc. (9th ed., 1913; nr. 137) has been extensively used, however, because the many sources it offers are very helpful in tracing the history of Magna Carta. For the interpretation of this document after McKechnie, the Magna Carta Commemoration Essays, ed. Henry Malden (1917; nr. 131) offer a wealth of scholarship; for our subject especially the contributions by Frederick M. Powicke ("Per Iudicium Parium Vel Per Legem Terrae,") pp. 96-121, by Sir Paul Vinogradoff ("Magna Carta, c. 39: Nullus liber homo, etc.,") pp. 78-95, and by H. D. Hazeltine ("The Influence of Magna Carta on American Constitutional Development,") pp. 180-226. This collection of articles was originally prepared for the 700th anniversary of the events at Runnymede, in 1915. The most recent book extensively used in this connection appeared for the 750th anniversary: James C. Holt, Magna Carta (1965; nr. 129). Besides having obvious merits of its own - it is universally regarded as the best contemporary study on the Great Charter - this book is very helpful in showing how little McKechnie's masterly interpretation has had to be changed during this past half century.

A few general histories of English law must also be used, notably the standard works by William Holdsworth, A History of English Law (16 vols., 7th ed. 1966; nr. 128), particularly vol. I, pp. 298-350, by Pollock and Maitland, The History of the English Law Before the Time of Edward I (2nd ed., 1922; nr. 123), by Maitland, The Constitutional History of England (1946; nr. 132), and by Theodore Plucknett, A Concise History of Common Law (5th ed., 1956), which still is the standard textbook for university courses in the subject.

There are fewer histories of American law. For the reasons for this see Lawrence M. Friedman, "Some Problems and Possibilities of American Legal

* The numbers refer to the bibliography, pp. 135-156, below.

History," (1970; nr. 170). The standard histories of the Colonial period by Andrews (The Colonial Period of American History, 1934-1938; nr. 21) and by Osgood (The American Colonies in the Seventeenth Century, 1940, and The American Colonies in the Eighteenth Century, 1924-1925; nrs. 37 and 38) do however contain much valuable information.

Further sources for this chapter, besides Stubbs and the works listed in sections 9 and 10 of the Bibliography (below, pp. 148-150), are the British Statues of the Realm, and the charters and constitutions of the American colonies and the United States reprinted in The Federal and State Constitutions, complied by Benjamin Poore (1877; nr. 135).

The course of British and American legal history has determined the present structure and operation of trial by jury. The resulting procedure is shown by the example of its administration in Illinois. Because this section will prepare the discussion of cases that came before the Illinois Supreme Court between 1880 and 1940, the Revised Statutes of 1874, then in force, will be used as the major source. To contrast this declaratory act of the legislature with the actual procedure in the police stations and the courts some secondary literature will be quoted, mainly Carl A. Ross, "The Jury System in Cook County, Illinois," (1910; nr. 146) and Louis B. Schwartz and Stephen R. Goldstein, Law Enforcement Handbook for Police (1970; nr. 152). See also section 11 of the Bibliography (below, p. 151).

Little original research will be carried out in this chapter. Original sources of the history and development of trial by jury will be quoted extensively and the most authoritative authors will be summarized.


HISTORY OF TRIAL BY JURY FROM THE CAROLINGIAN ROYAL INQUISITION
TO BLACKSTONE

The first enactment in Colonial America that safeguarded the rights of the people and contained a clause guaranteeing trial by jury was the Massachusetts "Body of Liberties" of 1641. (1) Article 29 of that document reads:

In all Actions at law it shall be the libertie of the plaintife and defendant by mutual consent to choose whether they will be tryed by the Bench or by a Jurie, unlesse it be where the law upon just reason hath otherwise determined. The like libertie shall be granted to all persons in Criminall cases. (2)

This provision was drawn up in consequence of an opinion of the deputies in the Massachusetts General Court (3) in 1635 that "some men should be appointed to frame a body of ground laws, in resemblance to Magna Carta, which, ... should be received for fundamental laws." (4) The Great Charter of King John was thus taken as a model for the construction of the American legal system from the very beginning.

Although trial by peers in the form of trial by jury was incorporated into the American judicial system from Magna Carta it was not an invention of the thirteenth century. Holt reminds us that the mentioning of this mode of adjudication by the Charter was "simply an assertion of a generally recognized axiom." (5) The earliest instance of trial by peers in England is found in chapter 31, § 7, of the "Leges Henrici Primi": "uniusque per pares suos judicandus est et ejusdem provinciae." (6) Frederick W. Maitland showed already in the late 1880s that trial by peers was more likely an importation of the prerogative procedure of the Frankish kings than an old Anglo-Saxon custom. Following Forsyth and Brunner in this respect (7), he argued that this procedure had been brought to England in 1066 and had first been extensively used by Henry II. (8) This is today the common view of the scholars in the field.

The same authorities hold that a capitulary (9) of Louis I ("The Pious"), son of Charlemagne and emperor of the Holy Roman Empire, mentioned the earliest precursor of the English jury. It was signed early in 829 and put into effect by August of that year. As a capitulary it was addressed to the commissioners of the king (the missi dominici) who went around the country to make inquests (inquisitiones). It seems that Louis at that time intended to reform his empire, but whatever the commissioners finally reported, there is little evidence that the emperor acted on their findings.

The first paragraph of the "Capitulare Missorum" is concerned with the Church and its relation to the treasury (fiscus). This matter is left open to future regulation. The second paragraph reads:

> Item volumus, ut omnis inquisitio, quae de rebus ad ius fisci nostri pertinentibus facienda est, non per testes, qui producti fuerint, sed per illos, qui in eo comitatu meliores esse cognoscuntur, per illorum testimonium inquisitio fiat, et iuxta quod illi testificati fuerint, vel contineantur vel reddantur. ... (10)

The goal of this inquest seems to have been purely fiscal: inquisitio here meant "assessment for taxation," (11) and the king obviously distrusted the witnesses produced for the occasion by those who had to account for their taxable property - apparently because liegemen, friends, and relatives had often testified to a rich man's lack of resources. The king wanted impartial witnesses: "illi qui in eo comitatu meliores et veraciores cognoscuntur". The number of these truthful men was not specified and probably varied for different localities. The area they were to come from was delimited by "in eo comitatu". For this particular purpose the jurisdiction was the county of the Frankish empire.

The assumption of the experts today is that by the eleventh century the custom of the inquisitio had become common in the Normandy, (12) where it was employed with great skill by the duke, William, for the consolidation of his power against the rebellious barons. It seems very natural that William would bring an instrument which had helped him to establish his authority in Normandy across the Channel after he had become "the Conqueror". In England he was faced with a strange and generally hostile population. His greatest accomplishment and "the most enduring administrative schievement of the middle ages," (13) the Domesday Book, was indeed in this tradition. It is only a summary of the accounts made by his commissioners, but in the "Inquisitio Eliensis," a private account of the land of Ely in Eastern England, we find a description of the actual procedure. It begins:

> Hic subscribitur inquisitio terrarum quomodo barones regis inquirunt, videlicet, per sacramentum vicecomitis ... et totius centuriatus, presbiteri, praepositi, vi. villanorum uniuscujusque villae. Deinde quomodo vocatur mansio, quis tenuit eam tempore Regis Eadwardi; quis modo tenet; quot hidae; quot carrucae in domino, quot hominum; quot villani; quot cotarii; quot servi; quot liberi homines; quot sochemani; quantum silvae; quantum prati; quantum pascuorum; quot molendina; quot piscinae; quantum est additum vel ablatum; quantum valebat totum simul; et quantum modo; quantum ibi quisque liber homo, vel sochemannus habuit vel habet. Hoc totum tripliciter; scilicet tempore Regis Aeduardi, et quando Rex Willemus dedit; et quomodo sit modo; et si potest plus haberi quam habeatur. (14)

The motive for the survey, as expressed in the document, is again purely fiscal ("et si potest plus haberi quam habeatur"). The inquisition was made by the barons of the king who had to rely on the information they could get from the notables of the shire. In contrast to the capitulary of King Louis the oath was particularly mentioned, although it is of course possible that in the Frankish empire such an oath had to be taken in connection with an inquisition. The oath here was of the nature of that of an expert witness of our own days who testifies before a public official about matters he is supposed to know intimately. It is not demanded in the document here under discussion that the sworn men should be impartial, but the make-up of the jury was rather inclusive (vicecomites scirae, presbiteri, praepositi, villani) and this might have served to check the bias of an individual or a special group.

The "Capitulare Missorum" of 829 and the "Inquisitio Eliensis" were not only similar but to some extent identical in their expressed purpose, in spite of the great distance in time and geography between them. The "Assizes of Claredon" of 1166 have a different aim. It must have been noticed by rulers before Henry II that they received more information through their inquisitions than they actually needed for taxation purposes. Henry II was the first king to use this fiscal instrument for judicial (or rather, police) inquiries:

> Inprimis statuit praedictus rex Henricus de consilio omnium baronum suorum, pro pace servanda et justitia tenenda, quod per singulos comitatus inquiratur, et per singulos hundredos, per xii. legaliores homines de hundredo, et per iv. legaliores homines de qualibet villata, per sacramentum quod illi verum dicent: si in hundredo suo vel villata sua aliquis homo sit rettatus vel publicatus quod ipse sit robator vel murdrator vel latro aliquis qui fuerit receptor robatorum vel murd-

ratorum vel latronum, postquam dominus rex fuit rex. Et hoc inquirant Justitiae coram se, et vicecomites coram se. (15)

No longer does the king appear as the sole source of law: "statuit praedictus rex Henricus de consilio omnium baronorum suorum." It is not specified that the twelve legaliores homines from the hundred or the four from the vill should possess a certain social status. But a "law-worthy man" was surely a freeman. The swearing-in of these men is expressly mentioned. The hundred was a subdivision of the county, and the vill of the hundred. (16) The whole procedure was therefore a very local affair. The task of the jurors was to present suspected delinquents to the judicial authorities of the realm. It is this obligation of presentment that has led commentators to see in the "Assizes of Clarendon" the beginning of the Grand Jury.

It is not easy to evaluate who benefited most from the undeniable democratization this document brought into the judicial procedure. The king could no longer have people arrested on the mere suspicion of one of his officers, but neither could the barons do so. Probably it was the general population, who in this kind of grand jury participated actively in the judiciary. This jury could not only present or indict a person, it could also in many cases determine what kind of trial the prisoner was to undergo. This eventually led to the emergence of the Petit Jury, and in order to understand this a brief survey of the different modes of trial and their development in twelfth century England is necessary.

The word "trial" is derived from Old French trier," to pick out, to sift." Trier, in turn, comes from Vulgar Latin tritare, intensive of terere," to rub, to grind," in the technical sense of "threshing" (Classical Latin triturare, English "triturate"). The original idea of "trial" must thus have been something like "separating the bad from the good." This could be done in a number of ways and since God and the Church knew best what good was and what bad, most early forms of trial were designed to provoke the verdict of heaven.

The main modes of deciding issues at law in England during the twelfth century were ordeal, wager of law, battle, and exoneration by witnesses.

The most ancient mode of trial and the one most commonly used for free men was the ordeal. (17) The idea is demonstrated by the ordeal of the hot iron. The accused had to take a hot iron into his bare hands (usually at a solemn moment of the mass) and walk nine feet with it. Then his hand was bandaged ("sealed") for three nights, and afterwards inspected. "If it is clean, God be praised; but if unhealthy matter is found where the iron was held he shall be deemed guilty and unclean." (18) It must be added, however, that Maitland investigated a period of eighteen years and found only one such ordeal that did not acquit the defendant. (19)

Wager of law (20) was essentially a character test. The accused person had to produce a number of people who declared upon oath that they believed that the defendant would never commit perjury and therefore his swearing that he was innocent must mean that he was not guilty. These compurgators did not swear to the facts but solely to the character of the indicted person. In actions of debt and detinue this character test was not abolished until 1833. (21)

Battle (22) was a mode of trial that could only be used in civil cases because the king did not battle in lawsuits. (23) Very often champions who traveled from trial to trial fought for the parties, and a real "battle business", complete with managers, seems to have sprung up around the custom. (24)

Exoneration by witnesses (25) was not a trial in the modern sense either. It was simply a question of which party could produce more people who would swear that the facts were as it alleged. A slip of the tongue could be fatal; this was important at a time when people took oaths most seriously. Some of the witnesses were examined but this custom fell into disuse and the examination and cross-examination of witnesses in the modern sense came from another tradition. (26)

Behind all these forms of trial was the idea that the court only meted out "medial judgment", i.e. a judgment that followed as a matter of course from the verdict of God as expressed in the tests and trials the accused had to undergo. The result was that prisoners could choose "between half a dozen different procedures according to the nature of their cases". (27) By the end of the twelfth century, however, only the ordeal was used extensively in criminal cases (28), the defects of the other ancient modes having gradually become apparent.

If the jury could declare whether an accusation was made maliciously or with good reason, whether the accused was likely to be involved in a crime, if, in other words, it could present or indict him (functions of a grand jury), why could it not decide whether he was guilty or innocent in the first place (functions of the petit jury)?

Developments in Rome made an answer to this question mandatory. In 1215 Pope Innocent III, during the Fourth Lateran Council, forbade the clergy to participate in ordeals. (29) Moreover, the pope intervened directly in the dispute between the barons and King John. In a letter dated March 19, 1215, he advanced the idea that the king should abandon judicial practices which in some cases at least had become rather arbitrary. Innocent quoted this his own letter in a later one (apparently to "the people of England" (30) ), which he probably signed on June 18, 1215. In it he advised John: "Ita quod si forte non posset inter eos concordia provenire; in curia sua per pares eorum secundum Regni consuetudines atque leges mota deberet dissensio terminari; ..." (31) Here we already find the two ideas of "trial by peers" ("per pares suorum dissensio terminari") and "law of the land" or "common law" ("Regni consuetudines"). John's letter patent of May 10, announcing his terms to the barons, was apparently based on the Pope's admonitions of March 19, and it is very instructive to notice the changes in wording:

> Rex omnibus ad quos littere presentes pervenirent salutem. Sciatis nos concessisse baronibus nostris qui contra nos sunt quod nec eos nec homines suos capiemus nec dissaisiemus nec super eos per vim vel per arma ibimus nisi per legem regni vel judicium parium suorum in curia nostra, donec consideracio facta fuerit per quatuor quos elegimus ex parte nostra et quatuor quos eligent ex parte sua et dominum Papam qui superior erit super eos, et de hoc securitatem eis faciemus quam poterimus et quam debimus per barones nostros. (32)

The formulation of this letter is sufficiently close to that of the "Articles of the Barons" (ca. June 15) and of Magna Carta itself that we can assume that it actually furnished the model for these later documents. Articles 28 and 29 of the "Articles of the Barons" read as follows:

> Ne aliquis Ballivus possit ponere aliquem ad legem, simplici loquela sua sine testibus fidelibus.
>
> Ne corpus liberi hominis capiatur, nec imprisonetur, nec dissaisietur, nec utlaghetur, nec exuletur, nec aliquo modo destruatur, nec Rex eat vel mittat super eum vi nisi per juditium parium suorum vel per legem terre. (33)

This corresponds to chapters 38 and 39 of the Magna Carta of 1215:

> Nullus ballivus ponat decetero aliquem ad legem simplici loquela sua sine testibus fidelibus ad hoc inductis.
>
> Nullus liber homo capiatur vel imprisonetur aut dissaisietur aut utlaghetur, aut exuletur, aut aliquo modo destruatur, nec super eum mittemus nisi per legale juditium parium suorum vel per legem terre. (34)

One must understand these provisions within the context of the considerable weakening of the ordeal by the pope and in connection with the counsels to John from Rome.

Magna Carta was thus not an edict by the king alone. It was a compromise between the king and the barons, arrived at after foreign intervention and intensive bargaining. In a sense the barons had the support of the Pope, but it would be misleading to assume that John was destitute of all followers: he had good counselors like Stephan Langton, archbishop of Canterbury, and William, the Earl Marshal, and although a great many of his subjects had deserted him for the barons, those mentioned in the preamble of Magna Carta were probably true to his cause.

Chapters 38 and 39, quoted above, are notably silent in regard to the number and venue of those who are to be the triers of fact. The provision that the judgment was to be a _legale juditium parium suorum_ is a novelty in this context but it reflects the general European feudal notion that a vassal had the right to be tried by his fellow vassals. (35) The goal of Magna Carta was no doubt to curb the royal power and to give the freemen back their ancient rights, but chapter 39 did not do what, judging from the circumstances, one should have expected it to do: establish a definite mode of procedure, binding on king and barons. It did, however, assert that judgment should precede execution, a principle that was by no means universally accepted at that time. (36) It is to the assertion of this principle that Holt ascribed the greatness of this chapter. (37)

What was meant by _pares_ in this context? "The 'peers' of a Crown tenant were his fellow Crown tenants, who would normally deliver judgment in the _Curia Regis_; while the 'peers' of the tenant of the mesne lord were the other freeholding tenants assembled in the Court Baron of the manor." (38) What the barons wanted, then, was simply to be judged by those who were at least their equals; it is possible that this did not exclude judgment by superiors. (39) Trial by peers was a general right of all freeholders. (40)

It would be misleading to assume that trial by peers as demanded in Magna Carta meant trial by jury. (41) Judgment by peers did not include recognition and presentment. (42) The peers were rather to act as domesmen, i.e. judges "appointed to doom (judge) on matters in controversy." (43) They passed a judicium but "the verdict of a jury, the testimony of a body of neighbour witnesses was in no sense a judicium." (44) The jury was not made up of peers, as is shown by the trial of Thomas de la Hethe, who had twenty-four knights on his jury. (45) It was just another form of ordeal:

> At first, the jury was no more regarded as "rational" than the ordeals which it replaced, and just as one did not question the judgment of God as shown by the ordeal, so the verdict of a jury was equally inscrutable. It is but slowly that the jury was rationalised and regarded as a judicial body. (46)

If the jury was simply an instrument by which deity could express its will, it did not need to be specially qualified for its job: God could express his verdict through anybody. But as its judicial functions developed and the whole system became rationalized the idea emerged that it would be an advantage if the jurors knew something about the circumstances of the case or had even witnessed the facts at issue themselves. They would thus be able to judge the matter better than somebody entirely ignorant of facts and circumstances. Plucknett declared that the character of the jury was that of witnesses:

> While Sir Thomas Smith was describing the jury as a purely judicial body, and statute was compelling the attendance of witnesses, jurors were still allowed to use their own knowledge in reaching a verdict, and might reach a verdict although no witnesses and no evidence had been produced. (47)

Brunner pointed out that the jury was a body of witnesses of the defendant's "notoriety" and that special testimony about the crime (in technical terms: evidence) was submitted to it. The evidence was formally subordinated to the general knowlege of the jury. (48) It was not until the days of Cromwell that the King's Bench, then called the Bancus Superior, decided that a juror may not secretly tell his fellow jurors about his personal kowledge of the cause, but that he had to submit it to the court publicly, like any other witness. (49) Vicinus facta vicini praesumitur scire was still valid. If the witnesses named in a disputed deed were still alive they were summoned to sit with the jury. (50)

The related idea that the jury had to come from the neighborhood of the place where the facts at issue had occurred also leads to the conclusion that the jurors were, in some respects at least, witnesses. The documents cited above mention various local administrative units in this connection, such as the county, the shire, the hundred, and the vill. (51) Lord Coke mentioned the township, the parish, and the hamlet "within which the matter of fact issuable is alleged" (52) and in England it was not until 1705 that it was declared sufficient for the jury to come from the county. (53)

## THE FORMULATORS

The eminent place held by Sir Edward Coke (1552-1634) as one of the fundamental formulators of American jurisprudence is today accepted by most researchers as a matter of fact. When, in 1648, the "Body of Liberties" of Massachusetts of 1641 (54) was to be revised, the General Court "sent to England for two copies of Sir Edward Coke's commentaries on Magna Carta, among a few other law tomes." (55) Almost from the day of publication of the second, third, and fourth parts of the Institutes (June, 1642), critics recognized that Coke's account of medieval English law was less than historically watertight. Holt pointed out, however, that a critique of Coke's interpretation of Magna Carta is a somewhat futile academic exercise because we ourselves, after centuries of progress in historical scholarship, do not know exactly what the words used in the Great Charter meant in 1215, very likely because in that compromise between the king and the barons the wording was often intentionally vague. (56) Coke's interpretation of Magna Carta was a formative force in the construction of the American legal system:

> In many ways, Coke was to become the juristic progenitor of the men who were to make the American Revolution. James Otis, Patrick Henry, John Adams - to name but a few - were all nurtured upon Coke's writings and the example of his career. (57)

> Sir Edward Coke, through his Institutes of the Laws of England had created a new myth and prepared Magna Carta for export overseas, and it soon became operative in another world. (58)

His method was to commet every phrase and even single words extensively, much as McKechnie was to do almost three hundred years later. What is meant, for example, by Per judicium parium suorum?

> By judgement of his Peers. Onely a Lord of Parliament of England shall be tried by his Peers being Lords of Parliament, and neither Noble men of any other Country, nor others that are called Lords, and are no Lords of Parliament, are accounted Pares, Peers within this Statute. (59)

> And it is here called Judicium parium, and not veredictum, because the Noble men returned, and charged, are not sworn, but give their judgment upon their Honour, and ligeance to the King, ... (60)

At another point in his Second Institutes, Coke elaborated on his conception of "by his peers":

By his Peers, that is, by his equals.
The general division of persons by the Law of <u>England</u>, is either one that is noble, and in respect of his nobility of the Lords house of Parliament, or one of the Commons of the Realme, and in respect thereof, of the house of Commons in Parliament: and as there be divers degrees of Nobility, as Dukes, Marquesses, Earles, Viscounts, and Barons, and yet all of them are comprehended within this word, <u>Pares</u>, so of the Commons of the Realm, there be Knights, Esquires, gentlemen, Citizens, Yeomen, and Burgesses of several degrees, and yet all of them of the Commons of the Realm, and as every of the Nobles is one a Peer to another, though he be of a several degree, so is it of the Commons; and as it hath been said of Men, so doth it hold of Noble Women, either by birth, or by marriage, but see hereof <u>Cap.</u> 29. (61)

The importance of this interpretation of Magna Carta lies in the fact that it formed the basis of the American Constitutional movement. (62) Max Radin, in his <u>Handbook</u> (63), pointed out that Coke not only created the myth of Magna Carta, but also formulated the "much more deleterious myth of the Common Law as a complete system 'locked in the brains of the judges' who by a mystical but not specified process declare law without making it". (64)

Coke opposed royal power with an appeal to the "ancient rights of Englishmen". His own account of his clash with James I gives us a good picture of the issue involved:

> King: "This means that I shall be under law, which is treason to affirm".
> Coke: "Bracton saith, quod Rex non debet esse sub homine, sed sub Deo et lege". (65)

Whether it is true or not that he was essentially a conservative with the outlook of a Tudor statesman (66), when the American Colonists found themselves in dispute with their king, they could again and again rely on the authority of the eminent British jurist. Moreover, Coke's appeal to the written laws and charters gave the Colonists the conviction that it was necessary for them to draw up such laws and charters themselves. The same is true for the successors of James who wrote elaborate charters for their colonies. American constitutional law was therefore highly codified from the beginning, and the best trained jurists of the colonies applied themselves to the task of writing constitutions as the law of the land.

Thus even if Coke "manipulated medieval 'precedents' and used them to support his 17th-century view of the common law" (67) and although both the historians and the lawyers have pointed out many inaccuracies in his interpretation of Magna Carta, (68) he created a myth and a model of procedure against royal prerogatives that were of utmost influence in America.

Because of his intellectual abilities and the political circumstances of his career, Lord Coke became the expositor of the common law to the American revolutionaries and lawyers. But he had written in the first half of the seventeenth century, and his language, frequently interspersed with Latin and law-French, could not be effectively used for political oratory in the late eighteenth century. The American revolutionaries needed catching phrases and inspiring formulations that would appeal to the public and prove their point about King George's supposedly illegal acts. They were fortunate that from 1765 to 1769 a four-volume compendium of Commentaries on the Laws of England was published in London. It was not as difficult to read as Coke's Institutes, the language was almost poetic and the key sentences were easy to remember. Its author was William Blackstone (1723-1780). In the third volume of his Commentaries he included a chapter "Of the Trial by Jury". (69) A few papagraphs will, without further analysis, illustrate his style and method.

> But I will not mispend [sic] the reader's time in fruitless encomiums on this method of trial; but shall proceed to the dissection and examination of it in all its parts, from whence indeed its highest encomium will arise, since the more it is searched into and understood, the more it is sure to be valued. And this is a species of knowledge most absolutely necessary for every gentleman in the kingdom: as well because he may be frequently called upon to determine in this capacity the rights of others, his fellow-subjects; as because his own property, his liberty, and his life, depend upon maintaining, in its legal force, the constitutional trial by jury. (70)
> Let us now pause awhile, and observe (with Sir Matthew Hale) in these first preparatory stages of the trial, how admirably this constitution is adapted and framed for the investigation of the truth beyond any other method in the world. (71)
> Upon these accounts the trial by jury ever has been, and I trust ever will be, looked upon as the glory of the English law. ... And therefore a celebrated French writer, (Montesquieu, Spirit of laws, xi, 6) who concludes, that because Rome, Sparta, and Carthage have lost their liberties, therefore those of England in time must perish, should have recollected that Rome, Sparta, and Carthage, at the time when their liberties were lost, were strangers to the trial by jury. (72)

The more technical sections are written in the same lucid and facile style. Blackstone's is not the penetrating intellect that could pry open the secrets of the law, but he had the undeniable ability to present the most complicated problems in a pleasing prose. In the long run he was much more popular in the United States than in Great Britain, no doubt partly because of these qualities. One of the methods of measuring this popularity is to compare the number and dates of the American and the British editions of his work.

The National Union Catalog, Pre-1956 Imprints (73) lists the editions of the Commentaries in vol. 59, on pages 640 to 657. Only complete editions and reimpressions will be taken into account here. A statistical analysis reveals the following data: British editions range from the first, in 1765-1769, to the fifteenth, in 1908. The first American edition was published in 1771-1772 and the most recent one in 1941. There are 62 British editions (including a Canadian one from 1862 since it appeared before the British North America Act of 1867), compared to 153 American ones. Even more surprising is their distribution in time:

Table 6   Distribution in time of British and American editions of Blackstone's Commentaries.

| Decade | British editions | American editions |
|---|---|---|
| 1765-1774 | 11 | 2 |
| 1775-1784 | 7 | 1 |
| 1785-1794 | 5 | 1 |
| 1795-1804 | 7 | 4 |
| 1805-1814 | 4 | 3 |
| 1815-1824 | 5 | 2 |
| 1825-1834 | 4 | 5 |
| 1835-1844 | 6 | 7 |
| 1845-1854 | 2 | 14 |
| 1855-1864 | 5 | 17 |
| 1865-1874 | 1 | 16 |
| 1875-1884 | 2 | 20 |
| 1885-1894 | 1 | 22 |
| 1895-1904 | 1 | 21 |
| 1905-1914 | 1 | 7 |
| 1915-1924 |  | 8 |
| 1925-1934 |  | 1 |
| 1935-1944 |  | 2 |

Source: National Union Catalog, vol. 59, pp. 640-657

From this, the mean years of all editions can be computed. They are:

Mean year of publication for Great Britain:   1814
Mean year of publication for United States:   1872

The same data can be plotted in a rectangular coordinate system with time as the abscissa and the number of editions as the ordinate:

Fig. 13   Distribution in time of British and American editions of Blackstone's Commentaries.

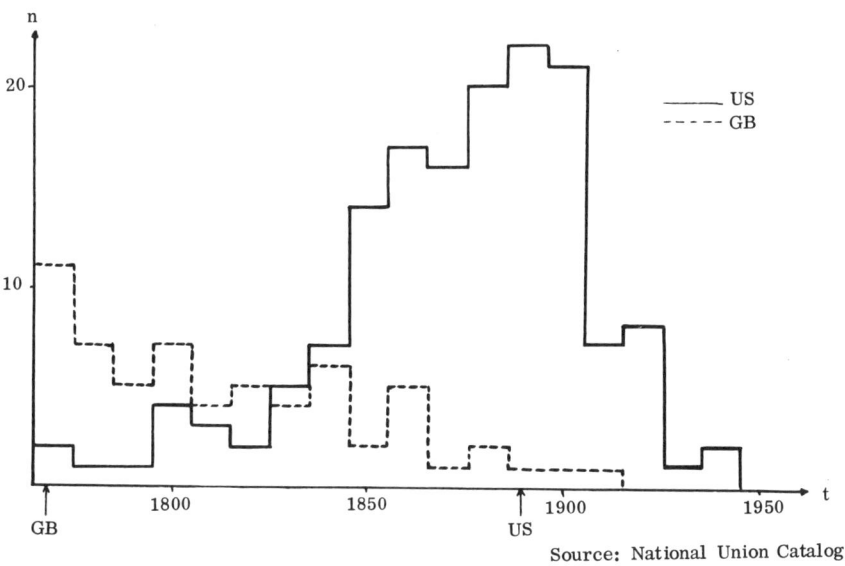

Source: National Union Catalog, loc. cit.

From this graph it is immediately apparent that not only were many more editions of Blackstone published in the United States than in Great Britain, but also that the highest number was only reached a century after the work had appeared in England. In its homeland it was most often reprinted at the beginning, and the mode, i.e. the most commonly occurring value of the collection of dates, lies therefore around 1770 (indicated by an arrow). The mode for the American editions, on the other hand, lies around 1890 (arrow).

The medians, i.e. the years in which half of the editions and reprints had been issued and half of them were yet to come, lie around 1809 for Great Britain and 1876 for the United States.

The average, or arithmetic mean, between mean, mode, and median as a measure of the central tendency of the collection of data comes out at 1798 for Great Britain and 1879 for the United States. The time lag of popularity was therefore eighty years.

The reverence with which Blackstone's work was treated in America throughout the nineteenth century can be seen in the forewords to the editions of the editions of the Commentaries which appeared during that time the United States.

55

In the Chitty edition of 1853, published in Philadelphia, the "Preface by the American Editor" of 1832 is reprinted, in which it was stated that

> The Commentaries of Blackstone continue to be the text book of the student and of the man of general reading, notwithstanding the alterations in the law since the time of their author. The great principles which they unfold remain the same, and are explained in so simple and clear a style, that, however much the details of the law may be changed, they will always be read with interest. (74)

Thomas M. Cooley wrote even more eulogizing "Suggestions Concerning the Study of Law" in his edition of the Commentaries (Chicago, 1884):

> The Commentaries of Mr. Justice Blackstone have now for more than a century been the wonder and delight of persons whose curiosity or interest has led them to investigate the constitution and laws of Great Britain, the condition of things from which they grew, and the reason upon which they rest. Lapse of time does not seem to diminish the attractions, or to lessen materially the practical value of these Commentaries. (75)

There can be no doubt that during the nineteenth century Blackstone was much more highly valued among United States students and lawyers than among their British colleagues.

> The fame of Blackstone in the 19th century was greater in the United States than in Blackstone's native land. After the Declaration of Independence the Commentaries were the chief source of knowledge of English law for the commonwealth of the west. A book which in the old country was and is a textbook became in the new an oracle of law. The results were not always good. What was a true exposition of the spirit of the law in the 18th century England was unreal in the Illinois of Abraham Lincoln. (76)

One of the reasons why Blackstone was so popular in the United States during the second half of the nineteenth century was certainly the way American law education was organized at that time, (77) and with the emergence of the case study method in the law schools Blackstone's fame declined. Nevertheless, in 1953 his statue was erected in front of the United States courthouse for the district of Columbia in Washington, D.C. (78)- to the amused astonishment of knowledgeable British visitors to that city.

It is no coincidence that both Coke and Blackstone heralded or reflected important developments on both sides of the Atlantic. One of the consequences of the constitutional upheavals which took place in England after 1628 was the so-called Great Emigration of 1628-1640 during which two hundred thousand people left England and some twelve hundred sea voyages were made to America. (79) The emigrants carried with them their grievances against the king, which included, among other things, that

> where also, by the Statute called The Great Charter of the Liberties of England, It is declared and enacted, That no Freeman may be taken or imprisoned or be disseised of his Freehold or Liberties or his free Customes, or be outlawed or exiled or in any manner destroyed, but by the lawfull Judgment of his Peers or by the Law of the Land; ... (80)

Trial by jury was also one of the central themes of British politics at the debates of the second convention parliament of February, 1689. This body adopted a Declaration of Rights and presented it to William and Mary, who accepted it. The Declaration was then embodied in the Bill of Rights of October of the same year, in which the illegal acts of James II were summarized, his abdication was announced, and William and Mary were declared king and queen.

One of the points of grievance against James was that

> of late years Partiall, Corrupt, and Unqualified Persons have been returned and served on Juryes in Tryalls, and particularly diverse Jurors in Tryalls for High Treason, which were not Freeholders, ... (81)

William of Orange thereupon promised that "jurors ought to be duly impanelled and returned, and jurors which pass upon men in trials for high treason ought to be freeholders." (82)


## TRIAL BY JURY IN AMERICA UNTIL THE ADOPTION OF THE FEDERAL CONSTITUTION

The Englishmen who crossed the Atlantic to settle in the American Colonies brought with them all the fundamental rights and liberties of free British subjects. Considering the general constitutional history of Great Britain this is not surprising. What intrigues the historian interested in the development of institutions is the uniformity of the formulations used in defining the legal relationship of the Colonies to the mother country. For a hundred and fifty years this relationship was described in unvarying terms: the settlers had "all the liberties of free-born British subjects," they could "enact laws as near as may be" to their British models, but they had to be "not contrary or repugnant" to those of England.

The charter granted for the settlement of America by Elizabeth I to Sir Walter Raleigh on March 25, 1584, affirmed that the Colonists took with them to the New World all the rights and liberties of British subjects:

> And wee doe graunt to the saide Walter Ralegh, ... and to all, and every of them, ... that they ... being either borne within our saide Realmes of Englands, ... shall and may have all the privileges of free Denizens, and persons native of England, ... (83)

The queen then authorized Raleigh to enact laws and statutes, a privilege already accorded to his half-brother, Sir Humphrey Gilbert in 1578 (84) with the same limitations: the laws and statutes must be "as near as may be, convenient" to those in Britain:

> So always as the said statutes, lawes, and ordinances may be as neere as conveniently may be, agreable to the forme of the lawes, statutes, government, or pollicie of England, ... (85)

These provisions are repeated in the First Charter of Virginia (1606) by James I:

> Also we do, for US, our Heirs, and Successors, DECLARE, by these Presents, that all and every the Persons being our Subjects, which shall dwell and inhabit within every or any of the said several Colonies and Plantations, and every of their children, which shall happen to be born within any of the Limits and Precincts of the said several Colonies and Plantations, shall HAVE and enjoy all Liberties, Franchises, and Immunities, within any of our Dominions, to all Intents and Purposes, as if they had been abiding and born, within this our realm of England or any other of our said Dominions. (86)

The Second Charter of Virginia (1609) contained in addition to this the clause that the laws of Colonies should be "as near as conveniently may be" (87) to those of England. The same formulation is again found at the end of the Colonial period, in the Proclamation of October, 1763, that the "laws and litigations" of America should be "as near as may be, agreeable to the laws of England". (88) In between there is a great number of Colonial charters and laws that use almost identical terms. (89)

Sometimes local circumstances made it advisable not to enact the same laws in America and in Britain. But even in this case, American laws were not be "contrary or repugnant" to those of England:

> ... and also to make, ordaine, and establish all Manner of Orders, Laws, Directions, Instructions, Forms, and Ceremonies of Government and Magistracy fitt and necessary for and concerning the Government of the said Collony and Plantation, so always as the same be not contrary to the Laws and Statutes of this our Realme of England, ... (90)

This is again a formulation that can be found in many charters, down to the Charter of Georgia of 1732. (91)

Trial by jury is one of the franchises which could conveniently be transferred to the new environment and we find allusions to it in various documents. A very comprehensive statement was made in this respect in the Massachusetts "Body of Liberties", mentioned above. (92) It contains interesting details on the right to trial by jury, jury selection, and the duties of the jurors:

> 29. In all Actions at law it shall be the libertie of the plaintife and defendant by mutual consent to choose whether they will be tryed by the Bench or by a Jurie, unlesse it be where the law upon just reason hath otherwise determined. The like libertie shall be granted to all persons in Criminall cases.
>
> 30. It shall be in the libertie both of the plaintife and defendant, and likewise every delinquent (to be judged by a Jurie) to challenge any of Jurors. And if his challenge be found just and reasonable by the Bench, or the rest of the Jurie, as the challenger shall choose it shall be allowed him, and tales de cercumstantibus impaneled in their room.
>
> 49. No free man shall be compelled to serve upon Juries above two Courts in a yeare, except grand Jurie men, who shall hould two Courts together at the least.
>
> 50. All jurors shall be chosen continuallie by the freemen of the Towne where they dwell.
>
> 57. Whensoever any person shall come to any very suddaine untimely and unnaturall death, Some assistant, or the Constables of that Towne shall forthwith summon a Jury of twelve free men to inquire of the cause and manner of their death, and shall present a true verdict thereof to some neere assistant, or to the next Court to be helde for that Towne upon their oath.
>
> 76. Whensoever any Jurie of triails or Jurors are not cleare in their Judgments or consciences concerning any cause wherein they are to give their verdict, They shall have libertie in open Court to advise with any man they think fitt to resolve or direct them, before they give their verdict. (93)

The "Fundamental Constitutions of Carolina" (1669) by John Locke, in which monarchial ideas were applied to American circumstances and which never had any legal force, also mentioned trial by jury. After the introduction, in section five, of landgraves and caziques into the American polity, section twenty-seven asserted that "No landgrave or cazique shall be tried for any criminal cause in any but the chief justice's court, and that by a jury of his peers". (94) Sections sixty-six and sixty-eight lay down the duties of the grand jury and the property qualifications for jurymen. (95) Section sixty-nine affirms that "Every jury shall consist of twelve men; and it shall not be necessary that they should all agree, but the verdict shall be according to the consent of the majority". (96) Section one hundred and eleven grants any freeman the right to trial by a jury of his peers in criminal causes. (97)

William Penn's own trial in England makes it understandable that he introduced trial by jury in his American possessions. In his "England's present interests considered" of 1675 he had already referred to Lord Coke in order to assert that "by the law of the land" meant "trial by peers":

> Chief Justice Coke well observes, in his Second Institutes, that per legem terrae, or by the law of the land, imports no more than a trial by process, and writ originally at common law; which cannot be without the lawful judgment of equals, or a common jury: therefore per legale judicium parium , by the lawful judgment of peers, and per legem terrae, by the law of the land, plainly signify the same privilege to the people. (98)

His "Concessions and Agreements of West New Jersey" (1677) are explicit on this point:

> Chapter XVII.
> That no Proprietor, freeholder or inhabitant of the said Province of West New Jersey, shall be deprived or condemned of life, limb, liberty, estate, property or any ways hurt in his or their privileges, freedoms or franchises, upon any account whatsoever, without a due tryal and judgment passed by twelve good and lawful men of his neighborhood first had: And that in all cases to be tryed, and in all tryals, the person or persons, arraigned may except against any of the said neighborhood, without any reason rendered (not exceeding thirty five) and in case of any valid reason alleged, against every person nominated for that service.
>
> Chapter XIX.
> That there shall be in every court, three justices or commissioners, who shall sit with the twelve men of the neighborhood, with them to hear all causes, and to assist the said twelve men of the neighborhood in case of law; and that they the said justices shall pronounce such judgment as they shall receive from, and be directed by the said twelve men, in whom only the judgment resides, and not otherwise.
> ...
>
> Chapter XXII.
> That the tryals of all causes, civil and criminal, shall be heard and decided by the verdict or judgment of twelve men of the neighborhood, only to be summoned and presented by the sheriff of that division, or propriety where the fact of trespass is committed. (99)

The same ideas are expressed in his "Pennsylvania Frame of Government" (1682). In the Preface he stated that "I do not find a model in the world, that time, place, and some singular emergences have not necessarily altered; nor is it easy to frame a civil government, that shall serve all places alike" (100) and trial by jury is mentioned in section eight of "Laws Agreed Upon in England, etc." (101)

The "New York Charter of Libertyes and Privileges" (1683), which was vetoed by the Duke of York in 1684 but substantially enacted under the guise of a new statute in 1691 also asserted this right:

> That Noe freeman shall be taken and imprisoned or be disseized of his ffreehold or Libertye or ffree Customes or be outlawed or Exiled or any other wayes destroyed, nor shall be passed upon adjudged or condemned But by the Lawfull Judgment of his peers and by the Law of his province. ...
>
> And none of the said Amerciaments shall be assessed but by the oath of twelve honest and Lawfull men of the Vicinage provided the faults and misdemeanours be not in Contempt of Courts of Judicature.
>
> All Tryalls shall be by the verdict of twelve men, and as neer as may be peers or Equalls And of the neighborhood and in the County Shire or Division where the fact Shall arise or grow Whether the Same be by Indictment Jnfermacon Declaracon or otherwise against the person Offender or Defendant.
>
> That in all Cases Capitall or Criminall ther shall be a grand Inquest who shall first present the offence and then twelve men of the neighbourhood to try the Offender who after his plea to the Indictment shall be allowed his reasonable Challenges. (102)

With such a legislative record and such charters behind them, one of the main complaints of the revolutionaries about king George III was that he had abridged their right to trial by jury. This was voiced in the "Declaration of Rights and Grievances" of 1765, a reaction to the Stamp Act, in article 7: "That trial by jury is the inherent and invaluable right of every British subject in these colonies". (103) Again, in "The Rights of the Colonists and a List of Infringements and Violations of Rights" of 1772:

> 8. The extending the power of the Courts of Vice Admiralty to so enormous a degree as deprives the people of the Colonies in a great measure of their inestimable right to tryals by Juries: which has ever been Justly considered as the grand Bulwark and security of English property. ... (104)

The first Continental Congress (1774) resolved that

> the respective colonies are entitled to the common law of England, and more especially to the great and inestimable privilege of being tried by their peers of the vicinage, according to the course of that law. ...
> Also the 12 Geo. 3 ch. 24 ... deprives the American subject of a constitutional trial by a jury of the vicinage. ... (105)

61

The value of this institution was similarly asserted in the "Address to the inhabitants of Quebec" of the same year. (106) The Virginia "Declaration of Rights" which had recourse to natural law, not to common law, and Thomas Jefferson's draft of a Virginia Constitution, both of the revolutionary year 1776, mentioned trial by jury. (107) Then the Declaration of Independence itself, of course, reproached George III "for depriving us, in many cases, of the benefit of trial by jury".

The frequency with which trial by jury was integrated into the declarations and constitutions of the several States between 1776 and 1787 shows the importance attributed to the institution at that time. They are therefore briefly mentioned here:

| | |
|---|---|
| 1776: | Delaware Declaration of Rights, sections 13 and 14; Delaware Constitution, art. 25. |
| | Maryland Constitution: Declaration of Rights, art. 3, 17, 18, 19, 21 and Maryland Declaration of Rights, section 29. |
| | North Carolina Declaration of Rights, sections 9, 12, 14. |
| | Pennsylvania Declaration of Rights, sections 9, 11, 25. |
| 1777: | Constitution of Georgia, articles 37-39, 51/52, 55, 61. |
| | Constitution of New York, §§ 13, 61. |
| | Constitution of Vermont, Ch. I, §§ 10, 13, Ch. II, § 22. |
| | Virginia Declaration of Rights, § 10. |
| 1778: | South Carolina Constitution, article 61. |
| 1780: | Massachusetts Constitution, articles 12, 13. |
| 1783: | New Hampshire Bill of Rights, §§ 17, 20, 21. |
| 1784: | New Hampshire Constitution, §§ 15-17. |
| 1786: | Vermont Constitution, Ch. I, § 14. |
| 1787: | Discussion of the original plan for the Northwest Ordinance by Thomas Jefferson. The plan dated back to 1784 and was discussed on Thursday, May 10, 1787, and Wednesday July 11, 1787, with respect to trial by jury. Approved Friday, July 13, 1787 (article II of the Northwest Ordinance of 1787). (108) |
| | Discussion of trial by jury in the Federal Convention on September 12, 1787, in the course of the debate on whether a federal bill of rights would be necessary. (108a) |

George Mason objected to the proposed Constitution of the United States because it did not contain a bill of rights and particularly because of the lack of provisions for a jury in civil causes. (109) James Iredell wrote a pamphlet "Answers to Mr. Mason's objections to the new constitution" in 1788 (110), in which he, a federalist, had this to say about trial by jury:

> There is no danger of the trial by jury being rejected when so justly a favorite of the whole people. The representatives of the people surely can have no interest in making themselves odious, for the mere pleasure of being hated, ... It is in the power of Parliament, if they dare to exercise it, to abolish the trial by jury altogether. But woe

> be to them who should dare to attempt it. It would undoubtedly produce an insurrection, that would hurl every tyrant to the ground who attempted to destroy that great and just favorite of the English nation. (111)

John Dickinson, known under the pen name of Fabius, had published a pamphlet in the same year and in the same series (112), in which he called trial by jury a "heaven-taught institution", "corner-stone of liberty", "palladium", and "our birth-right", reflecting all the stock epithets used for it by the revolutionaries.

The Federalist No. 83 by Publius (Alexander Hamilton) which was first published on May 28, 1788, was more sober in language but just as committed to the cause. It was also concerned with the objection against the proposed plan of government that trial by jury was not guaranteed in civil cases. The opening sentence asserted that

> The objection to the plan of the convention, which has met with most success in this state, and perhaps in several of the other states, is <u>that</u> relative <u>to the</u> <u>want</u> <u>of a</u> <u>constitutional provision</u> for the trial by jury in civil cases. (113)

It appears that the two sides in the constitutional convention were in few things as unanimous as in their esteem for trial by jury:

> The friends and adversaries of the plan of the convention, if they agree in nothing else, concur at least in the value they set upon the trial by jury: Or if there is any difference between them, it consists in this; the former regard it as a valuable safeguard to liberty, the latter represent it as the very palladium of free government. (114)

And, adding his own opinion:

> For my own part, the more the operation of the institution has fallen under my observation, the more reason I have discovered for holding it in high estimation; and it would be altogether superfluous to examine to what extent it deserves to be esteemed useful or essential in a representative republic, or how much more merit it may be entitled to as a defence against the oppressions of an hereditary monarch, than as a barrier to the tyranny of popular magistrates in a popular government. Discussion of this kind would be more curious than beneficial, as all are satisfied of the utility of the institution, and of its friendly aspect to liberty. (115)

Hamilton then proceeded to show that it would be very difficult to enact a constitutional guarantee of trial by jury in civil cases because of the great differences existing in the administration of justice in the various states, and because it would be almost impossible to delimit the boundaries between actions at common law and actions of equity. He concluded with the interesting observation that laws could not guarantee a just government: "The truth is that the general GENIUS of a government is all that can be substantially relied upon for permanent effects. Particular provisions, though not altogether useless, have far less virtue and efficacy than are commonly ascribed to them ; " (116)


## THE LEGAL PROCESS: ARREST, INDICTMENT, TRIAL, AND APPEAL

The rules and regulations governing the legal process in America today have thus a long history that shows a constant and progressive endeavor to protect the accused person from arbitrary "justice". Throughout this history the preservation of the trial by jury has been regarded as essential for an equitable judicature. It is not generally recognized that many so-called fundamental principles of Anglo-Saxon justice have only slowly developed over the centuries or were even unknown until relatively recent times. A striking example is the denial of legal assistance in cases of treason and felony in England because "it was thought to be an insult to the king's judges to suggest that the accused needed help in obtaining justice". (117)
Today a number of built-in safeguards theoretically ensure a suspected person of just and fair treatment during the entire legal process from arrest to appeal. The several steps in this process are described in this section. The main sources were a law enforcement handbook for police (118) and the Revised Statutes of Illinois.
A r r e s t. To be arrested is for most people a very serious infringement of their personal liberty, even if no further legal action ensues. Unjustified arrest may mean loss of time, reputation, credit, and other values. The Magna Carta had therefore already stipulated that "nullus ballivus ponat aliquem ad legem simplici loquela sua sine testibus fidelibus ad hoc inductis". (119) Today certain formalities must be fulfilled until police can arrest a suspect. In cases of crimes (felonies and misdemeanors), for example, a police officer must in most states produce a warrant for the arrest, naming specifically the person to be arrested and the reason for the arrest. An officer may arrest a person without such a warrant only if the crime was committed in his presence, or, in felonies, upon probable cause (i.e. if facts and circumstances are known to the policeman that suggest strongly that a person is engaged in the commission of a crime). Alternatives to arrest are warnings and summonses. (120) After the arrest a suspect must be brought before a magistrate (generally a justice of the peace, or a police magistrate) "without unnecessary delay". (121) The magistrate has to determine whether the arrest was lawful, he has to advise the prisoner of his rights, he must decide whether the prisoner can be held for trial on the basis of the evidence presented by the police, whether the prisoner can be released while awaiting trial and if so, what the amount of bail should be, or whether the accused should be sent to the

"untried department" of the local jail. In minor cases the magistrate can even try the defendant. If this sounds relatively failsafe and simple, it must be remembered that in practice a number of arbitrary decisions must be made: What does "in the presence of the police officer" mean, and what "without unnecessary delay"? At this crucial stage the suspect does not have the benefit of consideration of his case by his peers, or of any regulated trial at all.

In the first place, since the police themselves often make judgments about whether to arrest or merely warn, or question, or advise, and since arrest is itself an unhappy experience for the person arrested, the police decision is a kind of disposition of the case involving weighing of evidence, discretion, and the imposition or nonimposition of a sanction. In the second place, the overwhelming majority of cases that are prosecuted end in a plea of guilty, often resulting from a kind of bargaining between the prosecutor and defense counsel. ... Obviously the functions of prosecutor and defense in this important area of "plea discussions" is quite different from the way it is when they face each other in a trial operating under strict rules of evidence presented above. (122)

In passing, the problem of the "Invisible Man" may be noted: many blacks are arrested simply because white police officers can not see the individual behind the color, because "all Negroes look alike" to them.

Indictment. Even if a magistrate agrees that a suspect was arrested reasonably and that he should be held in custody until trial, the prisoner is not yet formally under accusation. There are various ways in which such a person can be charged with a crime. Technically one can distinguish between presentment, indictment, information, and affidavit or complaint: A presentment is "made by the grand jury of their own motion". An indictment "is preferred at the suit of the government", and is usually framed by the prosecuting officer and "by him laid before the grand jury, to be found or ignored". An information "is filed at the mere discretion of the proper law officer ..., without the intervention or approval of the grand jury ". An affidavit "is a charge made and preferred by an individual". Complaint "is often used interchangeably with affidavit". (123)

In most states the usual way of accusing a prisoner is by indicting him. In other states this has been abolished in favor of the information.

The grand jury, then, is the first group of peers that passes on the fate of a prisoner. In Illinois the way in which grand jurors are drawn and impaneled, and what their duties are, is clearly laid down in the following sections of chapter 74 of the Revised Code of Statutes of 1874:

9. If a grand jury shall be required by law or by the order of the judge for any term of court, it shall be the duty of the county board in each of the counties in this state wherein such court is directed to be holden, at least twenty days before the sitting of such court to select twenty-three persons, possessing the qualifications as provided in section 2 of this act, and as near as may be a proportionate number

from each town or precinct in their respective counties, to serve as grand jurors at such term; ...

below, p. 68) (Section 2, concerning the qualifications for jury duty, will be quoted

§ 16. A full panel of the grand jury shall consist of twenty-three persons, sixteen of whom shall be sufficient to constitute a grand jury.

§ 17. After the grand jury is impaneled, it shall be the duty of the court to appoint a foreman, who shall have power to swear or affirm witnesses to testify before them, and whose duty it shall be, when the grand jury, or any twelve of them, find a bill of indictment to be supported by good and sufficient evidence, to indorse thereon "A true bill; " where they do not find a bill to be supported by good and sufficient evidence, to indorse thereon "Not a true bill;" and shall, in either case, sign his name as foreman, at the foot of said indorsement, and shall also, in each case in which a true bill shall be returned into court as aforesaid, note thereon the name or names of the witness or witnesses upon whose evidence the same shall have been found.

§ 18. Before the grand jury shall enter upon the discharge of their duties, the following oath shall be administrated to the foreman, to-wit:
You, as foreman of this inquest, do solemnly swear (or affirm, as the case may be,) that you will diligently inquire into and true presentment make of all such matters and things as shall be given you in charge, or shall otherwise come to your knowledge, touching the present service; you shall present no person through malice, hatred or ill-will; nor shall you leave any unpresented through fear, favor or affection, or for any fee or reward, or for any hope or promise thereof; but in all of your presentments, you shall present the truth, the whole truth, and nothing but the truth, according to the best of your skill and understanding: so help you God.
And the following oath or affirmation shall be administered to the other jurors, to-wit:
The same oath that A B, your foreman, has just taken before you, on his part, you and each of you shall well and truly keep and observe on your respective parts: so help you God.

§ 19. No grand jury shall make presentments of their own knowledge, upon the information of a less number than two of their own body, unless the juror giving the information is previously sworn as a witness, in which case, if the evidence shall be deemed sufficient, and indictment may be found thereon in like manner as upon the evidence of any other witness who may not be of the jury.

The grand jury is not entirely independent from the executive. Grand jurors are often clearly influenced by the decision of the police and the District (or State's) Attorney to prosecute a suspected person. The District Attorney has been elected by the people to decide which cases should be prosecuted. "He also knows from experience how much it takes to satisfy a judge and to convince a jury". (124) He must lay all the relevant evidence before judge and jury, whether favorable to the government or to the defendant. But in most cases he also wants to be re-elected and he has no interest at all in going ahead with the prosecution of a case where his chances of winning are only slight. The grand jury knows all this, and therefore the screening out of cases which it thinks should not be prosecuted is often rather theoretical:

> The reason we say that grand jury "screening" is only theoretical is because the grand jury is usually so much under the influence of the D.A. that its decisions really are his decisions. (125)

This is strikingly proven also by a linguistic habit. A grand jury which "ignores" the District Attorney's decision is called a "runaway grand jury".
After indictment by the grand jury the case is in the hands of a trial court.

Trial. The proceedings before a grand jury and those in the trial court are presided over by a judge.

> The judge's job is to preside over the trial, to see that prosecutor and defense attorney operate fairly and in accordance with law, to tell the jury at the end of the trial the law bearing on the case, and, if the accused is convicted, to sentence the convicted man.
> It's up to the judge to say what evidence the jury can or cannot hear.
> ...
> At several points during the trial the judge has the job of deciding whether to acquit the defendant without letting the case go to the jury.
> ... The law is that a defendant is entitled to an acquittal without giving any defense or explanations, unless the prosecution first makes a convincing case against him. ...
> If the jury convicts, the judge has the responsibility to reconsider the whole case before judgment and sentence. This is brought about by defense counsel filing a "motion for new trial", listing all the mistakes he thinks have been made during the trial. (126)

The judge, then, is theoretically the administrator of the law; he does not "make" it. This is the job of the legislative branch of government. The courts (i.e. the judges) "are mere instruments of the law, and can will nothing", as John Marshall said. (127) There is of course a whole legal epistemology behind such a statement. It is important to realize that a judge m u s t assume the functions of a legislator if (as often happens) a case comes before him for which he can find no precedent and no legislative enactment. (128) Interminable and soul-searching discussions can be found in the literature about the question whether the judge makes the law or merely pronounces it. Reading such Scholastic argumentation one often wishes the Critique of Pure Reason had been more influential in the United States...

The manner in which a petit jury is to be drawn and impaneled in the State of Illinois is laid down in Chapter 78 of the Revised Statutes (again the 1874 edition will be quoted). The opening section declares that a jury list must be prepared annually:

> § 1. Be it enacted by the People of the State of Illinois, represented in the General Assembly, That the county board of each county shall, at or before the time of its meeting, in September, in each year, or at an any time thereafter, when necessary for the purpose of this act, make a list of a sufficient number, not less than one-tenth of the legal voters of each town or precinct in the county, giving the place of residence of each name on the list, to be known as the jury list.

Section 2 lists the qualifications of the jurors:

> § 2. At the meeting of the county board ... such board shall select from such list a number of persons equal to one hundred for each trial term ... and in the county of Cook, two hundred for each term of the circuit and superior courts of Cook county, and one hundred for the criminal court of Cook county for each trial term, to serve as petit jurors: Provided, that ... in making such selection the board shall take the names of such only as are:
> 
> First - Inhabitants of the town or precinct not exempt from serving on juries.
> 
> Second - Of the age of twenty-one years or upwards, and under sixty years old.
> 
> Third - In the possession of their natural faculties, and not infirm or decrepit.
> 
> Fourth - Free from all legal exemptions, of fair character, of approved integrity, of sound judgment, well informed, and who understand the English language.

Those persons and professions exempt from jury service are enumerated in section 4; they are: federal and state officials of various ranks, ministers, school teachers, physicians, "constant ferrymen", and members of the fire department. (129)

All persons selected for jury service must be checked off from the jury list. They may not again serve as jurors

> till every person named upon such list qualified to serve as a juror has been selected; and all subsequent selections of such jurors by such board shall be made from such list until all persons thereon qualified to serve have been selected, or until expiration of two years from the time of the making of such list, when a new list shall be made. ( § 5)

clerk, A list of persons selected must be kept in the office of the county

> who shall write the name and residence of each person selected upon a separate ticket and put the whole into a box to be kept for that purpose. ( § 7)

The jurors are then drawn in the following manner:

> § 8. At least twenty days before the first day of any trial term of any of said courts the clerk of such court shall repair to the office of the county clerk, and in the presence of such county clerk, after the box containing said names has been well shaken by the county clerk, and without partiality, draw from said box the names of a sufficient number of said persons, ... to constitute the petit jurors for that term ...

The prospective jurors are then summoned by the sheriff to appear in court:

> § 10. The clerk of the court shall, within five days after such drawing, issue to the sheriff a summons commanding him to summon as petit jurors a sufficient number, not less than thirty, of the persons so drawn, giving their residence, to appear at the place of holding such court. ...

> § 11. It shall be the duty of the sheriff to execute the summons by reading the same to, or leaving a copy thereof at the usual place of abode of each of the persons directed to be summoned to constitute the jury as aforesaid, and to make return thereof on or before the return day, to the clerk of the court in which said jurors are to serve, with an indorsement thereon, certifying on whom it has been executed, and the time when; ...

When the jurors appear in court the judge examines them, dismissing those who are exempt or disqualified, and appointing by lot those twenty-four who are to make up the panel;

> § 12. The judge shall examine the jurors who appear, and if more than twenty-four petit jurors who are qualified and not subject to any exemption, or any of the disqualifications provided in this act, shall appear and remain after all excuses are allowed, the court shall discharge by lot the number in excess of twenty-four. ...

It is an offense to actively seek a place on the jury or to solicit someone to become a juror:

> § 13. ... Any person who shall seek the position of a juror, or who shall ask any attorney or other officer of the court or other person to secure his selection as a juryman, shall be deemed guilty of a contempt of court. ... Any attorney or party to a suit pending for trial at that term who shall request or solicit the placing of any person upon a jury, shall be deemed guilty of a contempt of the court. ...

Section 14 lists the causes for challenge:

> § 14. It shall be sufficient cause of challenge of a petit juror that he lacks any of the qualifications mentioned in section two of this act; or if he is not one of the regular panel, that he has served as a juror on the trial of a cause in any court of record in the county within one year previous to the time of his being offered as a juror; or that he is a party to a suit pending for trial in that court, at that term. It shall be the duty of the court to discharge from the panel all jurors who do not possess the qualifications provided in this act, as soon as the fact is discovered: <u>Provided</u>, if a person has served on a jury in a court of record within one year he shall be exempt from again serving during such year, unless he waives such exemption: <u>Provided, further,</u> that it shall not be a cause of challenge that a juror has read in the newspapers an account of the commission of the crime with which the prisoner is charged, if such juror shall state, on oath, that he believes that he can render an impartial verdict, according to the law and the evidence: <u>And, provided, further,</u> that in the trial of any criminal cause, the fact that a person called as a juror has formed an opinion or impression, based upon rumor or upon newspaper statements (about the truth of which he has expressed no opinion), shall not disqualify him to serve as a juror in such case, if he shall, upon oath, state that he believes he can fairly and impartially render a verdict therein, in accordance with the law and the evidence, and the court shall be satisfied of the truth of such statement.

The names of those persons who are selected and not challenged successfully are put in a box and the actual jury of twelve persons is then drawn from this box and impaneled:

> § 20. ... and as often as it shall be necessary to impanel a jury, the clerk, sheriff, or coroner shall, in the presence of the court, draw by chance twelve names out of such box or other place, which shall designate the twelve to be sworn on the jury, and in the same manner for the second jury, in their turn, as the court may order and direct.

Many of the above provisions are impracticable in counties of several hundred thousand inhabitants. On June 9, 1897, the General Assembly approved therefore a Jury Commissioners Act, which is supplemental, not amendatory, to the Jurors Act. (130) It provided for jury commissioners in counties of 250'000 inhabitants and more (Cook county was then the only such county). It is the duty of these jury commissioners to prepare a jury list and to assist in the selection of jurors. They are chosen by the judges:

> Section 1. In every county of this State now containing, or which may hereafter contain, more than two hundred and fifty thousand (250'000) inhabitants, the judges of the several courts of record of such county, or a majority of them, shall choose three competent and discreet electors, who shall not be so chosen on account of party affiliations, who shall be known as the jury commissioners. ...

In counties with a population of less than 250'000, operating under the Jurors Act, a jury list of one-tenth of the legal voters is to be prepared annually (131); in the more populous counties such a list must be prepared every four years:

> § 2. The said commissioners upon entering the duties of their office, and every four years thereafter, shall prepare a list of all electors between the ages of twenty-one and sixty years, possessing the necessary legal qualifications for jury duty, to be known as the jury list. The list may be revised and amended annually, in the discretion of the commissioners. The name of each person on said list shall be entered in a book or books to be kept for that purpose, and opposite said name shall be entered the age of said person, his occupation, if any, his place of residence, giving street and number, if any, whether or not he is a householder, residing with his family, and whether or not he is a freeholder.

The jury commissioners then must select prospective jurors from these quadrennial jury lists. (132) After serving, a juror was exempt "during the life of the list". (133) The Jury Commissioners Act was amended by the Law of 1931 which further provided for the drawing of the jurors in the following manner:

> § 9. One or more of the judges ... shall certify to the clerk of the court the number of petit jurors required each month. The clerk shall then repair to the office of the jury commissioners and there, in the presence of the persons mentioned in section 8 of this Act, proceed to draw by lot the necessary number of names from those made available for such drawing as in section 8 of this Act provided. The clerk shall thereupon certify to the sheriff the electors whose names are so drawn, to be summoned according to the law.

The Jurors Act and the Jury Commissioners Act therefore provide an elaborate system of rules to ensure that those who serve on juries
- have certain basic qualifications ( § 2 of Jurors Act)
- do not serve too often ( § § 5, 14)
- are drawn impartially ( § 8, § 9 of Jury Commissioners Act),

- are examined by a judge ( § 12), and
- are capable of rendering an impartial verdict ( § 14).

Such a system is no luxury. To the average jury the many safeguards against arbitrary legal action that were outlined at the beginning of this section make it seem very unlikely that an entirely innocent person would be subjected to a trial.

A person charged with crime is in very serious trouble. He's got a lot going against him. There's a big, professional detective force [ i.e. the police ] looking for evidence against him. The judge and the jury are inclined to believe, as anybody would, that the accused is most likely guilty or else the police wouldn't have arrested him, the magistrate wouldn't have held him, the grand jury wouldn't have indicted, and the prosecuting attorney wouldn't be pushing for conviction. (134)

The defendant does of course have the benefit of assistance of counsel, whose main job, it seems, is to keep innumerable deadlines, to find his way through a maze of rulings and regulations, and to convince the jury with oratorial skill that his client is either innocent or that he deserves the smallest possible punishment. Judge Samuel F. Miller portrayed the rhetorical side of defense work when he said, in his opinion of the court in the Slaughter-House Cases:

> The eminent and learned counsel who has twice argued the negative of this question [ i.e. can the legislature of a state grant exclusive privileges to citizens or corporations? ], has displayed a research into the history of monopolies in England, and the European continent, only equalled by the eloquence with which they are denounced. (135)

It is this that makes the American courtroom scene so eminently usable for detective stories and motion pictures.

Appeal. If the statutory safeguards have been to no avail, if a defendant still believes that he has been treated unfairly, he can move his cause to an appellate court by appeal, certoriari, or writ of error. Such an appellate court decides whether a trial was conducted fairly and lawfully. In England the law of double jeopardy makes the re-trial of a person for the same crime impossible, in the United States a defendant can be tried over again if his conviction has been reversed. In most states, however, courts of appeal cannot control the sentencing.

In Illinois, Appeals to the Appellate Courts and to the State Supreme Court can come from City Courts, including the Municipal Court of Chicago, from the Superior Court of Cook County, from the Circuit Courts, and from County Courts. The State Supreme Court often decides of its own motion whether it will hear a case or not. (136) Under constitutional law it does not generally hear appeals and errors directed from trial courts in criminal cases below misdemeanors. The following table summarizes, by way of an example, how such criminal cases above misdemeanors have been disposed of by the Illinois Supreme Court in the decade of 1910 to 1920.

Table 7   Disposition of judgments of felonies in the Illinois Supreme Court, 1910 - 1919

|      | Affirmed | Reversed |
|------|----------|----------|
| 1910 | 14 | 9 |
| 1911 | 15 | 13 |
| 1912 | 14 | 9 |
| 1913 | 13 | 11 |
| 1914 | 15 | 18 |
| 1915 | 11 | 17 |
| 1916 | 17 | 12 |
| 1917 | 16 | 11 |
| 1918 | 14 | 13 |
| 1919 | 13 | 6 |
| Total | 142 | 119 |
| Percentage | 54.4 | 45.6 |

Source: Constitutional Convention, Bulletin No. 10: "The Justice Department, Jury, Grand Jury and Claim against the State", Springfield: Legislative Reference Bureau, 1919, Table 8 (after p. 896).

The Court thus affirmed about ten per cent more cases than it reversed. In view of the fact that the presumption must always be in favor of the inferior court (137) the high number of reversals is remarkable.

The diagrams below show the ways in which in Illinois cases can at present be moved from police magistrates and justices of the peace to the Appellate Courts and to the Supreme Court.

Fig. 14  Organization of the Illinois Courts - Cook County.

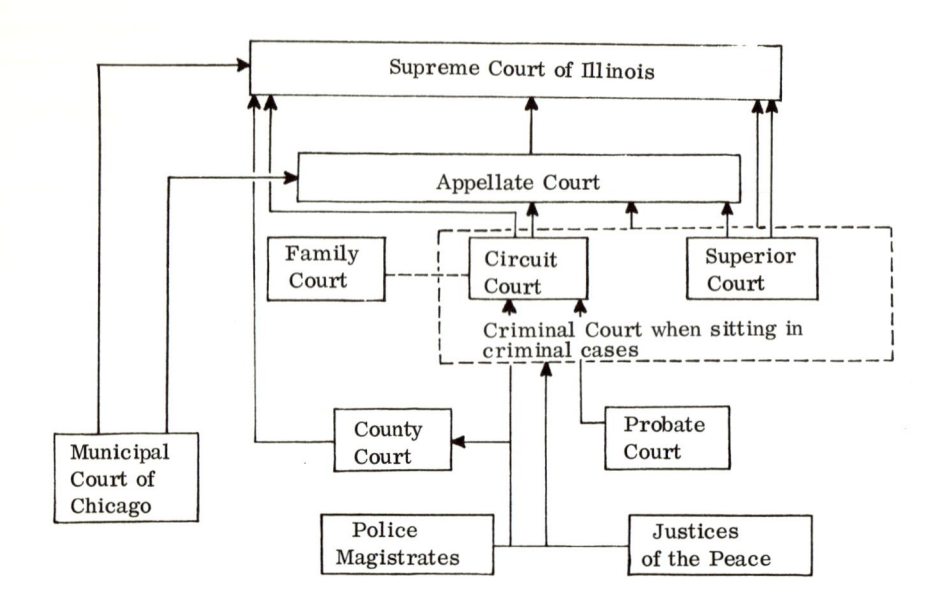

```
                    ┌─────────────────────────────────────┐
                    │     Supreme Court of Illinois       │
                    └─────────────────────────────────────┘
                         ▲   ▲       ▲           ▲   ▲
                         │   │       │           │   │
                    ┌────┴───┴───────┴───────────┴───┴────┐
                    │          Appellate Court            │
                    └─────────────────────────────────────┘
                         ┌──────────┐   ┌──────────┐   ┌──────────┐
                         │ Family   │   │ Circuit  │   │ Superior │
                         │ Court    │───│ Court    │   │ Court    │
                         └──────────┘   └──────────┘   └──────────┘
                                   Criminal Court when sitting in
                                   criminal cases
                                        ▲
                         ┌──────────┐   │   ┌──────────┐
   ┌──────────┐          │ County   │       │ Probate  │
   │Municipal │          │ Court    │       │ Court    │
   │Court of  │          └──────────┘       └──────────┘
   │Chicago   │               ▲
   └──────────┘          ┌──────────┐   ┌──────────┐
                         │ Police   │   │ Justices │
                         │Magistrates│  │of the Peace│
                         └──────────┘   └──────────┘
```

Source: Neil F. Garvey, The Government and Administration of Illinois, New York: Crowell, 1958, p. 221

Fig. 15    Organization of the Illinois Courts, exlusive of Cook County.

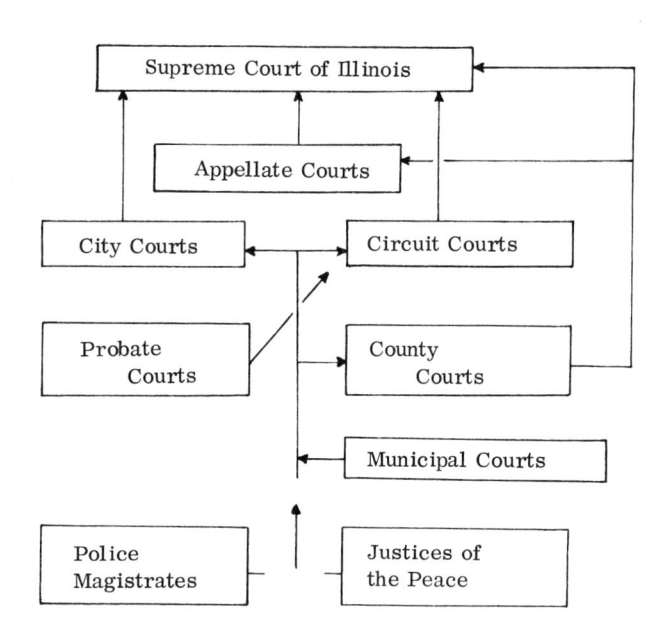

```
                    ┌─────────────────────────┐◄────────────
            ┌──────►│ Supreme Court of Illinois│             │
            │   ▲   └─────────────────────────┘             │
            │   │             ▲                              │
            │   │   ┌──────────────────┐                     │
            │   │   │ Appellate Courts │◄────────────────    │
            │   │   └──────────────────┘                │    │
    ┌───────────────┐        │  ┌────────────────┐      │    │
    │  City Courts  │◄───────┼─►│ Circuit Courts │      │    │
    └───────────────┘       ╱│  └────────────────┘      │    │
                           ╱ │                          │    │
    ┌───────────┐         ╱  │  ┌───────────┐           │    │
    │  Probate  │────────╱   ├─►│  County   │           │    │
    │  Courts   │            │  │  Courts   │           │    │
    └───────────┘            │  └───────────┘           │    │
                             │  ┌──────────────────┐    │    │
                             │◄─│ Municipal Courts │    │    │
                             │  └──────────────────┘    │    │
                             ▲                          │    │
    ┌───────────┐            │   ┌─────────────┐        │    │
    │  Police   │            │   │ Justices of │        │    │
    │Magistrates│────────────┘   │  the Peace  │        │    │
    └───────────┘                └─────────────┘        │    │
```

Source:  Garvey, op. cit.,
p. 218

CONCLUSION

What was the history and the development of the trial by jury?
From the beginning, there was in the United States an appeal to Magna Carta as the origin of the institution, but we can trace it back even further: to the Frankish empire of the ninth century. From there it had come to Normandy and William the Conqueror took it to Britain. The original purpose of the institution was fiscal; it was used for tax assessment and population censuses. Henry II was the first to use it for his judicial machinery. For a time trial by jury existed concurrently with other modes of adjudication (like the ordeal), but after the Fourth Lateran Council it became the most important way of accusing and trying a person. The idea behind the older forms of trial (medial judgment) was, however, not changed but integrated into the jury system. The jurors at this time were very

likely in a sense witnesses.

Fig. 16    Development of trial by jury until the 13th century

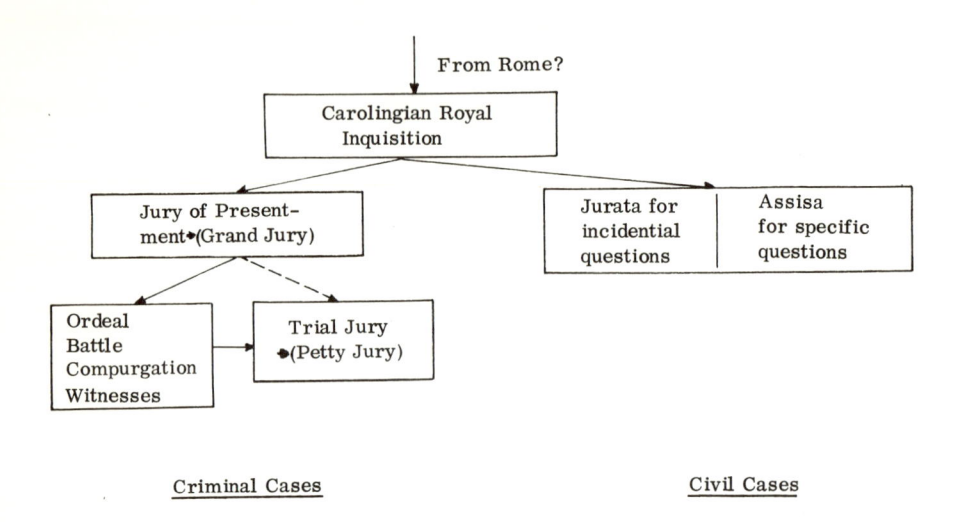

```
                    From Rome?
                        ↓
            ┌───────────────────────┐
            │  Carolingian Royal    │
            │     Inquisition       │
            └───────────────────────┘
           ↙            ↓              ↘
┌──────────────────┐   ┌─────────────┬──────────────┐
│ Jury of Present- │   │ Jurata for  │ Assisa       │
│ ment→(Grand Jury)│   │ incidential │ for specific │
└──────────────────┘   │ questions   │ questions    │
    ↙       ↘          └─────────────┴──────────────┘
┌─────────┐  ┌──────────┐
│ Ordeal  │  │Trial Jury│
│ Battle  │→ │→(Petty   │
│Compurg. │  │  Jury)   │
│Witnesses│  └──────────┘
└─────────┘
```

         Criminal Cases                    Civil Cases

The major mediators and transformers of trial by jury were Lord Coke and Blackstone. Coke was a most able and scientific jurist but he was also politically motivated in his research and he used the argumentation of the barons against John very conveniently in his own altercations with James and Charles. When, a hundred and fourty years later, the American colonists rebelled against yet another British king they could well use the learned expositions of the rights of the people by the eminent British jurist.

76

Fig. 17     The uses of legal argumentation in England and America

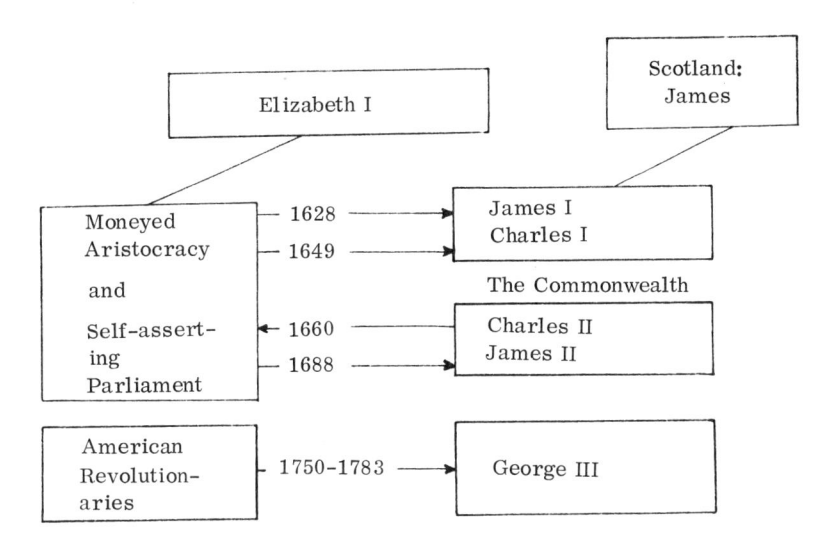

```
                    ┌──────────────┐              ┌──────────────┐
                    │  Elizabeth I │              │  Scotland:   │
                    └──────────────┘              │   James      │
                                                  └──────────────┘

┌──────────────┐      ── 1628 ──→       ┌──────────────┐
│  Moneyed     │                        │  James I     │
│  Aristocracy │      ── 1649 ──→       │  Charles I   │
│  and         │                        └──────────────┘
│  Self-assert-│                         The Commonwealth
│  ing         │      ←── 1660 ──       ┌──────────────┐
│  Parliament  │                        │  Charles II  │
│              │      ── 1688 ──→       │  James II    │
└──────────────┘                        └──────────────┘

┌──────────────┐
│  American    │
│  Revolution- │      ── 1750-1783 ──→  ┌──────────────┐
│  aries       │                        │  George III  │
└──────────────┘                        └──────────────┘
```

Blackstone became operative for different reasons. His message was very timely and his language excellently adaptable to the political contest in the American colonies. For more than a century after the Revolution he held a most prominent place with American jurists (and, consequently, politicians), at a time when he was incomparably less significant in Great Britain.

The formulations used in England to express certain legal relationships were apparently seamlessly woven into the fabric of the American polity. Outstanding early documents are the Massachusetts Body of Liberties of 1641, the declarations by Penn, practically all state constitutions from 1776 to 1789, and the Seventh and Fourteenth Amendments to the Constitution.

The American jury system thus stood from the very beginning under two tacit assumptions: that words have a definite meaning which does not change over the centuries and by being transplanted overseas to another continent, and that they can be used like tools, that they are instruments with which reality can be grasped and operated on. In the light of modern research in philosophy, psychology, and linguistics these assumptions can no longer claim universal acceptance. The American legal tradition was not merely verbal, it was proverbial, in the sense that certain formulations were repeated over and over again, without too much thought about semantic change. Instead of using language, as they thought, American jurists were used by it.

This is apparent if we look at a specific state, like Illinois. Every provision in the state statutes on jurors can be traced back and its origins shown in Continental Europe or England. The main qualifications for a juror are: he must come from the vicinage (county), he must be impartial, between 21 and 60 years of age, and he must be drawn at random. An industrial county on the shores of Lake Michigan and an medieval county in England may not have much in common and random selection may become a doubtful instrument of selection if it collides with impartiality. But these venerable provisions were always held, in America, to be essential to a fair administration of justice by trial by jury.

The three outstanding results of this section are:
- the jury system was not invented to solve conflicts but to assess taxes and count the population,
- it came down to our days through the interpretation, mainly, of Lord Coke who had his own political purposes, and of William Blackstone, who was a brilliant writer but a somewhat less gifted jurist, and
- it was kept operative by traditional formulations, not necessarily because it answered best the needs of justice.

At this point of the inquiry, then, we can summarize: In the United States and especially in the industrialzed portion of the Midwest there was a minority, set off distinctly from the dominant majority, and although the legal system did contain precedents which did not preclude special provisions for this situation, the rubble of philosophies weighing on it made it appear ill equipped to cope with the particular difficulties.

It is therefore very important to observe how the judges argued and acted in this situation and to what extent their reasoning facilitated or impeded the development of a legal system that could do justice also to the black population. This will be done in the remaining chapter of this book.

CHAPTER III

JUDICIAL REASONING ON TRIAL BY JURY

INTRODUCTION

How did judges interpret and use the instruments analyzed in chapter II in cases involving member of a minority, especially of the black population described in chapter I?

Cases involving the interpretation of the jury system, or of the status of the black population, or of both have been compiled in law reports, treatises, dictionaries, legal encyclopedias, search books, and digests. It is thus relatively easy to find a number of fundamentally important cases. But they are usually only briefly quoted or summarized and on the basis of this material one can do little more than learn the technicalities involved in the question of blacks and the trial by jury. It is therefore necessary to go back to the opinions contained in the Court Reports. See also section 12 of the Bibliography (below, pp. 152-153).

For this dissertation cases from the United States Supreme Court from 1756 to spring, 1972, and cases from the Illinois Supreme Court from 1829 to spring, 1972, were examined.

Theoretically, control cases involving members of the dominant society ("whites and the trial by jury") should be analyzed concurrently. This is, however, not possible within the scope of this book. Many questions treated here do moreover not even arise when a white defendant is before the court and a comparison is therefore often not possible. This does not detract substantially from our findings. To control at least the external data of the cases somewhat the following procedure has been adopted: One hundred random cases were picked out from the 403 volumes of the United States Reports and from the 456 volumes of the Illinois reports, each. This was done with the help of D. B. Owen, Handbook of Statistical Tables, Reading, Mass.: Addison-Wesley, 1962, section 20.2, "Random Numbers", pp. 517-558 which lists 40'000 random digits. These random cases were then compared with the cases on trial by jury analyzed for this chapter. The following are the most salient results:

79

Table 8    Comparison of random cases and cases on trial by jury

|  | Random | Trial by Jury |
|---|---|---|
| a. United States Supreme Court | | |
| coming up from Illinois | 7 % | 1 % |
| lower court judgment approved | 45 % | 56 % |
| reversed | 55 % | 44 % |
| b. Illinois Supreme Court | | |
| coming up from Cook County or Chicago | 45 % | 34 % |
| lower court judgment approved | 57 % | 55.5 % |
| reversed | 43 % | 44.5 % |

The distribution in time of the cases on trial by jury looks like this:

|  | Before 1880 | 1880-1940 | 1940-1972 |
|---|---|---|---|
| United States | 24 % | 52 % | 25 % |
| Illinois | 22 % | 52 % | 27 % |

About 100 cases were selected from the United States Supreme Court after cases which merely repeated precedents had been eliminated (84 are quoted in the text), and about 120 from the Illinois Supreme Court (101 are quoted).

These opinions can be analyzed on two levels: In a first step one can learn "what the law was". The decisions tell us what in the minds of the judges the law of the land said. In a second step one can see how judges argued. The opinions show how some of the best educated Americans interpreted basic problems of their society.

It is obvious that the first step cannot and must not be the main concern of this dissertation. The task of deriving "what the law is" from decisions and opinions has been done by professional jurists who have compiled decisions from all jurisdictions and tried to abstract what is essential in them. If, for example, one wants to know the law on the jury system, one can learn it from the two editions of the Corpus Juris, where a great number of decisions referring to that institution are collected and analyzed.

It is to the second step, therefore, that we turn our main attention. This makes it possible to see not only the mentality of the judge whose opinions we analyze, but also the mentality of a wider public. Judges pronounced their opinions in order to defend their decisions and they presumably chose those arguments which a wider public would accept. A change of these arguments over a period of time would then indicate a change in public opinion on certain values or policies. We must be careful to differentiate between majority and concurring opinions, and dissenting opinions. Dissenting opinions very often contain much more personal views of the judges than majority opinions.

This is how judges themselves described the nature of their decisions: In 1842 the U.S. Supreme Court held that

> In the ordinary use of language it will hardly be contended that the

decisions of Courts constitute laws. They are, at the most, only evidence of what the laws are; and are not of themselves laws. They are often re-examined, reversed, and qualified by the courts themselves, whenever they are found to be either defective, or ill-founded, or otherwise incorrect. The laws of a State are more usually understood to mean the rules and enactments promulgated by the legislative authority thereof, or long established local customs having the force of laws. (1)

And in 1893 the Illinois Supreme Court said:

> Since the decision in Smith v. Eames was announced, the rule stated in the paragraph last quoted has been referred to and followed and has been accepted as the settled law, and it must be now so regarded, except so far as it has been modified by the fourteenth section of the act of 1874 in relation to Jurors. (2)

But the validity of decisions and opinions as laws does not concern us here; it is the mode of reasoning and the values expressed in them that interest us.

COMMON LAW AND STATUTE LAW: HISTORICAL ARGUMENTATION

The preceding chapter has shown that there was an almost seamless transition from the jury of the British common law to the American jury. Early decisions confirm this. Chief Justice M'Kean of the Supreme Court of Pennsylvania held, in a decision dating from the year 1782, that "It is the opinion of the Court, however, that the common law of England has always been in force in Pennsylvania; ... " (3) But the British common law only obtained in America as far as it was "applicable" in the new environment. (4) After the formation of the United States this doctrine became somewhat refined. It was asserted that the basis of the American legal system was not the common law actually in force in Great Britain, but the common law as it existed at the time of the emigration of the first Englishmen to the various colonies. Thirty years after the decision by Chief Justice M'Kean this new doctrine was stated succinctly in a decision of the Supreme Court of the United States in a case coming from Vermont. In Pawlet v. Clark the Court declared in February, 1815:

> Independent, however, of such a provision we take it to be a clear principle that the common law in force at the emigration of our ancestors is deemed the birthright of the colonies unless so far as it is inapplicable to their situation, or repugnant to their other rights and privileges. (5)

This has remained the cornerstone of American jurisprudence:

> The common law of England is not to be taken in all respects to be that of America. Our ancestors brought with them its general principles, and claimed it as their birthright; but they brought with them and adopted only that portion which was applicable to their situation. (6)

The United States as a nation does not have a common law. In a case decided in 1879 the Supreme Court held that

> The Fourteenth Amendment does not profess to secure to all persons in the United States the benefit of the same laws and the same remedies. Great diversities in these respects may exist in two States separated only by an imaginary line. On one side of this line there may be a right of trial by jury, and on the other side no such right. Each State describes its own mode of judicial proceeding. (7)

If great diversity can exist in two different states of the Union there can be no federal common law of the United States. Congress could presumably enact a provision to integrate the common law into the American legal system on the federal level, as was said in the 1834 decision involving two Supreme Court reporters, Wheaton and Peters: "It is clear there can be no common law of the United States. ... The common law could be made a part of our federal system, only by legislative adoption". (8)

Still, even if strictly speaking only the several states have their common laws, there is a common basis for these state laws. There is a set of fundamental rules which is valid in all states and in the Union as a whole. This set of rules is called "the law of the land".

There is little difference between the law of the land and the common law as far as their cardinal ideas are concerned. An early definition of the law of the land is found in a case of 1819, where the issue was whether a charter granted by the British Crown in 1769 was dissolved by the Revolution or not. The answer of the Supreme Court was that a state legislature had no right to alter such charters unilaterally and that therefore the charter was still in force. Counsel for plaintiff in error, Daniel Webster, cited Lord Coke, chapter 39, referring to the lex terrae, and continued:

> By the law of the land is most clearly intended the general law; a law which hears before it condemns; which proceeds upon inquiry, and renders judgment only after trial. The meaning is, that every citizen shall hold his life, liberty, property, and immunities, under the protection of the general rules which govern society. Every thing which may pass under the form of an enactment, is not, therefore, to be considered the law of the land. (9)

This definition has had a long life. It is quoted verbatim, for example, in Powell v. Alabama, one of the famous Scottsboro trials of 1932. (10) It is easy to see how it came to be identical with the idea of "due process of law", (11) and the two terms are indeed today held to be synonymous.

The Illinois Supreme Court has had little opportunity to pronounce on these federal questions. The definition of the law of the land as due process of law was upheld in an 1867 decision. (12) The state does of course have its common law. It has been ruled that only common law modes of trial are possible under the authority of the state. (13) Another decision shows that the common law of Great Britain has not been incorporated unchanged. Its general principles are preserved, and some of them have even more privilege and legal force in Illinois than in the British common law:

> Nor has the common law distinction between principal challenges and challenges to the favor been kept up in this State, still many of the principles growing out of that distinction have been habitually recognized and enforced. Indeed, most of the objections to jurors which at common law were held to be ground of principal challenge, are held with us to be absolute disqualifications, ... (14)

The State of Louisiana, of course, did not inherit the common law from its former mother countries.

There was never any question as to the general validity of the common law in America. The introduction of another legal system was never seriously contemplated. But the notion that only those elements of the common law that were "applicable" in the New World should be in force there created the necessity of some criteria according to which it could be decided whether statutes that were part of the British common law could be held applicable and not repugnant to American circumstances. First attempts at formulating such criteria did not really solve the problem but merely restated it. In the already quoted decision of the Supreme Court of Pennsylvania of 1782, in Morris's Lessee v. Vanderen, Chief Justice M'Kean continued:

> that all statutes made in Great Britain, before the settlement of Pennsylvania, have no force here, unless they are convenient and adapted to the circumstances of the country; and that all statutes made since the settlement of Pennsylvania, have no force here, unless the colonies are particularly named. The spirit of the act of Assembly passed in 1718 supports the opinion of the court. (15)

The most important criterion governing the reception of British statutes in America was time. There was a distinction between statutes enacted before the settlement of the colonies, and those made later, a criterion adhered to by the Supreme Court of the United States in 1831, in Doe v. Winn, which was, like Morris's Lessee v. Vanderen, a proceeding for ejectment: "These statutes being passed before the emigration of our ancestors, being applicable to our situation, and in amendment of the law, constitute a part of our common law". (16) From a formalistic point of view it is easy to see why there was this distinction between statutes that were enacted before the settlement of a colony and those that were enacted later. Still, the question, what "applicable" meant was not answered.

In an early decision, the Court of Oyer and Terminer of Pennsylvania introduced the ratio legis as a test of admission of an English statute into America. It was a murder case in which four Italians were the defendants. (17) The mode of trial, according to common law, wa trial by jury, and counsel for defense demanded a jury de medietate linguae ("of the moiety of the tongue"). This kind of jury was authorized in England by 27 Edward III, statutes 2, c.8 and 28 Edward III, c. 13 of around 1354 and 1355, giving an accused foreign merchant the right to have his case tried by a jury composed half of Englishmen and half of his own nationals. The Court of Oyer and Terminer granted Mesca and co-defendants medietas linguae, but only because the defendants could cite a Pennsylvania precedent case in which this kind of jury was accorded to the accused (Ottenreed; February, 1764). It did not hold that 28 Edward III, c. 13, was in force in Pennsylvania:

> The reasons which gave rise to the 28 Edw. 3 do not apply to the present government, nor to the general circumstances of the country. Prisoners have here a right to the testimony of their evidence upon oath, and to the assistance of Council, as well in matters of fact as of law, which was not the case in England, in the year 1353, when that statute was enacted. We do not think, indeed, that granting a medietas linguae, will, at all, contribute to the advancement of justice; ... (18)

The statute could be deemed in force if it contributed to the advancement of justice, but because the American mode of procedure granted the accused so many rights to protect him from arbitrary conviction a trial de medietate linguae was no longer necessary as a safeguard against unfairness from the bench. Cessante ratione cessat ipsa lex. (19)

This kind of argumentation can be very dangerous. It could be used to abolish many procedural safeguards against abuse by saying that in a system of law "so full of that tenderness and humanity to prisoners, for which our English laws are justly famous" (20) such procedural safeguards are not necessary. Another disadvantage is that the courts have no clear standards - and, consequently, all the discretion - to decide whether a ratio legis which led to the enactment of a statute in England still prevailed in the United States, in other words, if it was still "applicable". The question of applicability remains, but it has been slightly shifted from the field of jurisprudence, in which most judges were presumably trained, to that of history, in which they were not (because the ratio was of course often extra-legal). This had the unfortunate consequence that judges often based their opinions on their views of a particular historical event, a view which was not usually founded on serious scholarship, but at best on a received interpretation, at worst on their own personal belief about some occurrence in the past.

Because historical argumentation is basic to American jurisprudence - the very idea of precedents demands such argumentation - this judicial interpretation of history can be exemplified by any amount of quotations from opinions. A few shall suffice.

Regarding the problem to what extent the American revolution had abolished the unquestionable validity of the British common law in America, one finds the sweeping judgment that the American revolution was not a social revolution. It did not alter the domestic condition or capacity of persons within the colonies, nor was it designed to disturb the domestic relations existing among them. (21)

Sometime historical judgments were buttressed by appeals to reason and common sense:

> As to the words from Magna Carta, incorporated into the constitution of Maryland, after volumes spoken and written with a view to their exposition, the good sense of mankind has at length settled down to this: that they were intended to secure the individual from arbitrary exercise of the powers of government, unrestrained by the established principles of private rights and distributive justice. (22)

Even if in some respects one can agree with the interpretation of Magna Carta in this opinion, written in 1819, one is forced to assume that the certainty with which it was pronounced was the certainty of the uninformed.

Another case in point is the majority opinion in Scott v. Sanford (1856). Chief Justice Taney elaborated on the problem of whether blacks were men or something inferior. He justified his view that blacks under the Constitution of the United States were inherently unfit to associate with whites on an equal footing by showing that the framers of the Constitution could not have meant to introduce egalitarian principles into it as far as Afro-Americans were concerned. Referring to the black population at the time of the Declaration of Independence, Taney said:

> They had for more than a century before been regarded as beings of an inferior order, and altogether unfit to associate with the white race, either in social or political relations; and so far inferior, that they had no rights which the white man was bound to respect; and that the negro might justly and lawfully be reduced to slavery for his benefit. He was bought and sold, and treated as an ordinary article of merchandise and traffic, whenever a profit could be made by it. This opinion was at the time fixed and universal in the civilized portion of the white race. It was regarded as an axiom in morals as well as in politics, which no one thought of disputing, or supposed to be open to dispute; ... And in no nation was this opinion more firmly fixed or more uniformly acted upon than by the English Government and English people. ... The opinion thus entertained and acted upon in England was naturally impressed upon the colonies they founded on this side of the Atlantic. (23)

The use of the word "civilized" in this passage is worth particular notice. This case was admittedly one of the nadirs of American jurisprudence and shall not be presented here as representative of its tradition. (24) Often some attempt at historical "proof" was made. But this historical proof was couched in personal views and, of course, in most cases only those portions of sources were cited which supported the decision. A further example, again from an opinion on the validity of the common law of Great Britain in the United States, shall illustrate this:

> Those who had been driven from their mother country by oppression and persecution brought with them, as their inheritance, which no government could rightfully impair or destroy, certain guaranties of the rights of life and liberty, and property, which had long been deemed fundamental in Anglo-Saxon institutions. In the Congress of the Colonies held in New York in 1765, it was declared that the colonies were entitled to all the essential rights, liberties, privileges, and immunities, confirmed by Magna Carta to the subjects of Great Britain. ... On the 14th of October, 1774, the delegates from the several Colonies and Plantations, in Congress assembled, made a formal declaration of the rights to which their people were entitled, by the immutable laws of nature, the principles of the English Constitution, and the several charters or compacts under which the colonial governments were organized. Among other things, they declared that their ancestors who first settled the colonies were, at the time of their immigration, "entitled to all the rights, liberties, and immunities of free and natural born subjects within the realm of England; " that "by such immigration they by no means forfeited, surrendered, or lost any of those rights, but that they were, and their descendants now are, entitled to the exercise and enjoyment of all such of them as their local and other circumstances entitle them to exercise and enjoy; " and that "the respective colonists are entitled to the common law of England, and more especially to the great and inestimable privilege of being tried by their peers of the vicinage, according to the course of the law". 1 Journal of Congress, 27-8-9.
> These declarations were subsequently emphasized in the most imposing manner, when the doctrines of the common law respecting the protection of people in their lives, liberties and property were incorporated into the earlier constitutions of the original States. (25)

To analyze this briefly: Some remarks about ancestors who were "driven from the mother country by oppression and persecution" are followed by a paraphrase of a declaration of the Continental Congress of 1765 and a quotation from the Journal of Congress. These declarations were "subsequently emphasized in the most imposing manner" in the constitutions of the original states. The point to be made here is not that the conclusions reached are untenable, but that the historical scholarship falls short of what today would be demanded of a university freshman in history (26) and that on the basis of such inadequate research fundamental questions of American jurisprudence were decided.

To return to the problem of "British laws in America": When on a certain question it had been decided whether or not a British statute was in force in America, a further difficulty arose. If the answer was negative, another British or an American statute had to be found, if it was positive it had to be decided what construction this British statute should receive. In common law jurisprudence, the cases decided by means of a certain statute are at least as important as the statute itself, for jurisdictional purposes. If a statute had been construed in British courts, did this construction accompany it over the Atlantic? The most concise answer to this question can be found in a contract case from Washington, D.C., decided by the Supreme Court in January, 1831. There, a statute of Elizabeth I was invoked and the Court ruled:

> The statute of Elizabeth is in force in this district. The rule, which has been uniformly observed by this Court in construing statutes, is to adopt the construction made by the courts of the coutry by whose Legislature the statute was enacted. This rule may be susceptible of some modification, when applied to British statutes, which are adopted in any of these States. By adopting them they become our own as entirely as if they had been enacted by the legislature of the state. The received construction in England at the time they are admitted to operate in this country - indeed, to the time of our separation from the British empire - may very properly be considered as accompanying the statutes themselves, and forming an integral part of them. But however we may respect subsequent decisions, and certainly they are entitled to great respect, we do not admit their absolute authority. If the English courts vary their construction of a statute which is common to the two countries, we do not hold ourselves bound to fluctuate with them. (27)

Here again, the idea of time is stressed. There is a clear distinction between Colonial times before 1776 and the time after the Declaration of Independence. The ascertainment of the interpretation of constructions made in England before the secession of her American colonies implies at least some historical interpretation.

In such a legal system historical research is fundamentally important, even if it doesn't go back to eighteenth-century Britain. In Hurtado v. California (1884), Justice Harlan, in his dissenting opinion, held that the search for British precedents was immaterial in the question whether a trial for crime on information only was constitutional in California:

> Declining to follow counsel in their search for precedents in England in support or in refutation of the proposition that the common law permitted informations in certain classes of public offenses ... let us inquire - and no other inquiry is at all pertinent - whether according to the settled usages and modes of proceeding to which, this court has said, reference must be had, an information for a capital offense was, prior to the adoption of the Constitution, regarded as due process of law. (28)

The ascertainment of what constitutes "settled usages and modes of proceeding"(which is synonymous with "due process of law") is no less a task for the historian than the interpretation of ancient and venerable constructions.

Thus justice is sought in American courts, not by some abstract philosophical inquiry, nor by direct appeal to higher or natural law. There exists a higher law - a heritage from Christianity and the Enlightenment - and it can be found in past charters, statutes, declarations of rights, decisions, and so on. If time has shown that such a decision or statute has served its purpose, if it is settled usage, then it is proven "applicable", just, and therefore "due process of law". Search into the past is the mainstay of the quest for justice.

There is a curious parallel between this notion of justice in American courts and Dewey's conception of an "idea". Dewey's answer to the question: What is an idea?:

> Essentially, says Dewey, it was a plan of action, a proposal to do this or that. If it worked, it was true, in the sense of fulfilling the purpose for which it was brought into being. If it failed to work, it was false.
> ...
> [ His ] philosophy was a philosophy of results. ( 29)

This philosophy of results, or of success, pervades American judicial reasoning to an astonishing extent.


## DEFINITION OF TRIAL BY JURY, RIGHT TO TRIAL BY JURY, AND THE DUTIES OF JUDGES AND JURORS

One of the most important particulars of the "settled modes of proceeding" was and is the trial by jury. In a somewhat verbose opinion of the court, Supreme Court Justice Joseph Story declared in 1830:

> The trial by jury is justly dear to the American people. It has always been an object of deep interest and solicitude, and every enactment upon it has been watched with great jealousy. ... One of the strongest objections originally taken against the constitution of the United States, was the want of an express provision securing the right of trial by jury in civil cases. As soon as the constitution was adopted, this right was secured by the seventh amendment of the constitution proposed by Congress; and which received an assent of the people so general as to establish its importance as a fundamental guarantee of the rights and liberties of the people. (30)

In spite of this and similar views, (31) trial by jury has not been held indispensable by the Supreme Court. In one decision the Court declared that trial by jury might be abolished; (32) what is preserved by the Constitution is merely the right to such a trial.

The essential elements of this mode of trial are that:

- It is a trial by twelve men,
- It is in the presence and under the superintendence of a judge vested with the necessary authority, and
- The petit jury verdict must be unanimous. (33)

The reason why this "fundamental guarantee of the rights and liberties of the people" - which on the basis of this definition does not seem much preferable to other forms of procedure - has "always been an object of deep interest and solicitude" is that it is understood to incorporate the egalitarian ideal and carry democracy into the administration of justice:

> It is part of the established tradition in the use of juries as institutions of public justice that the jury be a body truly representative of the community. (34)

The development of the American jury system must be seen within the framework of the political ideals of the country:

> But even as jury trial, which was a privilege at common law, has become a right with us, so also, whatever limitations were inherent in the historical common law concept of the jury as a body of one's peers do not prevail in this country. Our notions of what a proper jury is have developed in harmony with our basic concepts of a democratic society and a representative government. ... And, its exercise must always accord with the fact that the proper functioning of the jury system, and, indeed, our democracy itself, requires that the jury be a "body truly representative of the community", and not the organ of any special group or class. (35)

The jury as a body must be representative of the community. Nothing is said about the individual juror in this respect. This has important theoretical consequences. It is a rare case where the distinction between the qualification of the group and the qualification of a member of this group is clearly realized, as has been done in Thiel v. Southern Pacific Company in 1946:

> Jury competence is an individual rather than a group or class matter. That fact lies at the very heart of the jury system. (36)

The Supreme Court of Illinois has followed closely the United States Supreme Court in its definition of the trial by jury. A trial, according to on decision recently cited is

> a judicial examination in accordance with the law of the land, of a cause, either civil or criminal, of the issues between the parties, whether of law or of fact, before a court that has jurisdiction over it. (37)

A jury is no necessary incident to a trial. "A court is fully organized and competent for transaction of business without the presence of a jury. The definition of a court does not include a jury as necessary to its functions". (38) Section 8 of article II of the constitution of Illinois even provided "That the grand jury may be abolished in all cases".

Over a hundred years ago it was decided that "judgment of his peers" in the state constitution did indeed mean trial by jury and had always been held to mean this. (39) The details of this trial do not differ from those held essential by the United States Supreme Court. They are "certain specified things", (40) such as twelve jurors, indifference of the jury, unanimity and finality of decisions regarding facts. The superintendence of a judge is mentioned, too. (41)

The constitution of the state guarantees the right to trial by jury "as heretofore enjoyed". (42) There has been some discussion of the meaning of "heretofore" and it has been settled that this meant trial by jury according to the common law of England:

> It was said that the words "the right of trial by jury as heretofore enjoyed", meant, under the common law of England, certain specified things which can not be dispensed with or disregarded on the trial of a person charged with felony. These requirements are: "A jury of twelve men must be empaneled, and any less number would not be a common law jury. The jury must be indifferent between the prisoner and the people. They must be summoned from the vicinage or body of the county in which the crime was alleged to have been committed. The jury must unanimously concur in the verdict. (This latter is one of the old requirements of the common law). The final decision upon the facts is to rest with the jury, and the court cannot interfere to coerce them to agree upon a verdict against their convictions.-Cooley's Const. Lim. 394". (43)

The Constitution of the United States guarantees a trial by jury in all criminal cases except impeachment (44) and in suits at common law, where the value of controversy is more than twenty dollars (45). But in a very remarkable opinion the Supreme Court doubted that this secured the right to trial by jury in such cases to everybody living under the sovereignty of the United States. (46)

The case came upt to the Court in consequence of the American expansion in the Caribbean and the Pacific around the turn of the century. Did trial by jury follow the flag to those outlying seas? The Court was cautions in its opinion, but it entertained the view that Anglo-Saxon jurisprudence was not applicable to "alien races" until the "blessings of a free government under the Constitution" were extended to them.

> We suggest, without intending to decide, that there may be a distinction between certain rights, enforced in the Constitution by prohibitions against interference with them, and what may be termed artificial or remedial rights, which are peculiar to our own system of jurisprudence. Of the former class are the rights to one's own religious opinion and to a public expression of them, or, as sometimes said, to worship

God according to the dictates of one's own conscience; the right to personal liberty and individual property; to freedom of speech and of the press; to free access to courts of justice, to due process of law and to an equal protection of the laws; to immunities from unreasonable searches and seizures, as well as cruel and unusual punishments; and to such other immunities as are indispensable to a free government. Of the latter class are the rights to citizenship, to suffrage, ... and to the particular methods of procedure pointed out in the Constitution, which are peculiar to Anglo-Saxon jurisprudence, and some of which have already been held by the States to be unnecessary to the proper protection of individuals. ... If those possessions are inhabited by alien races, differing from us in religion, customs, laws, methods of taxation and modes of thought, the administration of government and justice, according to Anglo-Saxon principles, may for a time be impossible; and the question at once arises whether large concessions ought not to be made for a time, that, ultimately, our own theories may be carried out, and the blessings of a free government under the Constitution extended to them. We decline to hold that there is anything in the Constitution to forbid such action. (47)

A different view was held by Chief Justice Melville W. Fuller in Hawaii v. Mankichi (1903). Mankichi, a Japanese, had complained because he had been tried in Hawaii for manslaughter without the indictment of a grand jury. The case was complicated by the fact that this had been shortly after the islands had come under the sovereignty of the United States. The European law administered under Queen Liliuokalani had not known grand jury indictment. The Court based its majority decision on the distinction between fundamental and merely procedural rights. (48) Chief Justice Fuller dissented:

This is not a question of natural rights, on the one hand, and artificial rights on the other, but of the fundamental rights of every person living under the sovereignty of the United States in respect of that Government. And among those rights is the right to be free from prosecution for crime unless after indictment by a grand jury, and the right to be acquitted unless found guilty by the unanimous verdict of a petit jury of twelve. (49)

Trial by jury was never held indispensable to due process of law. (50) In a variety of proceedings it had never been used: the Illinois Supreme Court, for example, held that it did not extend to suits in chancery that are of an equitable nature (51) and to cases in equity in general (52). But can a defendant who has a right to trial by jury waive this right? Can he submit to a trial without a jury? This question vexed American jurists for a long time. In answering it they had to explain their basic understanding of this institution, and therefore the main positions shall be mentioned here.

One view holds that the Constitution guarantees only the right to trial by jury, not trial by jury itself. This right may be given up voluntarily:

Had the terms been, that "the trial by jury shall be preserved", it might have been contended, that they were imperative, and could not be dispensed with. But the words are, that the right of trial by jury shall be preserved, which places it on the foot of a lex pro se introducta, and the benefit of it may therefore be relinquished. (53)

Another opinion held that a defendant could indeed waive his right to a trial by jury, even over the objection of the District or State's Attorney, but that his lawyer could not do so against his will. (54) In a third decision the consent of government counsel and of the court was deemed necessary for a waiver:

> In affirming the power of the defendant in any criminal case to waive a trial by a constitutional jury and submit to trial by a jury less than twelve persons, or by the court, we do not mean to hold that the waiver must be put into effect at all events. ... Not only must the right of the accused to a trial by a constitutional jury be jealously preserved, but the maintenance of the jury as a fact finding body in criminal cases is of such importance and has such a place in our traditions, that, before any waiver can become effective, the consent of government counsel and the sanction of the court must be had, in addition to the express and intelligent consent of the defendant. (55)

Already in 1842 the Illinois Supreme Court had decided that a prisoner might waive his constitutional rights if he wanted to do so, but that in a capital case he was presumed to stand on all his rights. (56)

In a recent case it was held that with a plea of guilty the accused waived all trials as far as guilt was concerned and that this included trial by jury. Apparently the averment of facts in a plea of guilty is to be taken at face value, a somewhat surprising interpretation which can be understood, perhaps, in the light of a philosophy of results. The following quotation shows this way of reasoning:

> If a person accused of crime cannot waive a jury trial, then logically a plea of guilty should not be accepted and, in that event, there would be forced upon the accused as well as the State a jury trial to establish facts admitted by the confession of guilt. ... The provisions of the bill of rights which guarantee to an accused person the right to a trial by jury refer only to the form and manner of the trial and are not jurisdictional in character. ... It is contrary to the spirit of the common law itself to apply a rule founded upon a particular reason, when that reason utterly fails - cessante ratione cessat ipsa lex.
> We conclude that the defendant in a criminal prosecution, whether the charge be a felony or a misdemeanor, has the power, upon a plea of not guilty, to waive a trial by jury; ... Upon the trial court is imposed the duty to see that an accused person's election to forego such a trial is not only expressly but also understandingly made. The performance of that duty involves a responsibility which cannot be perfunctorily discharged. (57)

The judge must possess the authority to have a jury summoned and impanelled; to have the jury and the constable in charge swear an oath; to instruct the jury on the law and advise them in respect to the facts; to enter judgment and issue execution on their verdict; and to set the verdict of the jury aside if it is in his opinion against the law or the evidence, except on acquittal from a criminal charge. (58) If, in a capital trial, the jury is unable to reach a verdict, the judge can dismiss it and order a new trial. (59) The judge is therefore responsible for the technicalities of the trial. Whenever there is a question as to a statute or ruling applicable in a situation it is his province to decide "what the law is". He is not, however, required to "declare the law in hypothetical questions which do not belong to the cause on trial". (60) Neither is he to judge the wisdom or injudiciousness of the law he administers. Quoting again from Scott v. Sanford:

> It is not the province of the court to decide upon the justice or injustice, the policy or impolicy, of these laws. The decision of that question belonged to the political or law-making power; to those who formed the sovereignty and framed the Constitution. The duty of the court is, to interpret the instruments they have framed, with the best lights we can obtain on the subject, and to administer it as we find it, according to its true intent and meaning when it was adopted. ...
> No one, we presume, supposes that any change in public opinion or feeling, in relation to this unfortunate race, in the civilized nations of Europe or in this country, should induce the court to give to the words of the Constitution a more liberal construction in their favor than they were intended to bear when the instrument was framed and adopted. ... This court was not created by the Constitution for such purposes. Higher and graver trusts have been confided to it, and it must not falter in the path of duty. (61)

That this was not simply a convenient explanation for a political decision in 1857 can be shown by other, similar decisions; the doctrine is quite obviously that the courts only execute the laws enacted by the legislatures. In a case before the Illinois Supreme Court in 1926 an analogous argumentation to that of the Scott decision was used. The question was whether women could sit on juries. Only electors then had that privilege. (62) The Court held that even if women were generally allowed to vote, and as electors would be entitled to be jurors, the legislators had meant male persons only when they used the word "electors" in the statute. (63) The Court had no right now to include women:

> The only legitimate function of the court is to declare and enforce the law as enacted by the legislature. The office of the court is to interpret the language used by the legislature where it requires interpretation but not to annex new provisions or substitute different ones. (64)

In short, the court - a synonym for "the judge" - administers the law as enacted by the competent authorities sine ira et studio; where the language of the law is unclear the judge interprets it "with the best lights we can obtain on the subject". The superficially simple task of administering the law becomes extremely difficult. How is the judge to ascertain the exact meaning of a word without extensive historical research into the situation at the time of legislation, and without comprehensive semantic studies? The job would be complex enough in a country with a codified law, but in view of the amorphous mass of often contradictory rulings and statutes of the common law system it becomes insurmountably complex.

Judges have of course recognized this, too. In the Illinois Supreme Court report on the 1887 decision concerning the Haymarket incident of April 5, 1886, in which a German anarchist leader and his followers stood accused of murder, the syllabus was ten pages long, the statement of the case 88 pages, and the opinion of the court 166 pages. Reflecting on the proceedings, Justice Mulkey said:

> In view of the number of defendants on trial, the great length of time it was in progress, the vast amount of testimony offered and passed upon by the court, and the almost numberless rulings the court was required to make, the wonder with me is, that the errors were not more numerous and more serious than they are. (65)

The idea has not yet completely died out that the judge only administers a pre-existent law which by some mysterious process forms a logical system locked in his brain out of which he can pull, figuratively speaking, a file on every question and take out of it the only just ruling. Cases of astounding mismanagement by judges have come up to the appellate courts. In one such case one Thomas Izzo was convicted of murder in the Criminal Court of Cook County, and sentenced to 99 years imprisonment. (66) During this trial the judge had misstated the number of peremptory challenges, had given an inaccurate definition of felony, and had made technically incorrect statements in explanation of the phrase "reasonable doubt". The Supreme Court of Illinois affirmed the judgment, holding it clear from the subsequent voir dire examination that the jurors were under no misapprehension because of the mistaken remarks of the judge. (67)

In People v. Izzo the trial judge was obviously incompetent. In the Scott case it would seem that Chief Justice Taney was not (or, at least, not only) incompetent but that his judgment was swayed by considerations which had more to do with politics than with justice. The accusation that a judge was biased, that he favored one of the parties for reasons other than the evidence produced in open court, is under any system of law an extremely serious one. Judges do and may of course hold their own personal views on social, political, and economic affairs. Looking over the great number of cases analyzed for the present paper one can say that rarely have Supreme Court judges patently allowed their private prejudices to lead them in their decisions. In courts of first instance, on the other hand, such bias was often openly expressed. (68) A case in point is reported in Neal v. Delaware (1881). (69) Neal, a black man, had been sentenced to death in Newcastle county, Delaware, for rape. He appealed this sentence on the basis of the Rives decision (70), where the United States Supreme Court had awarded mandamus because the jury had been all white. In the trial of Neal, Judge Comegys admitted, no black man had sat on the jury, nor had any black man sat on any jury in Delaware up to that time; and he added:

> That none but white men were selected is in nowise remarkable in view of the fact - too notorious to be ignored - that the great body of black men residing in this State are utterly unqualified by want of intelligence, experience or moral integrity, to sit on juries. (71)

The defense motions to quash were overruled because the affidavits that black men had been excluded from jury service on account of their color were unsupported by witnesses. The defendant then asked for subpoenas of witnesses. One of these was a clerk who at the time was ex officio in the courtroom. The subpoenas were denied because the motion to quash had already been overruled. The opinion of the United States Supreme Court, written by John M. Harlan, contained strong words for such discrimination:

> It was, we think, under all the circumstances, a violent presumption which the State court indulged, that such uniform exclusion of that race from juries, during a period of many years, was solely because, in the judgment of those officers, fairly exercised, the black race in Delaware were utterly disqualified, by want of intelligence, experience or moral integrity, to sit on juries. (72)

It was an exceptional case where a black man too poor to employ counsel could appeal to the Supreme Court because of prejudice of the trial judge. In this regard only the strictest standards are therefore satisfactory. A well-founded suspicion of the prisoner that he cannot get a fair trial because of bias of his trial judge should be ground for a change of venue. The Supreme Court of Illinois has rendered a decision in this sense:

> The plaintiffs in error were convicted of larceny and insist that the court erred in denying their application for a change of venue on account of prejudice of the judge. The petition for a change of venue and the accompanying affidavits complied with the statute and the right to a change of venue was therefore absolute. (73)

The ruling that change of venue must be granted if a petition for it is accompanied by affidavits, without any corroboration by witnesses, may be called generous. The courts always have to be on guard against purely delaying tactics. An even more liberal ruling, in the sense that change of venue is mandatory if the defendant simply fears that his trial judge might be prejudiced against him - analogous to the peremptory challenge of jurors - would very likely be impracticable and could defeat its own purpose.

On the face of it the job of the jury seems much less exacting than that of the judge. The juror is not supposed to have a huge set of legislative enactments and judicial rulings at his fingertips, he is not to be versed in history and half a dozen other academic disciplines. He must simply listen to the evidence in court and then - on the basis of his common sense and intelligence - decide "what has happened", what the facts are.

The most important qualification for this duty is that of impartiality.

Sir Edward Coke derived this from the injunction in Magna Carta that a juror must be liber homo:

> Hee that is of the Jurie must be liber homo, that is not only a freeman, and not bound but also one that hath such freedome of mind as he stands indifferent as hee stands unsworne. Secondly, hee must be legalis, and by the Law every Juror that is returned for the trial of any issue or cause ought to have three proporties.
> First, hee ought to bee least suspitious, that is to bee indifferent as hee stands unsworne, and then hee is accounted in Law liber & legalis homo, otherwise he may be challenged and not suffered to be sworne. The most usuall triall of matters of fact is by 12. such men, for ad quaestionem facti non respondent Iudices & matters in Law the Judges ought to decide and discusse, for ad quaestionem iuris non respondent Iuratores. (74)

These qualifications are reflected in the Illinois Jurors Act, which has as its aim the unbiased selection of impartial jurors. A juror must be of the vicinage, between 21 and 60 years old, in the possession of his natural faculties "and not infirm or decrepit", free from all exemptions, "of fair character, of approved integrity, of sound judgment, well informed", and capable of understanding English (75); he must also be impartial (76). Particular technical knowlege is not required.

The jury has wide discretion: facts must not be conclusively proven, the jurors can infer them, (77) and they also have the right to decide on intentions. (78) The best juror is the proverbial man from the street.

The dictum of Lord Coke that "ad quaestionem facti non respondent Iudices, ad quaestionem iuris non respondent Iuratores" contains a certain philosophy of the law. The underlying assumption apparently is that there are two distinct and independent phenomena, one called "facts", and the other "laws". (79) A theoretical model of a case tried under this system would demand that the judge and the jury listen to the pleadings and evidence in court, and that the judge then tell the jury what the law is in respect to the possible interpretation of this evidence. The jury then retreats and in secrecy determines by discussion what the facts are. The jurors return into the courtroom and their foreman informs the judge of their findings (i.e. of the verdict). The judge then takes from his store of laws those that fit the facts best and on this basis pronounces his judgment.

The fundamental difficulty of this model is that "facts" and "laws" are often inseparably intertwined. This can be demonstrated best by the case of A killing B. The jury may be satisfied that indeed A did kill B. But this will not be enough for the judge. In order to determine what law he has to administer in this case he must know whether the killing was murder or manslaughter, whether it was justifiable homicide or under the influence of alcohol, whether it was an accident or assault with intent to kill. But by deciding these and related questions the jury decides what law shall be applied. Under the guise of determining the exact facts it determines the law. (80)

# PREJUDICE, THE PRESUMPTION OF INNOCENCE, AND THE PRESUMPTION OF GUILT

The postulate that the jurors must be unbiased can be very theoretical in a society that is deeply prejudiced against a minority. Can laws change such prejudice? Does it make any difference whether the laws of the community are discriminatory or not? Surprisingly, the traditional judicial view holds that it does not.

Martin Luther King expressed this when he wrote: "Laws only declare rights; they do not deliver them". (81) This argumentation was used by segregationists and integrationists alike (82) and it sums up some basic assumptions without questioning their validity. The relationship between social reality and the law has always been one of the fundamental problems of Western jurisprudence. The two polar views are:
- People have their conception of the world they live in and the laws are patterned in accordance with these conceptions. They change, of course, and so do in consequence the laws. (The general population begins to believe in the equality of races and t h e r e f o r e non discriminatory laws are enacted).
- People have their conception of the world they live in and the laws are instrumental in changing this conception by legitimizing certain attitudes. (Swimming at the same beach as whites becomes legal for blacks and t h e r e f o r e sharing of a beach will become socially acceptable also for whites and they will change their attitude).

The surprising thing about the judicial decisions supporting the first view is that they assert it with doubtless certainty. It is put down as if it were the unquestionable result of scientific investigation, not as if it were one of the great problems in the philosophy of law.

When Justice Henry Billings Brown said, in Plessy v. Ferguson (1896):

> The argument also assumes that social prejudices may be overcome by legislation, and that equal rights cannot be secured to the negro except by an enforced commingling of the two races. We cannot accept this proposition. ... Legislation is powerless to eradicate radical instincts or to abolish distinctions based upon physical differences, and to attempt to do so can only result in accentuating the difficulties of the present situation. (83),

he demonstrated just that. Justice John Marshall Harlan, in his dissenting opinion answered that the law did not bring social justice and equality anyway, so the whole argument was immaterial. (83a)

It is a fundamental tenet and one of the pillars of the humanism of the common law that a defendant is presumed innocent until the prosecutor and his witnesses can convince the jury of his guilt. In one of the Scottsboro cases the United States Supreme Court declared: "However guilty defendants, upon due inquiry, might prove to have been, they were, until convicted, presumed to be innocent". (84) In the original trial of Clarence Norris, another of the Scottsboro defendants, the lawyer had moved to quash the indictment because of arbitrary exclusion of blacks from the grand jury that had presented it. The motion was denied, however:

> In denying the motion to quash, the trial judge expressed the view that he would not "be authorized to presume that somebody had committed a crime" or to presume that the jury board "had been unfaithful to their duties and allowed the books to be tampered with". (85)

This same kind of presumption of innocence of government officials had been expressed in Brownfield v. South Carolina, a case which was reviewed in the Supreme Court in 1903. The defendant there alleged that the grand jury was composed entirely of whites, although four fifths of the population and of the registered voters of the county were black. He further alleged that these four fifths had been excluded on account of their race and color only. He did not sufficiently support his allegations and the trial judge noted: "In the absence of any showing to the contrary, I was bound to assume that the jury commissioners had done their duty". (86)

In other cases, however, this presumption of innocence had no force. The early case of Mima Queen (1813) is comparable, in some respects, to the Scottsboro cases and to Brownfield because in all these cases the defendant was black. The plaintiff in error, Mima Queen, and her child petitioned for freedom because their ancestors had come to Maryland from England as free black people. Three witnesses testified to this, mainly from hearsay, because the black woman possessed no papers proving her statements. The Supreme Court under Chief Justice John Marshall ruled that hearsay evidence was inadmissible and that the woman and her child had no right to be free; Justice Duvall dissented vigorously. The plaintiff in error also took exception against two jurors. The second juror was one James Reed. He had formed no opinion on the case but he admitted that in a doubtful case he would favor the plaintiff:

> James Reed, when called, was questioned, and appeared to have formed and expressed no opinion on the particular case: but on being further questioned, he avowed his detestation of slavery to be such that in a doubtful case he would find a verdict for the Plaintiffs; and that he had so expressed himself with regard to this very cause. He added that if the testimony were equal he should certainly find a verdict for the Plaintiffs. The court then instructed the tryers that he did not stand indifferent between the parties. To this instruction exception was taken. (87)

In plain language this meant only that Reed would favor the plaintiff if the prosecutor could not prove her allegations untrue and this attitude was clearly in the tradition of letting somebody go free until his guilt was conclusively proven. But the Supreme Court ruled that Reed was not "indifferent" between the parties and that therefore it was right that he had not been sworn:

> It is certainly much to be desired that jurors should enter upon their duties with minds entirely free from all prejudice. Perhaps on general and public questions it is scarcely possible to avoid receiving some prepossessions, and where a private right depends on such a question the difficulty of obtaining jurors whose minds are entirely uninfluenced by opinions previously formed is undoubtedly considerable. Yet they ought to be superior to every exception, they ought to stand perfectly indifferent between the parties, and although the bias which was acknowledged in this case might not perhaps have been so strong as to render it positively improper to allow the juror to be sworn on the jury, yet it was desirable to submit the case to those who felt no bias either way; and therefore the court exercised a sound discretion in not permitting him to be sworn. (88)

These few cases do not permit any generalized conclusions. But tentatively one might infer that the doctrine of presumption on innocence worked better in cases where public officials in the discharge of their duty were concerned than when a black defendant wanted to assert it as his right.

The Supreme Court of Illinois has not treated this question uniformly. On the one hand one finds decisions in which it is indeed held that a juror has the right to believe that a prisoner is innocent until proved guilty, on the other hand there are decisions which state clearly that a juror favoring the accused without further evidence is incompetent. Both opinions were expressed in cases that lie within ten years of each other.

The first one came before the court in 1886. Plaintiff in error was the Chicago and Western Indiana Railroad Company. (89) One of their employees, Ferdinand Bingenheimer, had lost a leg in an accident. A railroad car had started while Bingenheimer tried to get on it in order to wash it. Bingenheimer had recovered damages from the railroad company and Chicago and Western Indiana appealed the sentence in the Appellate Court of the First District, and from there to the State Supreme Court. One of the jurors had stated on the voir dire examination that he could try the case impartially but that he sympathized with Bingenheimer. The Court held that this was "simply an expression of kindly feeling common to all good people" and that the juror was competent:

> He stated distinctly he did not "know as there was any reason why" he could not "try this case fairly and impartially". It is true he did state, if he had any sympathy it would be with the "young man that lost his limb", and that he "would have no sympathy for the railroad". That is simply an expression of kindly feeling common to all good people, and certainly the possession of so kindly a spirit would not disqualify a citizen, otherwise competent, from acting in the capacity of a juror. (90)

Seven years later, however, in Coughlin v. People the same court held a different view. Daniel Coughlin and six co-defendants were indicted on June 29, 1889, for conspiracy to kill Dr. Patrick Henry Cronin and for murdering him. All defendants in the ensuing sensational trial were members of the "Clan-na-Gael", the Irish "United Brotherhood". The victim had been one of the leaders of this secret organization and had been sentenced to death by one of its committees. Coughlin and two co-defendants received life sentences, but he appealed because some of the jurors had shown, on their voir dire, that they were prejudiced against the organization and generally believed what they had read in the papers about the guilt of the defendants. The court ruled that "If the juror is ready to respond to the question, "Is the prisoner guilty, or is he innocent?" then he is incompetent". (91) This is in contradiction to the theory of presumption of innocence. According to this theory a juror should answer the question by saying: "The prisoner is innocent until you have convinced me of the contrary".

   A juror might be inclined to favor a defendant because he is prejudiced against the possible sentence. He will therefore only judge the accused guilty if the evidence proves this incontrovertibly. This has the same effect as a presumption of innocence.

   Often a juror would state on his voir dire that he could never judge a defendant guilty if it was possible that the prisoner would in consequence be put to death, or that he would do so only if the evidence was really conclusive. The leading Illinois case in this respect is that of Gates v. People (1853). George Gates had been sentenced to death in La Salle Circuit Court for murder. He appealed because all persons who conscientiously objected to the death penalty had been excluded from the jury that tried him. The Supreme Court held that this exclusion was constitutional and that the prisoner had no right to demand a jury containing members opposed to one of the possible sentences:

> A juror ought to stand indifferent between the prosecution and the accused. He should be in a condition to find a verdict in accordance with the law and the evidence. On this principle, it is a good cause of challenge to a juror in a capital case, that he has conscientious scruples on the subject of punishment by death, that will prevent him from agreeing to a verdict of guilty. ... It would be but a mockery to go through the forms of a trial, with such a person upon the jury. The prisoner would not be convicted, however conclusive the proof of his guilt. ... The challenges were properly allowed. (92)

   The question is not answered whether a jury from which all conscientious objectors of the death penalty have been excluded is still representative of the community. This might have been so in 1853 but there is serious doubt that such a jury in the 1960's meets the standard. But even in a recent (1966) decision, in People v. Hobbs, the court indulged in spiteful ad personam argumentation:

> What defendant seems to be asserting is a right to have some individuals on the jury who may be prejudiced in his favor, someone who is unalterably opposed to one of the possible penalties with which he is faced. One wonders whether he would seek with equal vehemence the right of the State to have some on the jury who sincerely and conscientiously believe in the Old Testament rule of an eye for an eye, or

death and death only for murder. Such an arrangement would make for a "balanced" jury. The mere statement of the proposition reveals its utter inadequacy. (93)

With such opinions from the bench of the State Supreme Court it is not surprising that conscientious objectors have had a very hard time getting on juries. In a 1967 case that went all the way up to the Supreme Court of the United States it is reported that the trial judge said on the voir dire examination: "Let's get these conscientious objectors out of the way without wasting any time on them". (94)

A juror can be biased against the plaintiff, or the defendant, or the crime, or the punishment. A prejudice against a possible form of punishment can result in a bias in favor of the defendant. Prejudice against a certain crime can have the opposite effect. A juror might be inclined to convict the defendant simply because of the cruelty of the crime he is indicted for. This would result in a presumption of guilt.

That a jury could be inclined to be against the defendant simply because he is the defendant in a trial has been shown above. (95) But a juror can also be prejudiced against a defendant for personal reasons. The most famous trial in which the defendant challenged some of the jurors because they were biased against him personally was that of Aaron Burr. (96) This could be called the "classical" case of presumption of guilt. The general population and especially their representatives in Congress had been subject to President Jefferson's propaganda against Burr. Because the charge was treason against the yet young Republic the tempers on both sides were aroused and in the prevailing atmosphere an unbiased trial seemed almost impossible.

When Senator Giles was called on the voir dire he was challenged personally by Burr. Burr claimed the same right of challenging grand jurors for favor that he had of challenging petit jurors, and was sustained in his position by the Chief Justice. His objection to Giles was that, on occasions in the Senate, he had pronounced his opinion on certain documents sent to that body by President Jefferson attributing to Burr treasonable designs, and upon such information advocating the suspension of the writ of habeas corpus. He stated that he could produce evidence, if necessary, of public utterances of Senator Giles confirming these views. Senator Giles was stricken from the panel.
Another former United States Senator, and afterwards Governor of Virginia, summoned as a grand juror, was Wilson Cary Nicholas. He was a personal enemy of Burr, and when his name was called Burr challenged him. Colonel Nicholas had served three years in the Senate when Burr presided over it, and had taken a very decided part in favor of the election of his successor. He had freely expressed his suspicions, both in correspondence and publicly, of Colonel Burr's probable objects in the west. He was rejected. ... The general belief in the guilt of the accused was manifested at the very beginning of the trial. ... A number of citizens summoned for service on the grand jury frankly admitted that they had prejudged the case, and in consequence of such disqualifi-

cations and excuses the original panel was reduced to fourteen. ...
Mr. Randolph was named as foreman, but upon being asked to take the
oath, requested to be excused from serving. He had formed an opinion
concerning the nature and tendency of certain transactions imputed to
Mr. Burr. He had a strong prepossession, but thought he could divest
himself of it upon evidence. Mr. Burr observed that he was afraid they
would be unable to find any man without this prepossession. "The rule
is, " said the Chief Justice, "that a man must not only have formed,
but declared an opinion, in order to exclude him from serving on the
jury". Mr. Randolph replied that he had no recollection of having
declared one, and he was thereupon sworn as foreman. (97)

Related to this personal prejudice is the bias against an identifiable
group (blacks, teenagers), and against big business or big labor. A case where a
juror was biased against a big business enterprise came before the Illinois Supreme
Court in 1871. (98) One of the jurors in that trial, Samuel Askey, averred that he
was prejudiced "against insurance companies generally" because he could not comprehend their operations. Although he thought that this would not affect his verdict the
court held him incompetent:

As to this juror, the feeling he entertained against insurance companies
was of a bigoted and reprehensible character. ... A juror should stand
indifferent between the parties. No bias should influence his judgment
and swerve him from strict impartiality. ... It is not necessary that
his unfavorable impressions should be so strong that they can not be
shaken by evidence. It is sufficient if proof be necessary to restore
his impartiality. A party should never be compelled to produce proof
to change a preconceived opinion or prejudice which may control the
action of the juror. (99)

More common are the cases in which a juror is biased against a
defendant because he belongs to a different race than he himself, or because he is
an immigrant from a particular country. Besides blacks, especially defendants with
a Latin background have felt this kind of prejudice. In an 1897 case an Italian commission merchant attacked, not individual jurors, but the manner of selecting the
jury. He alleged that a jury drawn from a population that is traditionally anti-Italian
could not try him fairly:

In the motion for a new trial the manner of selecting the jurors is
assigned as one of the causes for a new trial, and the defendant filed
numerous affidavits going to show he was prejudiced injuriously from
this cause. ... One of these affidavits states that he has been engaged
in the commission business in South Water Street, in said city, continuously for the past twenty years; that he now has his place of business
at No. 127 South Water Street; that he knows the people doing business
on that and neighboring streets in said city, and is well informed as to
their estimation of persons of Italian birth in general. ... he knows

> that there is a deep seated prejudice existing among said business men against the average person of Italian extraction; that judging from his said knowledge of such prejudice and the universality of its existence, as observed by him, he does not believe that a prisoner of Italian birth could receive a fair and impartial trial at the hands of a jury composed of citizens drawn wholly or largely from among the men doing business on said South Water Street. (100)

The Supreme Court ruled that this was ground for reversal of Borelli's death sentence for murder. It is reported in a 1926 appeal from a murder trial in the Circuit Court of Peoria County, in which the defendant was Mexican American, that one C.A. Donaldson had said before he was accepted as a juror: "They better not take me on that jury or I will hang that Mexican ---". (101) In this case, too, the Supreme Court reversed the death sentence imposed by the lower court.

The mass media may be another source of prejudice. The question came up to the Supreme Court of Illinois in Gray v. People (1861). Gray had been judged guilty of burglary and larceny in the Court of Common Pleas of Aurora and he objected to some jurors, alleging that they had been influenced by reports about the crime in the press.

> One juror, with others objected to, declared that he had not formed and expressed any opinion of the guilt or innocence of the defendants; that he had no bias or prejudice upon his mind, and could give the defendants a fair trial according to the law and the evidence. This possibly might be so, but he declared on his examination, that he believed the statements in the newspapers that there had been a housebreaking, and if the prisoners were the persons named in the newspaper, he had an opinion of their guilt or innocence. He has formed an opinion, if it should turn out that one of the defendants was Silas Gray. (102)

Section 14 of the Revised Statutes of 1874 then contained the provision

> that in the trial of any criminal cause, the fact that a person called as a juror has formed an opinion or impression, based upon rumor or upon newspaper statements (about the truth of which he has expressed no opinion), shall not disqualify him to serve as a juror in such case, if he shall, upon oath, state that he believes he can fairly and impartially render a verdict therein, in accordance with the law and the evidence, and the court shall be satisfied of the truth of such statement. (103)

Sixty-four years after the Gray case the Supreme Court of the State declared that newspaper reports make it almost impossible to find completely unbiased jurors. To reject a juror because he had heard a broadcast report or read a newspaper account of a crime and formed an opinion thereon would have the consequence that "No man of ordinary intelligence would be qualified to sit as a juror". (104)

103

One very important and interesting fact has been demonstrated in
People v. Ortiz, quoted above. Although juror C.A. Donaldson was prejudiced
against the defendant he declared himself competent to sit on the jury. It could,
however, been shown that Donaldson was really partial. The power of a prospective
juror to declare himself incompetent, on the other hand, is almost absolute: he only
has to aver that he prejudged the case and that he is not able to render a fair verdict.
There are only two restrictions to this. If he states that he is biased in favor of the
prosecution but the defendant accepts him anyway, the court has no right to refuse
him, (105) and the opinions of a juror must not merely be formed, but expressed.
In addition they must not be purely hypothetical. (106) If a juror who is not biased
is excused for prejudice, generally not much harm is done, provided another unbiased juror can be found. It is much more pernicious if a prejudiced juror can get
on a jury by claiming to be unbiased. People v. Ortiz demonstrated that it is possible
for a person to become a juror maliciously in order to help convict a hated defendant.

It may be interesting, at this point, to quote a voir dire examination
in which a prospective juror stated that he had formed but not expressed an opinion.
The whole of his testimony is in the record:

Q. By the district attorney: "Have you formed or expressed any
opinion as to the guilt or innocence of this charge?"
A. "I believe I have formed an opinion".
By the court: "Have you formed and expressed an opinion?"
A. "No, sir; I believe not".
Q. "You say you have formed an opinion?"
A. "I have".
Q. "Is that based upon evidence?"
A. "Nothing produced in court".
Q. "Would that opinion influence your verdict?"
A. "I don't think it would".
Q. By defendant: "I understood you to say you had formed an opinion,
but not expressed it?"
A. "I don't know that I have expressed an opinion; I have formed one."
Q. "Do you entertain that opinion?"
A. "I do". (107)

The court ruled that this juror was not incapable of trying the defendant
fairly. It also held that not all opinions disqualify, only those "as will raise the
presumption of partiality". (108) In a more recent opinion, in United States v. Wood
(1936) the United States Supreme Court further elaborated on the question of bias:
"The bias of a prospective juror may be actual or implied; that is, it may be bias
in fact or bias conclusively presumed as matter of law". (109) It also ruled that
impartiality, along with speed, publicity, information as to the charge, confrontation
with witnesses, compulsory process and assistance of counsel, is a "matter of
substance, not of form", (110) but that the real difficulty lay in the fact that "Impartiality is not a technical conception" but a state of mind . (111)

In Illinois, a mere doubt that a juror has sworn falsely on his voir dire
is not sufficient for reversal, "the evidence must clearly preponderate in establishing

the fact". (112) To determine the prejudice of a juror the same method may be used as in ascertaining the bias of a witness:

> It is true, a witness may be asked directly as to his feelings of hostility to the party against whom he testifies; but the party is not confined to that mode of proof. Generally, that mode of examination sheds but little light on the subject. Much the most reliable evidence of the feelings of a witness consist in the proofs of what he has said or done. (113)

According to one early opinion it is, however, doubtful whether a venireman can fairly judge his own qualifications as a juror:

> But there is much less difficulty in establishing than in applying the rule. This arises in a great measure from the want of a clear perception on the part of the jurors, as to what in reality constitutes such an opinion, and from the difficulty which they experience in explaining, so that it may be fully comprehended, the true condition of their mind on the subject of inquiry. ... A man may be charged with murder, and a juror may have no doubt but the person alleged to be murdered, was killed, and that the accused killed him, and yet have no sort of an idea whether the homicide were justifiable, excusable or felonious. No one will pretend that such a juror has an opinion of the guilt or innocence of the accused. (114)

Towards the end of the century, the court developed a unified theory of the weight of the contention of prospective jurors that they are, or are not, biased. In <u>Coughlin</u> v. <u>People</u> (1893) the Supreme Court held that the Criminal Court of Cook County erred in believing without further inquiry the statement of a venireman that he was competent:

> It makes the statement of the juror that he can render a fair and impartial verdict, according to the law and the evidence, competent, ... But the statute does not attempt to determine in the least what shall be the probative force of the statement of the juror when made, or how far it shall have the effect of relieving him of the disqualification arising from the existence in his mind of such opinion. The juror's statement becomes evidence, to be received and given such weight as, under the circumstances appearing, it is fairly and justly entitled to. ... The theory seemed to be that if a juror could in any way be brought to answer that he could sit as an impartial juror, that declaration of itself rendered him competent. Such a view, if it was entertained, was a total misconception of the law. (115)

This relativizes the contentions of prospective jurors somewhat but it is still true that a venireman is often his own judge of his qualifications as a juryman.

In extreme cases an opinionated trial judge may not even allow counsel for defense to question a venireman as to his prejudices because the judge does not want an unbiased jury. Such a case came before the United States Supreme Court in 1931. It was an appeal from a murder trial in the District of Columbia, in which a black man had been sentenced to death. His counsel, Mr. Reilly, was not allowed to ask the jurors if they were racially prejudiced. The <u>Supreme Court Reports</u> contains a transcription of the discussion between the judge and counsel for defense:

>"Mr. Reilly: At the last trial of this case I understand there was one woman on the jury who was a southerner, and who said that the fact that the defendant was a negro and the deceased a white man perhaps somewhat influenced her. I don't like to ask that question in public, but -
>The Court: I don't think that would be a proper question, any more than to ask whether they like an Irishman, or a Scotchman.
>Mr. Reilly: But it was brought to our attention so prominently. It is a racial question -
>The Court: It was not this jury.
>Mr. Reilly: No. But it was a racial question, and the question came up -
>The Court: I don't think that is proper.
>Mr. Reilly: Might I, out of an abundance of caution, note an exception.
>The Court: Note an exception." (116)

The opinion of the highest court of the land about this verbal exchange was:

>Despite the privilege accorded to the negro, we do not think that it can be said that the possibility of such prejudice is so remote, as to justify the risk in forbidding the inquiry. And this risk becomes grave when the issue is life or death. (117)


## JURY SELECTION


One of the oldest complaints of rulers and courts is that the jurors are not qualified enough, that those who are - in the eyes of the law - best equipped by birth and education for jury service shun that duty in order to have time for more profitable, if less civic, pursuits. The United States Supreme Court very earnestly pressed this issue when it stated in an 1887 case from Missouri:

>In our large cities there is such a mixed population, there is such a tendency of the criminal classes to resort to them, and such an unfortunate disposition on the part of the business men to escape from

jury duty, that it requires special care on the part of the government to secure their competent and impartial jurors. (118)

But the same court also sustained a complaint that jurors were too qualified. In <u>Glasser</u> v. <u>United States</u> the plaintiff complained because the women included on his jury had all attended evening classes of the League of Women Voters on the duties of a juror. Glasser maintained that these women were better equipped for jury service than the average American woman and were therefore not representative of the community. The Court sustained his argumentation and reversed the conviction in part. (119) Neither the most nor the least intelligent citizens can be purposefully selected for jury service, and neither the most intelligent nor the least intelligent can be purposefully excluded from it:

> Under our Constitution, the jury is not to be made the representative of the most intelligent, the most wealthy or the most successful, nor of the least intelligent, the least wealthy or the least successful. It is a democratic institution, representative of all qualified classes of the people. (120)

The courts and the law should thus influence the selection of the jury as little as possible. Its composition should be largely determined by chance.

States can and do of course put down some qualifications for jury service:

> States should decide for themselves the quality of their juries as best fits their situation so long as the classifications have relation to the efficiency of the jurors and are equally administered.
> Our duty to protect the federal constitutional rights of all does not mean we must or should impose on states our conception of the proper source of jury lists, so long as the source reasonably reflects a cross-section of the population suitable in character and intelligence for that civic duty. (121)

Section 2 of chapter 74 of the Illinois revised Statutes, quoted above, is an example for such state action.

During slavery no black man could be a juror in the South (122) and after emancipation this did not change substantially. In 1868 the Fourteenth Amendment was enacted, providing in section 1:

> ... No State shall make or enforce any law which shall abridge the privileges or immunities of citizens of the United States; nor shall any State deprive any person of life, liberty, or property, without due process of law; nor deny to any person within its jurisdiction the equal protection of the laws.

But the due process and the equal protection clauses here proclaimed had little effect upon legislatures and upon officials who openly discriminated against blacks although this was illegal. Congress therefore enacted in 1875 a Civil Rights Act, (123) entitled "An Act to Protect All Citizens in their Civil and Legal Rights". It was signed on March 1, 1875. In the preamble the equality of all men before the law is stressed. Section 1 goes on to declare that all persons have equal rights in inns, public conveyances, theaters, and places of public amusement. Section 2 holds persons violating section 1 liable to penalty, and section 3 delimits the jurisdiction of the courts. Section 4 is concerned with the selection of jurors:

> Sec. 4. That no citizen possessing all other qualifications which are or may be prescribed by law shall be disqualified for service as grand or petit juror in any court of the United States, or of any State, on account of race, color, or previous condition of servitude; and any officer or other person charged with any duty in the selection or summoning of jurors who shall exclude or fail to summon any citizen for the cause aforesaid shall, on conviction thereof, be deemed guilty of a misdemeanor, and be fined not more than five thousand dollars. (124)

Section 5, finally, gives the Supreme Court of the United States the right to review all cases under this act, without regard to the sum in controversy.
There are obviously at least the following methods of discrimination: a) A state can enact discriminatory laws, b) an officer as mentioned in section 4 of the Civil Rights Act of 1875 can overtly discriminate because the community expects this from him or because he is prejudiced himself, and c) such an officer can discriminate covertly because he knows such discrimination is illegal but he wants to practice it anyway.

a. Open discrimination by the law. This is prohibited by the Fourteenth Amendment. The equal protection clause was tested in the Supreme Court in Strauder v. West Virginia in 1879. Judgment was rendered on January 3, 1880. It was a murder case that had originated in Ohio county, West Virginia. (125) The Court held that a state statute which expressly restricted jury service to whites was unconstitutional in that it violated the equal protection guarantee of the Fourteenth Amendment. This case has been followed in many other decisions on various levels of the judiciary. The states were therefore very cautions not to enact laws that discriminated openly in the jury selection proceedings.

One way to circumvent the injunctions of the Fourteenth Amendment was by laws which restricted jury service to certain classes of citizens without patently excluding blacks. The best known such enactments granted the right to jury service to electors only, at a time when black people were, or remained, disfranchised. In Rogers v. Alabama the plaintiff complained because under the Alabama constitution then in force blacks could not vote and therefore no black man could sit on his grand jury. The motion to quash was stricken by the Alabama court for "prolixity", but the United States Supreme Court did not sustain this.

Another facet of the same issue was the grandfather clause. Such clauses were embodied in the state constitutions and restricted franchise to those who either qualified directly or whose ancestors in the 1860s had been electors, in which case they themselves did not have to qualify. For all practical purposes this excluded blacks. Grandfather clauses were declared unconstitutional in Guinn v. United States, a 1915 case from Oklahoma:

> The original clause so far as material was this: "The qualified electors of the State shall be male citizens of the United States, male citizens of the State, and male persons of Indian descent native of the United States, who are over the age of twenty-one years, who have resided in this state one year, in the county six months, and in the election precinct thirty days, next preceding the election at which any such elector offers to vote". And this is the amendment:
> "No person shall be registered as an elector of this State or be allowed to vote in any election herein, unless he be able to read and write any section of the constitution of the State of Oklahoma; but no person who was, on January 1st, 1866, or at any time prior thereto, entitled to vote under any form of government, or who at the time resided in some foreign nation, and no lineal descendant of such person, shall be denied the right to register and vote because of his inability to so read and write sections of such constitution. Precinct election inspectors having in charge the registration of electors shall enforce the provisions of this section at the time of registration, provided registration be required. Should registration be dispensed with, the provisions of this section shall be enforced by the precinct election officers when electors apply for ballots to vote". (126)

The United States Supreme Court disapproved strongly of such legislation:

> We have difficulty in finding words to more clearly demonstrate the conviction we entertain that this standard has the characteristics which the Government attributes to it than does the mere statement of the text. (127)

b. **Overt discrimination by officials.** Even if the state statutes did not discriminate themselves, they often gave the officers charged with jury selection wide discretionary powers which were not infrequently used for the purpose of excluding blacks. The above-quoted section 4 of the 1875 Civil Rights Act therefore became potentially important. The basis for rigorous enforcement of this section in the courts was laid when the Supreme Court decided in Ex parte Virginia that the statute was constitutional and within the powers conferred to Congress by the last section of the Fourteenth Amendment. Justice Strong said in the opinion of the Court:

> The indictment charged that he [ the petitioner ] being a judge of the county court of Pittsylvania County of that State, and an officer charged by law with the selection of jurors to serve in the circuit and county courts of said county in the year 1878, did then and there exclude and fail to select as grand and petit jurors certain citizens of said county

of Pittsylvania, of African race and black color, said citizens possessing all other qualifications prescribed by law, and being by him excluded from the jury lists made out by him as such judge, on account of their race, color, and previous condition of servitude, and for no other reason, against the peace and dignity of the United States, and against the form of the Statute of the United States in such case made and provided. ...

That Statute gave him no authority, when selecting jurors, from whom a panel might be drawn for a circuit court, to exclude all colored men merely because they were colored. Such an exclusion was not left within the limits of his discretion. (128)

Equally interesting is the dissenting opinion by Justice Stephen Field, who was joined by Nathan Clifford. In it were summed up the central arguments that would be used for a century against black jurors:

If, when a colored person is accused of a criminal offence, the presence of persons of his race on the jury by which he is to be tried is essential to secure to him the equal protection of the laws, it would seem that the presence of such persons on the bench would be equally essential, if the court should exist of more than one judge, as in many cases it may; and if it should consist of a single judge, that protection would be impossible. ...

If this position be correct, there ought not to be any white person on the jury where the interests of colored persons only are involved.
...

And if it can make the exclusion of persons from jury service on account of race or color a criminal offense, it can make their exclusion from office on that account also criminal; and, adopting the doctrine of the district judge in this case, the failure to appoint them to office will be presumptive evidence of their exclusion on that ground. (129)

Field proceeded by first pointing out that there are many classes of not disadvantaged citizens who cannot be called for jury duty. He declared that "no one" would claim that this impaired their rights as citizens. He next contended that the Fourteenth Amendment protected only civil rights and not those that "arise from the form of government and its mode of administration". This is curious because it seems to assert the right of the political authority to do what private citizens may not, namely discriminate.

The idea that a single black judge could preside over a trial is not even considered a serious alternative but only used to show to what "absurd" situations the decision of the Court might lead. The same is true for the rest of the argumentation quoted.

Sixty years after Ex parte Virginia a similar case came up to the Supreme Court from Texas. (130) The Court again ruled that the state statute was "not in itself unfair" but that the officials empowered with jury selection had used their discretion to discriminate. The judgment of the Texas court was reversed:

Here, the Texas statutory scheme is not in itself unfair; it is capable of being carried out with no racial discrimination whatsoever. But by reason of the wide discretion permissible in the various steps of the plan, it is equally capable of being applied in such a manner as practically to proscribe any group thought by the law's administrators to be undesirable and from the record before us the conclusion is inescapable that it is the latter application that has prevailed in Harris County. ... Where jury commissioners limit those from whom grand jurors are selected to their own personal acquaintance, discrimination can arise from commissioners who know no negroes as well as from commissioners who know but eliminate them. If there has been discrimination, whether accomplished ingeniously or ingenuously, the conviction cannot stand. Reversed. (131)

Again thirty years later the court had to deal with a very similar case. In Whitus v. Georgia (132) it ruled for the first time that the use of segregated sources for the jury list (in this instance, tax digests) made out a prima facie case of purposeful discrimination. It further decided that such opportunity of discrimination as was present had been used. Here, too, the judgment was reversed.

c. Covert discrimination by officials. In many states another provision, not openly discriminatory but easily abusable, demands that jury commissioners be personally acquainted with prospective jurors, a method also used by judges in their choice of the venire. (133) Jury commissioners were almost exclusively white and their personal knowledge of the black population was often limited and partial. In one of the Scottsboro decisions the Supreme Court took judicial notice of this fact:

> The general attitude of the jury commissioner is shown by the following extract from his testimony: "I do not know of any negro in Morgan county over twenty-one and under sixty-five who is generally reputed to be honest and intelligent and who is esteemed in the community for his integrity, good character and sound judgment, who is not an habitual drunkard, who isn't afflicted with a permanent disease or physical weakness which would render him unfit to discharge the duties of a juror, and who can read English, and who has never been convicted of a crime involving moral turpitude".
> In the light of the testimony given by defendant's witnesses, we find it impossible to accept such a sweeping characterization of the lack of qualifications of negroes in Morgan County. (134)

Similarly in Hill v. Texas (1942):

> One testified: "I personally did not know of a qualified negro that I thought would make a good juror". The other testified he did not know which of the negroes of his acquaintance could read and write. (135)

In an environment in which there is almost no social contact between blacks and whites the provision that a jury commissioner should be personally convinced of the qualifications of a prospective juror - which demands to a very large extent subjective value judgments - amounts to little less than open discrimination by the law.

    Not only do jury commissioners generally have wide discretion in the discharge of their duties, but they are also very leniently treated by the courts if they do not strictly follow the law. Statutes, the courts have decided, do not have to be strictly complied with, substantial compliance is enough. This has of course created more problems than it solved. A representative selection of cases in which the Supreme Court of Illinois rejected complaints about unfair jury selection under this "substantial compliance" doctrine follows:

    The office of the court of Winnebago county was divided between two officials. In <u>Mapes</u> v. <u>People</u> the plaintiff alleged that the wrong one drew his jury; this objection was held "trivial" by the Supreme Court. (136) This ruling was confirmed one year later, in <u>Wilhelm</u> v. <u>People</u>, when the court held that a positive injury to the defendant must be shown and that a mere irregularity was not sufficient cause for challenge to the array. (137) The presumption is that the official did his duty and the plaintiff must prove the contrary. (138) And again, in a murder case, in <u>Siebert</u> v. <u>People</u> (1892), after a verdict of guilty:

> While the statute was not strictly followed in the selection of a jury, and the record fails to show that the rights of the defendants were impaired, or that the defendants were in any manner prejudiced, we can not hold that the irregularity should result in a reversal of judgment. (139)

    An article by Charles A. Ross of the Chicago Bar that appeared in the <u>Illinois Law Review</u> in December, 1910, sheds further light on this problem. (140) It is based on a report presented by the jury commissioners of Cook County on November 18, 1908, in support of a request for additional clerks in the office of the commissioners. This report shows clearly that the jury commissioners did not even attempt to comply with the Jury Commissioners Act of 1897 in at least four particulars:

    1. They never made or maintained a quadrennial jury book as provided for in section 27 of chapter 78 of the Revised Statutes.
    2. They selected possible jurors from registration lists and from the city directory, i.e. from unauthorized lists which contained names of people who were not qualified to serve on juries.
    3. They did not interview the persons selected from these lists personally to find out their qualifications but sent them forms throught the mail.

The recipients had to fill out these forms and judge their own capabilities, viz. whether they were "in possession of their natural faculties, and not infirm or decrepit" and "of fair character, of approved integrity, of sound judgment, well informed, ..." The shortcomings and dangers of such a system are apparent. On the back of the note the addressee had to answer some questions, but the more important provisions of the First, Third, and Fourth items of section 2 of chapter 78 of the Statutes were not even covered. (141)

That this practice continued for at least the next forty years is shown by several cases. In People v. Lieber (1934) the court noticed:

> On the hearing of this motion to quash, Lieber produced oral and documentary evidence and identified the records of the criminal court with reference to the selection of the grand jury: ... (4) a photostatic copy of the original return of the sheriff showing purported service by mailing to the fifty-six persons and that three were not found and one was dead. The notations, "Accepted", "Excused" and "Not found" were affixed to the original return by the clerk. Twenty-five of the fifty-six summoned jurors were excused before the beginning of the term. When or by whom they were excused is not disclosed, but in any event they do not appear to have been excused by lot or in open court. (142)

In 1948 the court disapproved of this practice but decided that the defendant was not prejudiced if all the jurors appeared after being summoned by mail. (143)

The notice sent to prospective jurors during the first decade of this century looked like this:

Office of the<br>
JURY COMMISSIONERS<br>
of Cook County

Room 824 County Court House.
    Clark, Randolph and Washington Sts.
Office Hours: 9 A.M. to 5 P.M.
Saturdays: 9 A.M. to 12 Noon.

                                        Chicago ............
.................................................
                             .................................
                                     Ward ... Precinct...

    You are hereby notified that your name is included in the list of persons subject to be drawn for Jury service.
    You are required to report to this office in person or by letter within five days from date hereof, whether eligible for Jury duty or not.
    You are required to give your age, occupation, whether you are a householder living with your family, and whether you own real estate in Cook county.
    When drawn for Jury Service you will receive summons in due course from the court.
    The present Jury Law, in force July 1, 1897, provides that "At the end of each term of court the said Jury Commissioners shall ascertain the names of all persons who have served and all who have been excused as jurors during said term, and the names of such as have served shall be then checked off from the said jury list and shall not again be placed in either jury box until all others on said list shall have served or have

*Please bring this notice with you, or write your answer on back of this notice.*

been found to be disqualified or exempt, and the names of all who have been excused and who possess the qualifications for jury service shall be again in the jury box".

Persons Eligible for Jury Service.
   I. Citizens of the county of the age of 21 years or upward and under 65 years.
   II. In the possession of their natural faculties and not infirm and decrepit.
   III. Free from all legal exemptions, of fair character, of approved integrity, of sound judgment, well informed, who understand the English language.

Classes of Persons Exempt:
   The Governor, Lieutenant Governor, Secretary of State, Auditor of Public Accounts, Treasurer, Superindendent of Public Instruction, Attorney-General, members of the General Assembly during their term of office, all judges of courts, all clerks of courts, sheriffs, coroners, postmasters, mail carriers, practicing attorneys, all officers of the United States, officiating ministers of the gospel, school teachers during the term of school, practicing physicians, registered and assistant pharmacists, constant ferrymen, mayors of cities, policemen, active members of the fire department, embalmers, undertakers, and funeral directors, actively engaged in their business, and all persons actively employed upon the editorial or mechanical staffs and departments of any newspapers of general circulation, printed or published in this State: Provided, that every fireman who shall have faithfully and actively served as such in any volunteer fire department in any city of this State, for the term of seven years, may thereafter be exempt from serving on juries in all courts. The Judges and Clerks of Election shall be exempt from jury duty during the term of their service and for two years thereafter. Members of the Illinois National Guard and Illinois Naval Reserve shall be exempt from jury duty during their term of service and for an equal period thereafter.

   If exempt under any of the claims named above, or qualified to serve, your statement should be made on the back of this notice.

.....................
.....................
.....................
Jury Commissioners.

(Verso.)

CHICAGO, ...........

JURY COMMISSIONERS,
   County Court Building
       Chicago.

   Gentlemen:
   My age is ..................... years.
   My occupation is .................................................
   I am ............... married, ................ residing with my family.

I .................... own real estate in Cook county.
Remarks ...................................................................
..........................................................................
..........................................................................
..........................................................................
..........................................................................
..........................................................................
..........................................................................
..........................................................................
Sign Name ................................................................
Business Address .........................................................
And Present Residence Address ............................................
(144)

> 4. Jurors who had served were exempt from further service until all other qualified people of Cook County had served, instead of until the list was exhausted.

Ross went on to inquire whether the improper construction of the law of 1897 by the commissioners amounted to an impairment of substantial rights of the defendants. "The true rule seems to be that as to all essential provisions they are mandatory, but provisions as to time and manner of performing the duties are directory". (145) This view he supported by cases from various jurisdictions. Reviewing the practice of more than a decade, the author concluded that

> the law of 1897 has never had a fair chance. That law seems susceptible of a construction that would prevent the Cook County system from being a by-word and a hissing. (146)

This law was only amended, twenty years after the article in the Illinois Law Review, by the law of 1931. But the court has in this century become noticeably stricter:

> Courts have been very liberal in excluding mere irregularities where an attempt has been made to comply with the law in providing juries, but they cannot hold valid and legal a jury where no attempt has been made to select it in accordance with the requirements of the statute. (147)

> The showing in this record is that the county board absolutely disregarded the provisions of said sections 1 and 2 aforesaid. In the first place, they failed to get a full ten per cent list as provided in section 1. In the second place, they made absolutely no attempt whatever to comply with section 2 as to making a selected list of one hundred persons for each trial term of the circuit court and other courts of record of the qualifications mentioned in that section. (148)

But the "substantial compliance" rule lived on:

> The evidence also showed that at the September, 1927, session the county board failed to make a new list and selection in accordance with the Jurors act. ...
> There is nothing to show that any substantial right of the plaintiff in error was impaired by the failure of the board of supervisors to strictly comply with the statute in reference to making up the jury list. In absence of a showing that no attempt was made to comply with the statute, a verdict of a jury will not be set aside, or a judgment thereon reversed, because a challenge to the array of jurors was overruled, unless the record shows that substantial rights of the defendant were thereby impaired. (149)

Even today a defendant can not automatically rest assured of the proper administration of the Jurors Act, as a case from 1954 demonstrated:

> It is also undisputed that the judge had not appointed jury commissioners under the provisions of section 1 of the Jury Commissioners Act at the time of the trial of this case at the circuit court; that jury lists had not been made up as directed by section 2 of that act; that the jurors present in Court had not been drawn pursuant to section 8 and 9 and that the jurors had been selected, drawn and summoned pursuant to the provisions of an act concerning jurors. ... A defendant charged with a crime is entitled to substantial compliance with the law relative to the selection of the grand jury which presents the formal accusation against him. (150)

In a 1960 case new names were placed in the jury box before the prior names had been exhausted, the sheriff had not served all persons on the prior venires before the fourth special venire was called, and the Court had ordered the summoning of bystanders to complete the jury, rather than calling another special venire. (151)

One of the ways to obey the letter of the law and still discriminate was by tokenism. Jury commissioners have probably never in open court admitted that they had no intention to select more than one black to sit on the panel, but such intent speaks quite clearly from the sources:

> Commissioner Wells: "... We had no intention of placing more than one negro on the panel. ..."
> Commissioner Tennant: "... I did not have any intention of putting more than one on the list".
> Commissioner Douglas: "... We liked this one, and our intentions were to get just one negro on the grand jury. ..." (152)

It is not easy to see how the court did arrive at the judgment, on this testimony:

> A careful examination of these statements in connection with all the other evidence leaves us unconvinced that the commissioners deliberately and intentionally limited the number of Negroes on the grand jury list. (153)

To this, the dissenting opinions answered:

> Clearer proof of intentional and deliberate limitation on the basis of color would be difficult to produce. (154)

To quote testimonies from just one more case, in which both the problem of personal acquaintance and the question of tokenism are very clearly at issue:

> One commissioner said: "I was not personally acquainted with any negro citizen of Dallas County that I thought was qualified to sit on the Grand Jury, at that time. I did not know one personally that I would recommend, myself, at that time.
> "... The reason that I did not submit the name of a negro in my 6 names that I submitted was because I did not know any negro citizen that I felt was qualified with reference to education and business ability to serve on this Grand Jury".
>
> Another said:
> "We did not select a negro when I served as a Commissioner; we did disregard color, race or creed; I did not know plenty of negroes that I said would be qualified. I know a lot of negroes that are qualified lawyers, doctors, Superintendents of Schools and that sort of thing but the particular thing is that their occupation precludes them from serving. You could not ask a doctor or lawyer to serve 3 months of their time, either white of colored; that limited us as to the number that we could select. I knew a lot of white and colored people that were qualified.
> "I did not select a negro on this Grand Jury Panel but I tried." This commissioner had sought a Negro High School Principal for the list.
>
> The third said: "The reason a negro was not selected was not because we discriminated; I only appointed those that I knew to be qualified.
> ...
> "If the name of any qualified negro citizen - been submitted at that time, who had given his permission and said that he had time to serve, I certainly would have submitted his name along with the other 15 names, if it was somebody that would have been acceptable to me". (155)

Both these cases came up to the United States Supreme Court from Dallas County, Texas, and both were murder cases that resulted in verdicts of guilty.

# CHALLENGES, VICINAGE, CHANGE OF VENUE, AND MIXED JURIES

In criminal trials both the prosecutor and the defendant have the right to except against a juror or the whole jury if they believe that this juror or this jury are not impartial. This kind of exception is called challenge.

> The right of challenge comes from the common law with the trial by jury itself, and has always been held essential to the fairness of trial by jury. (156)

Challenges can be subdivided into challenges to the whole panel, i.e. challenges to the array, and challenges to individual jurors.
Challenges to the Array. If one party believes that the drawing and impaneling of the whole jury has been unfair, that officials have favored the opposite side, the panel of jurors can be challenged:

> And you shall understand, that the Jurors names are ranked in the Pannell one under another, which order or ranking the Jurors is called the Array, ... so as to challenge the Array of the Pannell, is at once to challenge or except against all the persons so arrayed or impanelled, in respect of the partialitie or default of the Sherife, Coroner, or other Officer that made the returne. (157)

In Illinois such a challenge to the array must be supported by affidavits or proof of the illegality of the panel, and in order to be reviewed in a higher court it must be preserved in the bill of exceptions, together with the supporting evidence and the ruling of the trial court on it. (158) If no affidavits and no evidence are produced, this is fatal:

> This challenge was signed by the attorney for Hotchkiss but not sworn to. It was not accompanied by any affidavit nor was any evidence offered in its support. This failure to support the challenge either by evidence or by affidavits was a fatal omission and justified the trial court in overruling the challenge. (159)

To be successful in a reviewing trial, a plaintiff must show, here too, that substantial rights were injured by overruling a challenge to the array:

> A case will not be reversed because a challenge to the array of jurors was overruled, unless the record shows that substantial rights of the defendant were thereby impaired. (160)

In blatant cases, however, this is not necessary:

Where no attempt is made to comply with the legal method provided for summoning jurors, a challenge to the array must be sustained even though no prejudice to the defendant is shown. (161)

Challenges to Individual Jurors. These challenges are divided into peremptory challenges and challenges for cause.

Peremptory Challenges. Both sides may challenge a limited number of jurors without giving any reason. In the flowery language of William Blackstone:

> In criminal cases, or at least in capital ones, there is, in favorem vitae, allowed to the prisoner an arbitrary and capricious species of challenge to a certain number of jurors, without showing any cause at all; which is called a peremptory challenge; a provision so full of the tenderness and humanity to prisoners for which our English laws are justly famous. This is grounded on two reasons: 1. As every one must be sensible, what sudden impressions and unaccountable prejudices we are apt to conceive upon the bare looks and gestures of another; and how necessary it is that the prisoner (when put to defend his life) should have a good opinion of his jury, the want of which might totally disconcert him; the law wills not that he should be tried by any one man against whom he has conceived a prejudice even without being able to assign a reason for such a dislike. 2. Because, upon challenge for cause shown, if the reason assigned prove insufficient to set aside the juror, perhaps the bare questioning his indifference may sometimes provoke resentment; to prevent all ill consequences from which, the prisoner is still at liberty, if he pleases, peremptorily to set him aside. (162)

In a joint trial of more than one prisoner, each defendant may challenge his full number,

> and thus, in effect, the prisoners in such a case possess the power of peremptory challenge to the aggregate of the numbers, to which they are respectively entitled. This is a rule clearly laid down by Lord Coke, Lord Hale, and Serjeant Hawkins, and, indeed, by all the elementary writers. (163)

But nothing in the Constitution of the United States requires Congress to grant the defendants in criminal cases peremptory challenges: "Trial by an impartial jury is all that is secured". (164) In Illinois it was specifically ruled that both the defendant and "the People" have the right of peremptory challenge. (165)

Peremptory challenge can be a very convenient way for a District or State Attorney to remove blacks from a jury panel. If less than 15 percent of the population are black there is a very high possibility that a panel of 23 will contain three blacks or less. If the number of persons who can so be challenged is six, this means that all blacks can be removed from the jury without giving any reason. It is unlikely that more than one drawn then from the box will be black. It is of course all but impossible to prove that a State Attorney exercised his peremptories in order to racially discriminate and if no such showing can be made objections are not available.

> He says he was deprived of due process and equal protection because the State exercised the right so as to "systematically" exclude negroes. Even aside from the absence of any showing that the prospective jurors were excused solely because of race, there is no merit whatever in the contention. There was no exclusion of negroes per se from the panel itself; and, of course, there were in fact several among the number. The fact that the State's exercise of peremptory challenges resulted in excluding them from the petit jury did not deprive defendant of any constitutional right. ... The right of peremptory challenge is a substantial one which should not be abridged or denied. It may, by its very nature, be exercised or not exercised, according to the judgment, will or caprice of the party entitled thereto, and he is not required to assign any reason therefor. (166)

About the only way to ascertain if a prosecutor used his peremptory challenges in order to discriminate is by statistics. If it can be shown that a State Attorney for years excluded all blacks from his juries there is a strong assumption that these challenges were used for illegal purposes and the United States Supreme Court made clear in a recent (1965) case from Alabama that it will not tolerate this:

> This system, it is said, in and of itself, provides justification for striking any group of otherwise qualified jurors in any given case, whether they be Negroes, Catholics, accountants or those with blue eyes. Based on the history of this system and its actual use and operation in this country, we think there is merit in this position. ... The persistence of peremptories and their extensive use demonstrate the long and widely held belief that peremptory challenge is a necessary part of trial by jury. ...
> The essential nature of the peremptory challenge is that it is one exercised without a reason stated, without inquiry and without being subject to the court's control. ...
> The presumption in any particular case must be that the prosecutor is using the State's challenge to obtain a fair and impartial jury to try the case before the court.

"But", the Court forcefully continued,

> when the prosecutor in a county, in case after case, whatever the circumstances, whatever the crime and whoever the defendant or the victim may be, is responsible for the removal of Negroes who have been selected as qualified jurors by the jury commissioners and who have survived challenges for cause, with the result that no

Negroes ever served on petit juries, the Fourteenth Amendment claim takes on added significance. (167)

And, using even stronger language:

It would appear that the purposes of the peremptory challenge are being perverted. (168)

Challenges for Cause. A juror may be challenged for cause because of blood relationship with one of the parties, because he has a pecuniary interest in the outcome of the trial, if it can be shown that he is prejudiced, or for similar reasons. At common law such challenges were divided into two classes, principal challenges and challenges to the favor. (169) The causes for challenge under Illinois law are laid down in section 14 of chapter 78 of the Revised Statutes, quoted above. (170) If a juror is legally exempt but no party challenges him, his verdict is valid. (171) A defendant cannot complain about the overruling of his challenges for cause if his peremptory challenges were not exhausted. (172) Neither the prisoner nor the State may use their challenges to ensure participation of friendly or favorable jurors in the trial:

The right to challenge is the right to reject, not to select a juror. If from those who remain, an impartial jury is obtained, the constitutional right of the accused is maintained. (173)

Another of the built-in safeguards of the American jury system against biased jurors is the provision that the jury must come from the neighborhood of the place where the alleged crime was committed. In the historical section of this dissertation it was shown how the visne in this context had come to mean county and how this notion was imported into America. (174)

Early United Stated Supreme Court decisions are not very revealing as far as the interpretation of this facet of the jury system is concerned. The doctrine of the neighborhood jury was regarded as an absolute injunction and the Court had little occasion to rule on it. In the case of Queen v. Hepburn (175) the defendant excepted to a juror who was called as a talesman and who was an inhabitant of Alexandria county, Virginia, not of Washington, D.C., where the trial was held. The lower court had decided that he was a proper juror and he was sworn. Counsel for defense then objected and took exception to the opinion of the court. The Supreme Court ruled that it could not sustain the objection and exception on review because they should have been made before the juror was sworn. (176)

In the Illinois Supreme Court a certain development in this question is observable. The first case that came before it in this matter was Bell v. People (in 1837), in which the court held valid a provision in the enabling acts of the Municipal Court of Chicago of that year. It stated: "That the grand and petit jurors of said Municipal Court, shall be selected from the qualified inhabitants of the city". (177) In 1882, however, the same court held unconstitutional an act dividing the jurisdictions of the justices of the peace of Cook County into the City of Chicago and the territory within the county but ouside the city:

> This would be the opening through which all kinds of obnoxious legislation in this subject would pass. ... This is a local and special law relating to their jurisdiction, and is clearly unconstitutional. (178)

In accordance with a United States Supreme Court decision (179) counties were defined as

> mere political divisions of the territory of the State, as a convenient mode of exercising the political, executive and judicial powers of the State. ... Were it not for the constitutional restrictions, the General Assembly might ... change county lines, and even abolish counties and create new ones, to suit public convenience or interest. (180)

As long as these counties exist a suspect must be tried within the county where the alleged crime occurred and by a jury from that county. In 1884 the Supreme Court ruled that the trial of a liquor seller in Kane county was unconstitutional because the alleged sales had taken place in Cook county, although within 70 rods of the Kane county border. (181) In <u>Miller</u> v. <u>People</u> (1900) the opinion of the court in <u>Bell</u> v. <u>People</u> (1837) was distinguished and it was declared that a city grand jury must be drawn from the body of the county, not from within the city in which the court had jurisdiction. (182) The argumentation appealed to the history of the institution. The same was true in <u>Chicago</u> v. <u>Knobel</u> (1908)

> Under the common law, in both civil and criminal cases, the jury were to be selected from the <u>visne</u> or neighborhood, - from among the neighbors and equals of the litigants or the accused,- and by long usage this came to mean from the <u>body of the county</u>. (183)

With this, the doctrine was formed. In 1912 the court held that the jurisdiction and judgeship that Albert D. Rodenburg held in the town of Centralia were unconstitutional because Centralia lies partly within Marion county and partly within Clinton county. There would have been no legal way under these circumstances to select a jury, because it would have been necessary to select it from two counties. (184) Finally, in 1928 the court put down the rule that "A grand jury selected wholly from within the limits of a city is no legal grand jury and an indictment returned by it is not good". (185)

The rule that a jury should come from the immediate neighborhood of the court is well-founded in history and, as was demonstrated, intended as one of the safeguards against prejudiced jurors. Certain circumstances, however, can give the concept of the neighborhood jury quite the opposite effect. Especially after a particularly gruesome crime or after one of which a prominent member of the community has been the victim, the public may be so enraged that it is often impossible for a defendant to receive a fair trial. The system knows an escape in this case: the accused can move for a change of venue.

This is a purely procedural question on the state level and the United States Supreme Court has been very cautious not to overstep its jurisdiction. Rulings on change of venue by this tribunal are therefore relatively rare. One such case was that of Marcellus Thomas, a black man sentenced to death for murder in Harris county, Texas. One black had sat on Thomas' jury, but the defendant claimed that it was impossible for him to get a fair trial in Harris county on account of local prejudice. The trial court then heard testimony from the population and decided that racial prejudice existed but did not justify a change of venue. The United States Supreme Court held that on the record before it the presumption must be that the lower courts did their duty and affirmed the conviction:

> As before remarked, whether such discrimination was practiced in this case was a question of fact, and the determination of that question adversely to the plaintiff in error by the trial court of criminal appeals was decisive, so far as this court is concerned, unless it could be held that these decisions constitute such abuse as amounted to an infraction of the Federal Constitution, which cannot be presumed, and which there is no reason to hold on the record before us. On the contrary, the careful opinion of the court of criminal appeals, setting forth the evidence, justifies the conclusion of that court that the negro race was not intentionally or otherwise discriminated against in the selection of the grand and petit jurors. (186)

Illinois had originally had very liberal regulations governing change of venue. Until 1861 change of venue was granted simply if the accused swore that he feared an impartial trial was impossible. After that year a petition for change of venue had to be supported by affidavits and could be traversed by counter-affidavits. (187) A case in point was that of William J. Jamison (1893). Jamison, a black man, had shot one Charles A. Aaron at his home and was sentenced to death in the Circuit Court of Adams county. He alleged bias in the community and produced six affidavits which showed that there was indeed considerable prejudice, that the jail had even been beleaguered by citizens armed with sledgehammers, a rope, and other threatening instruments, and that a fair trial was very unlikely. (188) The State's Attorney filed affidavits of 367 citizens traversing the affidavits of the defense and stated substantially that he

> did not believe that any feeling existed among any considerable number of persons in the county, other than an earnest desire that impartial, even-handed justice might be done to the defendant on the one hand and to the people on the other. ... it is unreasonable to suppose that so large a number of men, most of whom appear to have been among the most prominent and widely know citizens of their respective localities, would be so reckless as to come forward, as they have done, and make affidavit that no such prejudice existed to their knowledge. (189)

On this evidence the Supreme Court ruled that the Circuit Court did not err in denying the defendant change of venue. Another leading case in this connection was that of Ray Pfanschmidt. Pfanschmidt had been sentenced to death in the same courts as Jamison, also for murder. He had killed and dismembered both his parents, his sister, and a boarding school teacher. Afterwards he had burned the house and the corpses. The case stirred of course considerable interest and antagonism in the county. Change of venue was denied in the lower courts because the defendant could not conclusively prove that it was impossible for him to receive a fair trial. "In view of the gruesomeness of the crime and the great publicity given to its every aspects", the Supreme Court ruled, change of venue should have been granted:

> It was not necessary for plaintiff in error to show beyond reasonable doubt or by a preponderance of evidence that he could not receive a fair and impartial trial, but a change of venue should be granted if the showing was such as to raise a reasonable apprehension that he could not receive a fair trial. (190)

The judgment was reversed.

It has already been noted that prejudice of the judge was an absolute ground for change of venue if the petition was accompanied by affidavits. (191) Another case that received a kind of prominence was that of People v. Arthur (1924). George Opal Arthur had also been sentenced to death for murder, in the Circuit Court of Piatt county. In this case the Supreme Court ruled that if a prisoner had to be removed from the county jail because the public threatened to lynch him, this was showing enough that public opinion was so strongly against him that change of venue should be granted. This decision therefore distinguished that of Jamison v. People, quoted above.

> We should not discuss in detail the ruling of the court on the motion for a change of venue. The showing in support of it was a strong one. The public feeling was so inflamed against the defendant that the sheriff deemed it wise for his safety to remove him from the court for a time. In our opinion the motion for a change of venue should have been granted, and it was error to overrule it. (192)

A rather curious argumentation was used in the more recent case of People v. Allen (1952). Frank Allen had taken indecent liberties with an eleven year old child. The Supreme Court ruled that a change of venue was not mandatory despite heated public feelings as "the nature of the alleged crime would be equally repulsive in any county". (193) The question was not whether the population abhorred the crime - any right-minded citizen presumably would - but whether this abhorrence would be transferred to the defendant. It was the identification of the prisoner with the crime before he was judged guilty that was vicious. The decision reaffirmed the ruling in Arthur:

> The nature of the alleged crime would be equally repulsive in any county. ... in fact, counsel did not utilize all his peremptory challenges in the course of selecting the jury, which took a little over a day. ... There was no direct evidence of threats made against

defendant, or publications denouncing him; nor was he removed from one jail to another to avoid lynching, as the defendant was in People v. Arthur, 314 Ill. 296. (194)

At the core of the Anglo-Saxon conception of justice and of the jury system, is the idea that one's peers can best judge one's actions. But the political and social development of the Anglo-Saxon world during the seven hundred and fifty years since Magna Carta has created a problem of which nobody dreamt in 1215, 1628, or even 1760. The problem can therefore not be solved by appeal to the authority of "the barons", or Coke, or Blackstone. For philosophical reasons, the Constitution is no help either. And although this problem is very real and touches the quick of the jury system, American jurisprudence and the judiciary have never allowed the pertinent questions to be asked, let alone answered them. The problem is: Who is, today, whose peer?

In a closely stratified, or in a very homogeneous, society as that of England from before Magna Carta till long after Blackstone the answer was easy. If "peer" was not a purely technical term denoting a member of the peerage (duke, marquess, earl, viscount, or baron) it could certainly be interpreted as meaning that a merchant was a merchant's peer or equal, a freeman a freeman's, a villein a villein's, and an Italian an Italian's (lex de medietate linguae). But who is a black American dockworker's equal? A white dockworker, a black housewife, a black professor, a white professor, or only a black American dockworker? The judiciary answers: all of these, because everybody is equal before the law. The logic - although not very impressive - is apparent. Everybody is equal before the law, therefore everybody is equal in court, and no matter who sits on the jury panel, they are all each other's and the defendant's equals. This argumentation not only contradicts social reality but also official decisions from the judiciary itself.

Americans do not form a "classless" society in which everybody is everybody's equal. The word "class" is to be understood in its technical meaning: minors form a class, and so do women, and Mexican-Americans, and college professors. It can hardly be claimed that all women, or all blacks, are equal among themselves, for the simple reason that every person belongs to a variety of such classes. One can be a woman, and black, and a college professor at the same time. What the dominant reference group of such a person is (her "identification"), whom she cares to call her equals, must be empirically investigated for every single instance of this combination. To suppose that a random sample of twelve people from the six million inhabitants of Cook county would yield even one "equal" does not seem to be very rational. One would have to go through a very careful selection process, in collaboration with the accused. But, it is immediately objected by the judiciary, the court must not take into account age, race, sex, and social status of the veniremen. Everybody is equal before the law.

This objection could be maintained more easily if there were not numerous opinions in which the courts have openly taken cognizance of the fact that the population is not homogeneous. Most obviously, women were excluded until the 1930's because only electors could sit on the jury. Not only sex, but race and social stratification, too, were taken into account by the courts if this was opportune.

During World War II the Supreme Court heard an appeal in connection with the government policy of interning Japanese and Japanese-Americans for fear of a Japanese attack on the Continental United States. The plaintiff, an American citizen by the name of Hirabayashi, claimed that the government had no right to intern him because it could not legally take notice of the fact that he was of an East-Asian (or any other) race. Not so, said Justice Harlan Fiske Stone in his opinion of the court:

> Distinctions between citizens solely because of their ancestry are by their very nature odious to a free people whose institutions are founded upon the doctrine of equality. ...
> Because racial discriminations are in most circumstances irrelevant and therefore prohibited, it by no means follows that, in dealing with the perils of war, Congress and the Executive are wholly precluded from taking into account those facts and circumstances which are relevant to measures for our national defense. ... (195)

If in this case the "perils of war" could be cited as the reason for governmental racial discrimination, the same is not true of other appeals. In the decision of the Court in Fay v. New York (1947) that "This court, however, has never entertained a defendant's objection to exclusions from the jury except when he is a member of the excluded class" (196) the existence of classes among the population is apparently not questioned by the Court. A further case of racial classification by the judiciary is found in Hernandez v. Texas (1954):

> The petitioner's initial burden in sustaining his charge of group discrimination was to prove that persons of Mexican descent constitute a separate class in Jackson County, distinct from "whites". One method by which this may be demonstrated is by showing the attitude of the community. Here the testimony of responsible officials and citizens contained the admission that residents of the community distinguished between "white" and "Mexican". ... On the courthouse grounds at the time of the hearing, there were two men's toilets, one unmarked, and the other marked "Colored Men" and "Hombres Aqui" ("Men Here"). (197)

The opinion of the Illinois Supreme Court in Jamison v. People, already quoted, that

> It is unreasonable to suppose that so large a number of men, most of whom appear to have been among the most prominent and widely known citizens of their respective localities, would be so reckless as to come forward, as they have done, and make affidavit that no such prejudice existed to their knowledge. (198)

clearly takes cognizance of social stratification.

The main purpose of chapter I of this thesis was to demonstrate how much the black community of Illinois differed from the rest of the population. Their historical background and experience obviously justifies classifying them as a distinct group, different from the native whites and the immigrants. The Fourteenth Amendment and the Civil Rights Act of 1875 gave them the right not to be excluded from juries on account of their race only. But these enactments did not give a black defendant the right to inclusion of his own race on the jury. This interpetation has been unvarying during the hundred years since the enactment of these two laws. Strauder v. West Virginia has already been cited. (199) Justice Stephen J. Field said, in his dissent in Neal v. Delaware (1881):

> All persons within the jurisdiction of the State, whether citizens or foreigners, male or female, old or young, are embraced in its comprehensive terms [ i.e. the Fourteenth Amendment's ]. If to give equal protection to them requires that persons of the classes to which they severally belong shall have the privilege or be subject to the duty - whichever it may be - of acting as jurors in the courts in cases affecting their interests, the mandate of the Constitution will produce a most extraordinary change in the administration of the laws of the States; it will abolish the distinctions made in the selection of jurors between citizens and foreigners, and between those of our race and those of the Mongolian, Indian or other races, who may be at the time within their jurisdiction. A Chinaman may insist that people of his race shall be summoned as jurors in cases affecting his interests, and that the exclusion is a denial to him of the equal protection of the laws. Any foreigner, sojourning in the country, may make a similar claim for jurors of his nation. It is obvious that no such claim would be respected, and yet I am unable to see why it should not be sustained, if the construction placed upon the Amendment by the majority of the Court in this case be sound. (200)

In 1947 the Court declared: "Society also has a right to a fair trial. The defendant's right is a neutral jury. He has no constitutional right to friends on the jury". (201) It is not evident why a black jury or one composed entirely of women should not be able to try a defendant in fairness also to society.

CONCLUSION

How did judges interpret and use trial by jury in cases involving members of a minority, especially blacks?
The unbroken British-American legal tradition has always been

recognized by American judges. They quoted freely from British laws, statutes, and legal writers if they thought they could decide a case by appeal to these authorities. The whole way of argumentation in American courts was traditionally historical in that the questions that came up were decided by precedent cases and sometimes by very old legislative enactments. There is a link between this historical argumentation and a certain philosophy of results which can be discerned in the opinions of the judges.

The Supreme Court has repeatedly held that trial by jury is not indispensable to the American understanding of justice. But the notion of democracy is incorporated in the institution and it has therefore always been held in high esteem and "jealously safeguarded" by the courts.

The presumption of innocence usually worked better when an official in the discharge of his duties claimed it as his right than when a black defendant was on trial. In the latter case the presumption was obviously often one of guilt. Similarly, lower courts have often allowed District Attorneys to use peremptory challenges to eliminate blacks - it is easy to see who is black - while it was very difficult for minority defendants to exclude prejudiced jurors, because such prejudice is not easily recognizable. If bias can be shown challenge for cause is available. Challenge to the array is only sustained by the courts if substantial rights of the defendant are impaired by the jury selection procedure, but it is not very clear what those substantial rights are.

Open discrimination by the law is prohibited by the Fourteenth Amendment, and its rigorous enforcement by the federal judiciary has made cases of this description rare. Open discrimination by officials, however, has been treated very leniently by the lower courts, although it is also prohibited, by section 4 of the Civil Rights Act of 1875. Covert acts of discrimination by officials have often come before the courts; this is a problem which Hamilton recognized in his Federalist No. 83:

> The sheriff who is the summoner of ordinary juries, and the clerks of courts who have the nomination of special juries, are themselves standing officers, and acting individually, may be supposed more accessible to the touch of corruption than the judges, who are a collective body. It is not difficult to see that it would be in the power of those officers to select jurors who would serve the purpose of the party as well as a corrupted bench. (202)

The judiciary has always vehemently been opposed to granting a distinct group of citizens (blacks or women, in particular) the right to have a jury composed entirely or partially of members of their own group, although the jury de medietate linguae was used in British and early American courts and could be cited as a precedent in legislation. All that is secured to minorities is the right not to be discriminated against in the selection procedure.

CONCLUSION

Was there a basic pervasive pattern of judicial reasoning on the equality of races which underlied, or governed, the black man's experience in America? The most striking immediate result of this dissertation is that it presents two essentially different profiles of America. The country that appears from the statistics seems to have little in common with the country the judges were talking about in their decisions and opinions. The salient features of these two profiles of a nation shall be briefly reviewed here in order to facilitate comparison.

## THE UNITED STATES AS REFLECTED IN THE STATISTICS

1. Total population doubled during the half century from 1890 to 1940. In many places the make-up of the population changed profoundly. In the East North Central division, the core of the Midwest, the black population increased 400% during this period. In a nation that was about 55% urban, 90% of these Midwestern blacks lived in cities; urban problems were to become prominent in the United States. In-migration into the Midwest was at times 500 to 600 or even 1'000 blacks per 1'000 resident black population. This is well reflected in the population pyramids. (pp. 18-23, 37-40, above)

2. The construction of a vast railway system created a complex situation: it made migration possible on this scale but it also favored a socio-economic climate that made the escape from the South to the North a very problematic move. In the process the "race question" was nationalized: it was no longer a purely Southern matter but became a national problem. (pp. 23-25)

3. In four major fields of life - politics, economy, health, and crime- statistics show clear differences between the black and the white communities. In the South, where most of the blacks lived, there was a strong tendency towards one-party rule and concomitant nondemocratic political practices; nationwide there were great divergencies in economic status and incomes between blacks and whites; connected to this was the poor physical and mental health of the black population, the high death rates, and the frequency of tuberculosis and violent deaths; even on an adjusted basis, arrest rates for blacks were several times as high as those for whites. (pp. 26-40)

## THE UNITED STATES IN THE MINDS OF THE JUDGES

1. A random selection of persons from the body of a county can yield unbiased, impartial, representative jurors who "hear before they condemn". Judges

only administer the law but do not make it. (pp. 93-97, 106/7)

2. Laws cannot change prejudice but they can enforce just treatment of minorities in the courts. Laws can secure the participation of these minorities in the judicial process on an equal footing with the majority and they can effectively suppress discriminatory actions by officials. There are numerous remedies which safeguard the defendant against unjust procedures in the courts. (pp. 97, 107-112, 118-122)

3. Officials are generally honest and unprejudiced. Although they make little effort to comply with the laws governing their official functions, the burden of proof rests with the defendant if he alleges unconstitutional practices. Even if officials are found guilty of discrimination they are very leniently treated by the courts. (pp. 112-117)

4. A prisoner can get a change of venue only if he proves that the trial judge is prejudiced or if his life is threatened by a mob. The presumption is in all other cases that he can get a fair trial. (pp. 121-125)

5. Social stratification exists but it can generally be disregarded and is in any case not relevant for the composition of a peer group. (pp. 125-127)

Simplifying but slightly, one can say that the black defendants lived in the world as it appears from the statistics while the white judges lived in a separate reality. As long as there are few contacts between the two there is little harm in this situation. But as soon as judges try to become operative in the defendant's world, and even regulate life in it, problems arise. Judges invade another culture and try to come to grips with it by using logics (language) within the framework of their particular legal heritage and traditional procedures.

## LOGICS AND LANGUAGE

Judges have to abstract important facts in order to fit the cases before them into their concepts. Miller (1) spoke of a resulting moral overstrain due to tensions between high ideals and low achievement and the attempted resolution of this overstrain through language:

> In language, the consequence of moral overstrain has been the development of numerous rhetorical devices that have served either to justify or to veil the disparity between social practice and social ideals. (2)

The rhetorical devices are: "not deciding at all; deciding, but on non-racial grounds, and deciding through unique application of legislatic reasoning". (3) This last point - legalistic reasoning - is closely related to the concept of legal fiction. Abstraction is necessary, simply because of the complexity of reality; but to what extent and in what fields may one abstract safely without defeating one's fundamental goals? It is permissible to claim that everybody is equal? Is it permissible to assume that people are n o t equal?

Unless a legal system contains premises about differences among races, as it may about differences between sexes or between young and old, the social realities that reflect such differences are likely to be treated in law under non-racial terms. Thus as these terms promote a non-racial law they often obscure a very racial reality. (4)

Only a law that contains premises about race can grant a black jury to a black defendant.

## LEGAL HERITAGE AND TRADITIONAL PROCEDURE

1. The law as a whole was introduced into America from 17th century and 18th century Britain. Individual laws and statutes were adopted in the New World if they proved applicable, if they worked. (pp. 51-57, 81-88)
2. Trial by jury was fundamentally important for the American idea of justice, but it was not thought to be indispensable for the judicial machinery. It did, however, embody the democratic ideal. It was generally held to be a specifically Anglo-Saxon mode of procedure, not applicable to other races and cultures with more "primitive" forms of government. There are dissenting opinions to this. (pp. 88-92)
3. The instrument of the neighborhood jury was originally created for tax assessment and was only much later used for judicial purposes. Nobody at first expected the jurors to be unbiased or to render a rational verdict. Such ideas developed slowly and in accordance with the more general political and social theories of the western world. The institution as we know it today was introduced into America on the strength of the argumentation of Lord Coke, William Blackstone, and the American revolutionaries. (pp. 44-57)
4. The rights and duties of Americans originated in England in the seventeenth century. All important provisions of trial by jury can be found in documents dating from that time. Many of the fundamental freedoms and the particulars of trial by jury were repeated in revolutionary documents in the second half of the eighteenth century in America. (pp. 57-64)
5. The whole elaborate system of procedures in American law is largely a verbal culture. (pp. 64-72)

To what extent should judges be guided by abstract philosophical and historical reasoning and to what extent by the findings of statisticians and social scientists? In the final analysis this question can only be answered by each judge individually for himself. There were abortive attempts at a better integration of social sciences into the judicial process. (5) But it seems certain that the philosophical and the scientific way of reasogn must complement each other. Each has its obvious advantages and its equally patent disadvantages. The judge who is guided solely by philosophical premises is less apt to be subject to personal bias than his colleague who lets his own experience color his judgment, he can make use of what the best thinkers of our culture have found out about law and justice,

and his rulings have a systematic and solid foundation. On the other hand, he may
suppress his own conscience, his compassion and other humane values for the cold
logics of legalistic reasoning, he may select his authorities to suit his purposes and
his philosophy, and his arguments may not be appropriate to the case before him.
He may lose touch with the down-to-earth problems of the people he judges.

Historical judicial reasoning has been one of the constants of American
social and political life; local differences exist and it can also be shown that there
was a development during longer periods of time. This is apparent if we compare,
for example, Hurtado v. California (1884) and Cassell v. Texas (1950) (6) Hurtado
and Cassell had both been judged guilty and sentenced for murder. The following
sources of law were cited and quoted (in this order) in the Hurtado opinion: a
Supreme Court of California decision, a Supreme Court of Wisconsin decision, Magna
Carta, the Constitution of the United States, Chief Justice Shaw, the Bill of Rights
of Massachusetts, Coke, Blackstone, a statute of Edward III, Sir Francis Winninton,
a statute of Henry VII and the Dudley Act of Henry VIII, Lord Holt, Sir Bartholomew
Shower, Justice Buller of the United States Supreme Court, a Maryland case of
1765, Reeve's History of English Law, Chancellor Kent, various U.S. Supreme
Court decisions, Cooley's Constitutional Limitations, "the laws of the Medes and
the Persians", Magna Carta again, Bacon, the Assizes of Clarendon and of North-
ampton, Justice Stephen's History of the Criminal Law of England, Sir James
Mackintosh's History of England, allusions to the Roman empire, Burke's Tract of
Popery Laws, an Illinois Supreme Court case, again several U.S. Supreme Court
cases, the usus loquendy of the Constitution and the Fifth Amendment, the Fourteenth Amendment, Webster, a Mississippi Supreme Court case, the constitution
of Connecticut of 1818, Swift's Digest, and again Blackstone.

Justice Harlan, in his dissent to this opinion, used Hutch, History of
the Massachusetts Bay, Story on the Constitution, Lord Chatham, the Journal of
Congress, the constitutions of Massachusetts (1780), New Hampshire (1784), Mary-
land and North Carolina (1776), South Carolina (1778), Virginia (1776), Delaware
(1792), the Northwestern Ordinance (1789), the United States Constitution and its
Amendments, Supreme Court cases, Magna Carta, Coke, Hallam, Mackintosh,
Erskine's speech of 1784 "in defence of the Dean of St. Asaph", Blackstone, Hawkins,
Woodeson's Lectures on the Laws of England, Bacon, Lord Hale, Jacob's Law
Dictionary, Broom's Common Laws of England, the spirit of the framers of the
Constitution, Anglo-Saxon liberties, Madison, cases from the Supreme Judicial
Court of Massachusetts, Chief Justice Shaw, Chancellor Kent, the Declaration of
Rights of the first Continental Bill of Rights of 1774, Bancroft, Hurd, Wilson,
Field, Sawyer, Cooley, and all state constitutions in force at that time.

In Cassell v. Texas the petitioner complained that his rights under
the Fourteenth Amendment had been violated by the exclusion of blacks from the
grand jury that had indicted him. Here we find a very different kind of argumentation
in the opinions of the court and of the dissenting justice. The court first examined
the census figures of Dallas county, where the trial had been held; it also found
out that in the five and a half years preceding the trial, 17 of the 252 members of
the jury panels in that county had been black (i.e. 6.7%). The discrepancy between
this 6.7% and the 15.5% of the total population that were black was then explained
by the statutory qualifications jurors must possess: grand jurors must be voters,

which requires payment of a poll tax; only 6.5% of the Dallas poll tax payers were black. (7) On these grounds, the Court held, the judgment could not be reversed. (8) But it then held that the jury commissioners had discriminated in the jury selection procedure. (9) In support of their opinion the justices used only U.S. Supreme Court cases, a Texas statute, United States Code title 18, § 243, and the 1875 Civil Rights Act, § 4, as well as the census reports. The judgment of the lower court was reversed.

In their concurring opinion, justices Frankfurter, Burton, and Minton held that

> To find in such honest even if pragmatic selection of grand jurors the operation of unconstitutional standards would turn this Court into an agency for supervising the criminal procedure of forty-eight States. (10)

> If one factor is uniform in a continuing series of events that are brought to pass through human intervention, the law would have to have the blindness of indifference rather than the blindness of impartiality not to attribute the uniform factor to man's purpose. (11)

Justice Clark, concurring, repeated two traditional tenets of the jury system:

> Any presumption as to the purpose of the judges, or of the commissioners whom the judges appointed instructed and supervised, must be that they intended no racial limitation. (12)

> The burden of showing facts which permit an inference of purposeful limitation is on the defendant. (13)

Justice Jackson did not agree with the decision of the Court:

> The use of objections to the composition of juries is lately so much resorted to for purposes of delay, however, and the spectacle of a defendant putting the grand jury on trial before he can be tried for a crime is so discrediting to the administration of justice, that it is time to examine the basis for the practice. (14)

Jackson concluded:

> I doubt if any good purpose will be served in the long run by identifying the right of the most worthy Negro to serve on grand juries with the efforts of the least worthy to defer or escape punishment for crime.
> ...
> I would treat this as a case where the irregularity is not shown to have harmed this defendant, and confirm the conviction. But in this and similar cases, I would send a copy of the record to the Department

of Justice for investigation as to whether there have been violations of the statute and, if so, for prosecution. (15)

        The argumentation and the decision in <u>Cassell</u> are probably not more "just" than those of <u>Hurtado</u> but they have the advantage of being more controllable than the hodge-podge of authorities and sources of law presented in the earlier case.

This is therefore the answer to the basic question, the pattern for which we have been looking: The use of mental concepts of a certain kind to regulate life in a society which may not accord with these concepts or even contradict them in important particulars. The most noble and sincere premises may defeat their own purpose if life "out there" does not fit the description.

This can explain to a large extent contradictions inherent in the jury system (for example that between the idea of random selection and the idea of impartiality). Judges try to regulate life from above, in direct consequence of "government of law, not of men", and "equal justice under law", which implies that law is something a b o v e men, something superhuman. The judges, who see themselves as guardians and representatives of this law, tend to act accordingly (traditional robes, daises, arcane language, etc.). And no matter what the statistics say, the world that exists in the minds of the judges is no less real than the one of the social scientists; it has very direct and personal consequences for the defendants. But the demand for more technical education of the judges in the fields of social science and statistics is a doubtful remedy. Judges must rather try to arrive at sure ethical standards which guide them in their decisions and opinions.

BIBLIOGRAPHY

AN ANNOTATED GUIDE TO THE LITERATURE AND THE SOURCES

This guide contains those books and articles that proved most helpful during the research and writing of this dissertation. It therefore lists much material that is nowhere in this paper mentioned directly and does not appear in the footnotes.
It has been judged superfluous to cite the chapters of Myrdal (nr. 15) that correspond to the various sections of this bibliography. Parts III to VI (pp. 205-569) and Appendixes 4 and 6 (pp. 1071-2 and 1079-1124) cover the subjects treated in sections 5 to 8 and 12 of this bibliography.
Abbreviations: U = University, P = Press, GPO = Government Printing Office.
Books have not been annotated where the contents are completely obvious from the title or subtitle.

1. BIBLIOGRAPHIES

1.1. BLACKS IN THE UNITED STATES

The standard bibliographies are those by Work and by Miller. No student of black American history can do without them.

(1)  McPherson, James M. et al., Blacks in America: Bibliographical Essays, Garden City, N.Y.: Doubleday, 1971. At the moment the most recent available bibliography in the field. Very well organized.
(2)  Miller, Elizabeth W., The Negro in America: A Bibliography, Cambridge, Mass.: Harvard UP, 1966. Still the standard work. Although it is selective rather than comprehensive, it gives a wealth of information, especially concerning articles in periodicals. A revised and enlarged edition was compiled by Mary L. Fisher. It contains a new foreword by Thomas F. Pettigrew and was edited by Harvard UP in 1970.
(3)  Sweet, Charles E., The Negro and the Establishment: Law, Politics, and the Courts, Bloomington: Indiana U Library, 1969. A six-page brochure on the central subject of this dissertation.
(4)  Szabo, Andrew, Afro-American Bibliography, San Diego: State College, 1970. A classified catalog of the holdings of the San Diego State College Library which has a large Afro-American Department.
(5)  Work, Monroe N., A Bibliography of the Negro in Africa and America, New York: Wilson, 1928. Exhaustive (660 pp.) up to its time.

## 1.2. LEGAL RESEARCH

The historian with no training in law should use these books, which help him through the maze of legal literature.

(6)  Davies, Bernita J., and Francis J. Rooney, <u>Research in Illinois Law</u>, New York: Oceana, 1954.
(7)  Hicks, Frederick C., <u>Materials and Methods of Legal Research</u>, Rochester, N.Y.: Lawyers' Co-op., 1942 (3rd ed.) Extremely useful as an introductory treatise.
(8)  Klein, Fanny J., <u>Judicial Administration and the Legal Profession</u>, Dobbs Ferry, N.Y.: Oceana, 1963. Part I: The Courts, Part II: The Lawyers. Annotated.
(9)  <u>Law Books and their Use</u>, Rochester, N.Y.: Lawyers' Co-op., 1927. Illustrative examples of various sources.
(10) Schwerin, Kurt (comp.), <u>Guide to Legal Collections in Chicago</u>, Chicago: Northwestern U School of Law, 1955.
(11) Surrency, Erwin C., Benjamin Field, and Joseph Crea, <u>A Guide to Legal Research</u>, New York: Oceana, 1959. A step-by-step introduction.

In addition to these books the student should always have the law dictionaries by B l a c k and by B o u v i e r at his elbow.

## 2. GENERAL BACKGROUND

These books provide a first survey of the problems involved in American "race relations".

(12) The American Negro Reference Book, ed. John P. Davis, Englewood Cliffs, N.J.: Prentice-Hall, 1966. Contributions by the leading authorities in various fields of research about the black experience.
(13) DuBois, William E. B. (comp.) Encyclopedia of the Negro: Preparatory Volume with Reference Lists and Reports, New York: Phelps-Stokes, 1946.
(14) Montagu, Ashley, Race, Science, and Humanity, Princeton: Van Nostrand, 1963. A collection of articles from the years 1926 to 1962, mainly around the author's central belief that the myth of race is "the modern form of the older belief in witchcraft". (Preface, p. iii) Both the popular and the taxonomic concepts of race are "a confused and dangerous idea". (p. vi). Should be read in conjunction with Saller (no. 17)
(15) Myrdal, Gunnar, An American Dilemma, New York: Harper, 1944. No longer the absolute authority, but still the turning point in the history of research concerning blacks in the United States.
(16) Pettigrew, Thomas F., A Profile of the Negro American, Princeton: Van Nostrand, 1964. A good introductory analysis. See especially Part II: Racial Differences.
(17) Saller, Karl, Rassengeschichte des Menschen, Stuttgart: Kohlhammer, 1969. (Urban-Bücher 125) Shows the relative irrelevance of the biological concept of "race".
(18) Silberman, Charles E., Crisis in Black and White, New York: Random, 1964.
(19) UNESCO, Le racisme devant la science, Paris: UNESCO, 1960.
(20) UNO, The Main Types and Causes of Discrimination, Lake Success, N.Y.: United Nations Organization, 1949.

# 3. HISTORY

Sources and analyses of American history with especial regard to the role of the black population. The forces and institutions that helped shape "black American history", particularly from 1865 to 1945.

(21)  Andrews, Charles M., The Colonial Period of American History, 4 vols., New Haven: Yale UP, 1934-1938; 6th printing, 1964.
(22)  Bennett, Lerone, Jr., Before the Mayflower: A History of the Negro in America, 1619-1962, Chicago: Johnson, 1962.
(23)  Bentley, George R., A History of the Freedmen's Bureau, Philadelphia: U of Pennsylvania P, 1955. A balanced account, presenting the successes and mistakes of the Freedmen's Bureau.
(24)  Bergman, Peter M. and Jean McCarroll, The Negro in the Continental Congress, New York: Bergman, 1969. A compilation from 34 vols. of the Journals of the Continental Congress. Vol. I: till 1789, vol. 2: 1789-1801, vol. 3: 1801-1807.
(25)  Black Protest: History, Documents and Analyses, 1619 to the Present, ed. Joanne Grant, Greenwich, Conn.: Fawcett, 1968. Letters of black migrants (Scott), p. 180, and the Race Riot of Chicago (Drake and Cayton), p. 187.
(26)  Broom, Leonard, and Norval D. Glenn, Transformation of the Negro American, New York: Harper and Row, 1965. Good synopsis of black life from 1865 to 1960. See especially ch. 8 "Characteristics of the Negro Population" for a brief account of demographic problems (pp. 157-171).
(27)  A Documentary History of the Negro in the United States, ed. Herbert Aptheker, 2 vols., New York: Citadel, 1951. 179 documents for "Colonial Times Through Civil War", 35 more documents for "Reconstruction To 1910".
(28)  DuBois, William E. B., Black Reconstruction, New York: Russell and Russell, 1935. The contents are evident from the lengthy sub-title: An Essay toward a History of the Part which Black Folks Played in the Attempt to Reconstruct Democracy in America, 1860-1880.
(29)  Franklin, John H., Reconstruction: After the Civil War, Chicago: U of Chicago P, 1962. An interpretative and narrative history of the Reconstruction era, based upon a thorough acquaintance with the sources.
(30)  Hasse, Adelaide R. (comp.), Index of Economic Material in Documents of the States of the United States, Carnegie Inst. Publs. no. 85, 1907-1922. The volume on Illinois covers the years 1809 to 1904. It was published in 1909 and is divided into two parts: 1. Collected Documents, Descriptive Works, Indexes, etc. 2. Topical Analysis. In this second part some historically interesting material is listed under the title "Population, Negro". There is a "Report on the expediency and practicability of preventing free negroes settling in state" of 1829, an 1851 "Report on Missouri compromise", and, among others, the Illinois State Historical Library Publication 9 (pp. 414-432) "Illinois: Legislation on slavery and free negroes, 1818-1865".
(31)  Hirshson, Stanley P., Farewell to the Bloody Shirt: Northern Republicanism and the Southern Negro, 1877-1893, Bloomington: Indiana UP. 1962. The

institutions beyond the control of the black victims. Shows the failure of the Republican Party of Lincoln to protect the blacks. Concentrates on the Presidents of the period between Garfield and Harrison.

(32) Logan, Rayford W., The Negro in American Life and Thought: The Nadir, 1877-1901, New York: Dial, 1954. Comprehensive analysis. On the Supreme Court, see pp. 97-116.

(33) Meier, August, Negro Thought in America, 1880-1915, Ann Arbor: U of Michigan P, 1963. The emergence of DuBois and Washington.

(34) Negro Protest Thought in the Twentieth Century, edd. Francis L. Broderick and August Meier, Indianapolis: Bobbs-Merrill, 1965. 54 selections from Washington to Farmer.

(35) The Negro Since Emancipation, ed. Harvey Wish, Englewood Cliffs, N.J.: Prentice-Hall, 1964. Speeches and writings by 15 black leaders from Frederick Douglass to Elijah Muhammad on various topics of the black experience.

(36) Nevins, Allan, The Emergence of Modern America, 1868-1875, vol. 8 of A History of American Life, ed. Arthur M. Schlesinger, New York: Macmillan, 1927. Contains a good "critical Essay on Authorities", (pp. 408-432). Chicago is described on pp. 79/80, 84/85.

(37) Osgood, Herbert L., The American Colonies in the Seventeenth Century, 3 vols., Gloucester, Mass.: Smith, 1957. (New York: Columbia, 1940)

(38) - The American Colonies in the Eighteenth Century, 4 vols., Gloucester, Mass.: Smith, 1958. (New York, Columbia UP, 1924-1925).

(39) Scott, Emmett J., Official History of the American Negro in the World War, Chicago: n.p., 1919. Inside view of a conservative black confidant of B.T. Washington. Much primary material is quoted verbatim. Scott was Special Assistant to the Secretary of War.

(40) Tindall, George B., South Carolina Negroes, 1877-1900, Columbia: U of South Carolina P, 1952. This was a dark time for South Carolina blacks but there were progressive developments which facilitated or made possible progress in the 20th century.

(41) Wharton, Vernon L., The Negro in Mississippi, 1865-1890, Chapel Hill: U of North Carolina P, 1947. Sees black migration in two stages: A movement to towns and from plantation to plantation (a flow of blacks from the upper South into Mississippi), and the Exodus to Kansas. There were already a few labor agents from the Midwest in the South at this time (p. 113).

(42) Williams, George W., History of the Negro in the United States from 1619 to 1880, 2 vols. in one, New York: Putnam, 1882. An extensive (1048 pp. of text) history. Of particular interest is ch. 28: Exodus, causes and effect. Southern treatment of blacks, not Northern politics was responsible.

(43) Woodward, Comer V., Origins of the New South, 1877-1913, Baton Rouge: Louisiana State UP, 1951.

## 4. BLACK EXPERIENCE

Life in the United States as seen by blacks. Besides fiction and autobiographies there are some scholarly interpretations (Woodward). This section also contains analyses of the American scene during the first half of this century (Lynd, Mecklin) and the reaction of the black community to it (Drake).

(44)   Baldwin, James, Notes of a Native Son, Boston: Beacon, 1949. Autobiographical. Youth in Harlem, escape to Paris and Switzerland.
(45)   - Nobody Knows My Name, New York: Dial, 1954. Essays of a rather disillusioned man, after his exile in Europe.
(46)   Bennett, Lerone, Jr., The Negro Mood and Other Essays, Chicago: Johnson, 1964. Essays on the black establishment, liberals, etc.
(47)   Burns, W. Haywood, The Voice of Negro Protest in America, London: Oxford, 1963.
(48)   Cash, William J., The Mind of the South, New York, Knopf: 1941. The South at its best is proud and courteous; its vices are: too great an attachment to racial values and fictions, and fear and hate of the black man. The Old and the New South.
(49)   Clark, Kenneth B., Dark Ghetto: Dilemma of Social Power, New York: Harper, 1965. Out of Clark's experience with HARYOU (Harlem Youth Opportunities Unlimited). "Psychology and Pathology of the Ghetto".
(50)   Cleaver, Eldrige, Soul on Ice, New York: McGraw, 1968. Incisive.
(51)   Drake, St. Clair, "Negro Americans and the Africa Interest", in Davis, Reference Book (no. 12), pp. 662-705.
(52)   DuBois, William E.B., Dusk of Dawn: An Essay toward an Autobiography of a Race Concept, New York: Harcourt Brace, 1940. 1868-1940 were not only 72 years in the life of DuBois, but also 72 important years in world history. Central themes: Concept of race, white world, black ("colored") world.
(53)   - The Souls of Black Folk, Chicago: McClurg, 1903.
(54)   Glenn, Norval D., "Negro Prestige Criteria: A Case Study in the Bases of Prestige", in American Journal of Sociology, vol. 68, no. 6 (May, 1963), pp. 645-659. "All other pertinent factors remaining constant, the importance of a variable as a prestige criterion varies directly with how unequally the variable is distributed". (p. 657).
(55)   Gloster, Hugh M., Negro Voices in American Fiction, Chapel Hill: U of North Carolina P, 1948. A history from the Reconstruction to around 1940. Linking black literature to the social and political questions of the day.
(56)   Johnson, Charles S., Shadow of the Plantation, Chicago: U of Chicago P, 1934. Inside view of the black rural South. Much quotation of black rural workers and their families (ca. 600). The basic hopelessness of this type of existence.
(57)   Justice Denied, edd. William M. Chace and Peter Collier, New York: Harcourt, 1970. Sub-title: The black man in white America.
(58)   Lincoln, C. Eric, "The American Protest Movement for Negro Rights", in

Davis, Reference Book (no. 12), pp. 458-483.
(59) Lynd, Robert S. and Helen M. Lynd, Middletown in Transition: A Study in Cultural Conflicts, New York: Harcourt Brace, 1937.
(60) - Middletown: A Study in Contemporary American Culture, New York: Harcourt Brace, 1929. The "classical" studies of small-town America. No. 59 could be called "Middletown Revisited".
(61) Mecklin, John Moffatt, The Ku Klux Klan: A Study of the American Mind, New York: Harcourt Brace, 1924. Written at the height of the "modern" Klan. The subtitle shows the partisan attitude of the author. Mecklin holds that the Klan is nothing alien to American life and that the failure by the public and the press to realize this compounded the problem.
(62) The New Negro: An Interpretation, ed. Alain L. Locke, New York: Boni, 1925. A vivid picture of the Harlem Renaissance. Fiction, Poetry, Drama, Music. Contributors include James Weldon Johnson, Langston Hughes, E. Franklin Frazier, Melville J. Herskovits, William E. B. DuBois, Arthur A. Schomburg, Countee Cullen, Angelina Grimké.
(63) Redding, Jay S., On Being Negro in America, Indianapolis: Bobbs-Merrill, 1951. Autobiographical. The ultimate solution of the "race problem" lies in a Christianity that is concerned with man rather than with God. Basically pessimistic.
(64) Rowan, Carl T., South of Freedom, New York: Knopf, 1952. "I have tried to tell the 'little things' that circumscribe the lives of black folk." (Preface, p. vii)
(65) Shabazz, El-Hajj Malik el-, (Malcolm X, Malcolm Little) The Autobiography of Malcolm X, New York: Grove, 1965. An impressive document of a search for identity.
(66) Slavery Defended, ed. Eric L. McKitrick, Englewood Cliffs, N. J.: Prentice-Hall, 1963. The View of the Old South (Sub-title).
(67) Washington, Booker T., Up From Slavery, New York: Burt, 1901.
(68) What the Negro Wants, ed. Rayford W. Logan, Chapel Hill: U of North Carolina P, 1944. Answer: First-class citizenship, full democracy, full equality.
(69) White, Walter, How Far the Promised Land, New York: Viking, 1955. By a black man who looked white and believed in the American Dream and in American Democracy.
(70) Woodward, Comer V., The Strange Career of Jim Crow, New York: Oxford, 1955. Widely heralded as one of the best books about the South.
(71) Wright, Richard, White Man, Listen!, Garden City, N. Y.: Doubleday, 1957.
(72) - Black Boy: A Record of Childhood and Youth, New York: Harper 1937. Impact of the "South" on a black who hates it intellectually but has a deep affection for it. He finally goes North.

## 5. POPULATION AND MIGRATION, HISTORY AND BIOGRAPHY OF CHICAGO AND THE MIDWEST

Demography of blacks in the United States. A survey of geographical data about the Midwest (Garland) and narrative accounts of life in the Midwest and Chicago during the first half of this century. The slums and ghettoes of Chicago.

(73) Dedmon, Emmett, Fabulous Chicago, New York: Random, 1953. An informal account of the origins and growth of Chicago.
(74) Dowd, Jerome, The Negro in American Life, New York: Century, 1926. Includes an account of the Chicago riots of 1919, based on the Report of the Chicago Commission on Race Relations (nr. 88), pp. 31-38. Criminality is dealt with on pp. 41-53 and migration on pp. 245-262.
(75) Drake, St. Clair and Horace R. Cayton, Black Metropolis, New York: Harper and Row, 1945. A social survey with historical background of the black ghettoes of Chicago during the 1930's.
(76) Duke, Charles S., The Housing Situation and the Colored People of Chicago, Chicago: n.publ., April, 1919. Concentrates on suggested remedies. Bibliography of housing in Chicago, 1910-1920 (pp. 33-35).
(77) Farrell, James T., Studs Lonigan, New York: Vanguard, 1932. A somber picture of Chicago in the 1920s.
(78) Garland, John H., The North American Midwest: A Regional Geography, New York: Wiley, 1955. A geographical analysis. See also: Geographical Review, vol. 33 (1943), pp. 86-99 and vol. 36 (1946), pp. 105-120.
(79) Heberle, Rudolf, Ueber die Mobilität der Bevölkerung in den Vereinigten Staaten, Jena: Gustav Fischer, 1929.
(80) Herrick, Robert, Memoirs of an American Citizen, New York: Macmillan, 1905. Herrick was professor at the University of Chicago. The city at the time of the Haymarket incident.
(81) Hutton, David G., Midwest at Noon, Chicago: U of Chicago P, 1946. The Middle West ("A Country of Extremes") as seen by an Englishman. Narrative.
(82) Illinois Negro History Makers, compp. Carl G. Hodges, et al., Chicago: Illinois Emancipation Centennial Commission, 1964. A brief history of blacks in Illinois, pp. 7-37, and statistics covering the years 1790 to 1960 (pp. 51-91).
(83) Kennedy, Louise V., The Negro Citizen Turns Cityward, New York, Columbia UP, 1930. Migration improved the black laborer's social and economic status (wider choice of occupations and higher wages) but created problems of urbanization.
(84) Kuznets, Simon, and Dorothy Swaine Thomas (directors), Population Redistribution and Economic Growth, United States, 1870-1950, consisting of the following volumes: I Lee, Everett S., et. al., Methodological Considerations and Reference Tables, Philadelphia: The American Philosophical Society, 1957. II Kuznets, Simon, et. al., Analyses of Economic Change, Philadelphia: Am. Philos. Soc., 1960. III Eldridge, Hope T. and Dorothy S. Thomas, Demographic Analyses and Interrelations, Philadelphia: Am.

142

Philos. Soc., 1964.
(85) Merriam, Charles E., Chicago: A More Intimate View of Politics, New York: Macmillan, 1929. A critical appraisal by the famous Chicago professor and politician (and loser of the mayoral race) of local politics.
(86) National League on Urban Conditions among Negroes, A Challenge to Democracy: The Migration of a Race, Annual Report 1916-1917 (vol. 7, nr. 1, Nov. 1917): pp. 21-23, "The Work in Chicago, Ill." Reports on what the Urban League did in 17 cities to help blacks who had recently migrated there.
(87) - The National League on Urban Conditions among Negroes: Methods of Work and Principles: The Local Organizations, Vol. 2, nr. 3, March, 1913. Should be read to understand no. 86. Hints for those who want to establish a local organization.
(88) The Negro in Chicago: A Study of Race Relations and a Race Riot, Chicago: U of Chicago P, 1922. By the Chicago Commission on Race Relations.
(89) Osofsky, Gilbert, Harlem: The Making of a Ghetto. Nergo New York, 1890-1930, New York: Harper, 1966. A thorough investigation of a particularly illuminating example of residential succession.
(90) Scott, Emmett J., Negro Migration During the War, New York: Oxford UP, 1920. By one of the highest ranking officials in the administration during the war. Scott was directly concerned with the black population redistribution during 1917/1918.
(91) Spear, Allan H., Black Chicago: The Making of a Negro Ghetto, 1890-1920, Chicago: U of Chicago P, 1967. The author examines the "forces that conditioned the development of separate Negro community life" and analyzes the "impact of this development upon Negro racial ideology". (Preface, pp. viii/xi). There is a deplorable lack of manuscripts.
(92) Taeuber, Karl E. and Alma F. Taeuber, Negroes in Cities: Residential Segregation and Neighborhood Change, Chicago: Chicago UP, 1965. Part I: The pattern of Negro residential segregation, Part II: The process of neighborhood change.
(93) - "The Negro Population in the United States", in Davis, Reference Book (no. 12), pp. 96-161.
(94) U.S. Commissioner of Labor, "The Slums of Baltimore, Chicago, New York, and Philadelphia", in Seventh Special Report, Washington, GPO, 1894. This investigation was authorized by Congress on July 20, 1892. It offers a wealth of statistical material on occupations, earnings, sanitary conditions and other essential facts to show life in these slums.
(95) U.S. Department of Commerce, Bureau of the Census, Negroes in the United States, 1920-1932, Washington: GPO, 1935.
(96) - Negro Population, 1790-1915, Washington: GPO, 1918.
(97) - Negroes in the United States, Washington: GPO, 1916. (Bulletin 129). The usual statistics on population, occupations, agriculture, mortality, and religion. These books are mainly time-savers, in that one does not have to thumb through all the volumes of all the censuses to find material relating to blacks.

## 6. POLITICS

A general analysis of the American political system as a mechanism to mediate conflicts (Dahl) and attempts to place blacks within this mechanism (Carmichael, Masnata). The more practical problems of voter participation, representation, and the integration of blacks within the existing political framework.

(98) Bunche, Ralph J., "The Negro in Chicago Politics", in National Municipal Review, vol. 17, no. 5 (May, 1928), pp. 261-264. William Hale Thompson's debt to the black population of Chicago. Ralph Bunche praises the great number of blacks in Cook County and Illinois politics.

(99) Carmichael, Stokely and Charles V. Hamilton, Black Power: The Politics of Liberation in America, New York: Random House, 1967.

(100) Dahl, Robert A., Pluralist Democracy in the United States: Conflict and Consent, Chicago: Rand McNally, 1967. The task of the political structure is to be mediator in the inevitable conflicts within the citizenry. Chapter 6 is on the Supreme Court.

(101) Lewinson, Paul, Race, Class, and Party, New York: Oxford, 1932. There was little progress for blacks in the South between the Civil War and 1930, as far as political participation was concerned.

(102) McClosky, Herbert, "Political Participation", in International Encyclopedia of the Social Sciences (1968), vol. 12, esp. pp. 256-264. The internal and external forces that determine participation by the individual in a political system. Bibliography pp. 264/265.

(103) Masnata, François, Pouvoir blanc, révolte noire: Essai sur la tradition démocratique aux Etats-Unis, Paris: Payot, 1968.

(104) Moon, Henry L., Balance of Power: The Negro Vote, Garden City, N.Y.: Doubleday, 1948. The attempt of blacks in the 1940s to get allies: Northern Democrats and Labor. The success of such action rests upon an economy of abundance.

(105) Smith, Samuel D., The Negro in Congress, 1870-1901, Chapel Hill: U of North Carolina P, 1940. The careers of the blacks who served in Congress, including some unsuccessful aspirants to Congress. Smith believes they were the cream of their race and their accomplishments helped those who wanted to see blacks out of politics.

(106) Wilson, James Q., Negro Politics: The Search for Leadership, New York: Free Press, 1960. Black politics in Chicago up to 1960. The questions about blacks and the machine are more important than those about black/white relationships.

(107) - "The Negro in American Politics: The Present", in Davis, Reference Book (no. 12), pp. 431-457.

## 7. ECONOMY

Books which appeared between 1920 and 1946 on the subject of blacks and the economy: The status of the black population within the economy and the possibilities of a separate black economy between 1917 and 1945. Also included is a study by Glenn which is a modern interpretation of the discriminatory practices of empolyers, unions, and employees.

(108) Bakke, Edward W., Citizens Without Work: A Study of the Effects of Unemployment upon the Workers' Social Relations and Practices, New Haven: Yale UP, 1940. A sociological inquiry written during the depression of the 1930s.

(109) Cayton, Horace R. and George S. Mitchell, Black Workers and the New Unions, Chapel Hill: U of North Carolina P, 1939. This study endeavors "to show how prejudice forms and is formed by economic relationships" (Introduction, p. ix). The author views black economy as "an escapist mechanism, with even less validity than Garvey's Black Republic". (p. 433).

(110) Glenn, Norval D., "Occupational Benefits to Whites from the Subordination of Negroes", in American Sociological Review, vol. 28, no. 3 (June, 1963), pp. 443-448. Discrimination exists because a majority gains by it.

(111) Greene, Lorenzo J. and Carter G. Woodson, The Negro Wage Earner, Washington, D.C.: The Association for the Study of Negro Life and History, 1930. Fields of Employment and social mobility of blacks, 1890-1930. The stress is on the shift from agriculture to industry.

(112) Harris, Abram L., The Negro as Capitalist: A Study of Banking and Business among American Negroes, Philadelphia: American Academy of Political and Social Science, 1936. Much informative material on black banks in the United States.

(113) Lewis, Edward E., The Mobility of the Negro: A Study in the American Labor Supply, New York: Columbia Ph. D. diss., 1931. Concentration on the rural South, 1919-1924.

(114) Miller, Herman P., Rich Man, Poor Man, New York: Crowell, 1964. A "by-product" of the author's 17 years with the Bureau of the Census. Chapter 6: "Race, creed and color: the income of minorities".

(115) Northrup, Herbert R., Organized Labor and the Negro, New York: Harper, 1944. Trade unions are beneficial for blacks.

(116) Röpke, Wilhelm, "Das Agrar-Problem in den Vereinigten Staaten", in Archiv für Sozialwissenschaften und Sozialpolitik, vol. 58 (1928), pp. 478-516, vol. 59 (1928) pp. 96-130. Geographical and historical development of American agriculture and its state in the 1920s.

(117) Spero, Sterling D. and Abraham L. Harris, The Black Worker, New York: Columbia UP, 1931. A treatise on the relationship of unions and the black workers.

(118) Weaver, Robert C., Negro Labor: A National Problem, New York: Harcourt Brace, 1946. Chapter 10 is on the Philadelphia, Los Angeles, and Chicago transport strikes and the use of federal agencies to promote fair employment.

See also next entry:
(119) Weckler, Joseph E., "Prejudice is not the Whole Story", in The Public Opinion Quarterly, vol. 9 (Summer, 1945), pp. 126-139. On the strikes growing out of the project to upgrade black traction employees in Philadelphia, Los Angeles, and Chicago. Only in Chicago could this be done quietly and quickly. In the other cities the management and the unions had "ulterior motives" for not upgrading blacks and in part used race prejudice for their own goals. "Mobilized public opinion had no apparent effects on either management or employees in Philadelphia and Los Angeles". (p. 139).
(120) Wesley, Charles H., Negro Labor in the United States, 1850-1925, New York: Vanguard, 1927.

## 8. HEALTH AND CRIME

A few works on the sociological aspects of health and crime.

(121) Gibbs, Jack P., and Walter T. Martin, Status Integration and Suicide: A Sociological Study, Eugene: U of Oregon Books, 1964. The major theorem is that "the suicide rate of a population varies inversely with the degree of status integration in that population" (p. 27). The authors conclude that "the predictive power of the major theorem, while not perfect, is well beyond chance expectancy". (p. 199).

(122) Hollingshead, August B., and Frederick C. Redlich, Social Class and Mental Illness, New York: Wiley, 1966.

(123) Pettigrew, Ann H., and Thomas F. Pettigrew, "Race, Disease, and Desegregation: A New Look", in Phylon, 24: 315-333 (Winter, 1963). See also no. 16, chapters 4-6 (pp. 72-158): "Health, Intelligence, and Crime".

(124) Wolfgang, Marvin E., Crime and Race: Conceptions and Misconceptions, New York: Institute of Human Relations. 1964. By a Jewish Committee.

## 9. LEGAL HISTORY

General histories of English law, interpretations of Magna Carta, and American constitutional history, particularly regarding due process of law and civil rights.

(125) Cross, Arthur Lyon, "An Unpopular Seventeenth-century View of Magna Carta", in American Historical Review, vol. 29, no. 1 (Oct., 1923), pp. 74-76. It was not unknown during the seventeenth century that Coke's interpretation of Magna Carta was unsound.

(126) Hazeltine, H. D., "The Influence of Magna Carta on American Constitutional Development", in Malden, Commemoration Essays (no. 131), pp. 180-226.

(127) Heller, Francis H., The Sixth Amendment to the Constitution of the United States: A Study in Constitutional Development, New York: Greenwood, 1969 (reprint of a 1951 U of Kansas diss.). On the background of the Sixth Amendment in English Law, the Colonial Experience, trial by jury, vicinage, etc. Well documented and helpful bibliography, pp. 176-188.

(128) Holdsworth, Williams S., A History of English Law, 16 vols., edd. A. L. Goodhart and H. G. Hanbury, London: Methuen, 1966 (reprint of the 7th ed., London 1956).

(129) Holt, James C., Magna Carta, Cambridge: Cambridge UP, 1965. The best modern book on Magna Carta.

(130) McKechnie, William S., Magna Carta: A Commentary on the Great Charter of King John, Glasgow: Maclehose, 1905. The turning point in the historiography about Magna Carta, as is shown, for example, by Holt (no. 129).

(131) Magna Carta Commemoration Essays, ed. Henry E. Malden, London: Royal Historical Society, 1917. Originally prepared for the 700th anniversary of Magna Carta in 1915, delayed by the War.

(132) Maitland, Frederick W., The Constitutional History of England: A Course of Lectures Delivered, Cambridge: Cambridge UP, 1908. These lectures were held in 1887/8. Still a necessary starting-point for anybody interested in the field. For the History of Procedure, see. pp. 115-132.

(133) Plucknett, Theodore F. T., A Concise History of Common Law, London: Butterworth, 1956 (5th ed.). Universally regarded as the best concise history of the common law. See particularly ch. 4, pp. 106-138.

(134) Pollock, Sir Frederick and Frederick W. Maitland, The History of English Law Before the Time of Edward I, Cambridge: Cambridge UP, 1923 (2nd ed., 1st ed. 1895). More Maitland's than Pollock's work. With respect to trial jury it does not go beyond Forsyth (no. 142), but it is written with the well-known thoroughness and verve ot its author.

(135) Poore, Benjamin P. (comp.), The Federal and State Constitution, Washington, D. C.: GPO, 1877.

(136) Powicke, Frederick M., "Per Iudicium Parium Vel Per Legem Terrae", in Malden, Commemoration Essays, (no. 131), pp. 96-121.

(137) Stubbs, William, Select Charters and Other Illustrations of English Constitutional History from the Earliest Times to the Reign of Edward the First,

Oxford: Clarendon, 1913 (9th ed.). The analyses of the texts are hopelessly outdated, but the book is very useful for the primary sources presented.

(138) Thompson, Faith, <u>Magna Carta: Its Role in the Making of the English Constitution, 1300-1629</u>, Minneapolis: Minnesota P, 1950.

(139) Vinogradoff, Sir Paul, "Magna Carta, c. 39: Nullus liber homo, etc.", in Malden, <u>Commemoration Essays</u> (no. 131), pp. 78-95.

## 10. TRIAL BY JURY

Besides the books and articles listed below, the reader should acquaint himself with what Tocqueville (ch. 15 of Democracy in America) and Montesquieu (ch. 6 of book 11 of Spirit of Laws) had to say about the institution.

(140) Brunner, Heinrich, Die Entstehung des Schwurgerichtes, Berlin: Weidmann, 1872. The basic text for Maitland.

(141) Finkelstein, Michael O., "The Application of Statistical Decision Theory to the Jury Discrimination Cases", in Harvard Law Review, vol. 80, no. 2 (Des., 1966), pp. 338-376. "Mr. Finkelstein uses mathematical analysis to show the extreme improbability that nondiscriminatory selection occured in situations in which courts have been unwilling to find a violation of the fourteenth amendment". (Introduction by the editor).

(142) Forsyth, William, History of Trial by Jury, London: Parker and Son, 1852. Trial by Jury was unknown to Anglo-Saxons before the Conquest (ch. 4, sect. 1), but they had something "which prepared the way for its introduction" (p. 55). Basically the "modern" view of the development of trial by jury.

(143) Harker, Oliver A., "The Illinois Juror in the Trial of Criminal Cases", in Illinois Law Review, vol. 5 (1911), pp. 468-475. The jury in Illinois has the right to determine law and facts, and this right should be abridged.

(144) Johnson, Julia E., Jury System, vol. 5 no. 6 of The Reference Shelf, New York: Wilson, 1928. The pros (pp. 7-14) and cons (pp. 14-22) of the present jury system. The rest of the book is a collection of articles: general, in favor, and against the jury system. Good bibliography (pp. 23-42).

(145) Kalven, Harry, Jr., and Hans Zeisel, The American Jury, Boston: Little Brown, 1966. Judge-jury disagreement. The basic question is: How would cases be dealth with if there were only judges, no jury? A scientific survey of 3576 cases.

(146) Ross, Carl A., "The Jury System of Cook County, Illinois", in Illinois Law Review, vol. 5, no. 5 (Dec., 1910), pp. 283-299. The mismanagement of the jury system in Cook County at the beginning of this century.

(147) Schwartz, Bernard, The Bill of Rights, 2 vols., New York: Chelsea, 1971. Sub-title: A documentary history. Documents from Magna Carta to the Official Notice of the ratification of the Bill of Rights in 1792. Sources with brief introductions.

(148) Thayer, James B., "The Jury and Its Development", in Harvard Law Review, vol. 5 no. 6 (Jan., 1892), pp. 249-273, no. 7 (Feb., 1892) pp. 295-319, and no. 8 (March, 1892), pp. 357-388. A history of trial by jury from 829 to ca. 1700. Based on Brunner (no. 140).

## 11. LEGAL PROCESS

The legal process from Arrest to Appeal.

(149) Hall, Livingston, and Yale Kamisar, Basic Criminal Procedure, St. Paul: West, 1966.
(150) Orfield, Lester B., Criminal Procedure from Arrest to Appeal, New York: New York University P, 1947.
(151) Puttkamer, Ernst W., Administration of the Criminal Law, Chicago: U of Chicago P, 1953. The technical side of criminal law.
(152) Schwartz, Louis B., and Stephen R. Goldstein, Law Enforcement Handbook for Police, St. Paul: West, 1970. "The aim of this handbook is to provide police departments and policemen with brief, informal, interesting reviews of some main concerns in police operations". (Preface, p. iii). Simple style, illustrated.
(153) Skolnick, Jerome H., Justice Without Trial: Law Enforcement in Democratic Society, New York: Wiley, 1966. The police of Westville, Cal. See especially ch. 4: "Operational Environment and Police Discretion" including a section on "The racial bias of police", pp. 80-86.

## 12. BLACKS AND THE LAW, CIVIL RIGHTS AND THE COURTS

From the Black Codes to the Warren Court.

(154) Abraham, Henry Julian, Freedom and the Court: Civil Rights and Liberties in the United States, New York: Oxford UP, 1967. Introduction into the problem of civil rights of the individual vs. those of the community of which he is part. Reviews Bill of Rights, due process, freedom of expression and religion, and race relations (pp. 245-312).

(155) Brown, G. Gordon, Law Administration and Negro-White Relations in Philadelphia: A Study in Race Relations, Philadelphia: Bureau of Municipal Research, 1947. This study grew out of the famous strike of the workers of the Philadelphia Transport Co. (cf. nos. 118, 119). It offers statistical material and opinions of informants on: Blacks in Philadelphia, crime and delinquency, the Philadelphia police force, blacks and the police, blacks and the legal process (pp. 136-152).

(156) Discrimination and the Law, ed. Vern Countryman, Chicago: U of Chicago P, 1965. Centers on discrimination in employment, education, public accomodations and housing. The jury system is mentioned in the introduction ("The Growth of the Law") by the editor.

(157) Greenberg, Jack, Race Relations and the American Law, New York: Columbia UP, 1959. See especially Parts I and II: "The Capacity of Law to Affect Race Relations", (pp. 1-10) and "A Legal Overview", (pp. 31-78).

(158) Guild, June P., Black Laws of Virginia: A Summary of the Legislative Acts of Virginia Concerning Negroes from the Earliest Times to the Present, Richmond, Va.: Whitlet and Shepperson, 1937.

(159) Mangum, Charles S., The Legal Status of the Negro, Chapel Hill: U of North Carolina P, 1940. Not a philosophical treatise, "but a statement of the law as it has been interpreted by courts all over the nation" (p. vii). The questions of the jury system receive extensive attention (pp. 308-342).

(160) Miller, Loren, The Petitioners: The Supreme Court of the United States and the Negro, New York: Pantheon, 1966. Various famous trials in detail (Scottsboro, Plessy, Strauder, Scott).

(161) Stephenson, Gilbert T., Race Distinctions in American Law, London: Appleton, 1910. The part on the jurors (pp. 247-272) deals with the present (i.e. beginning of the twentieth century) legislation in the North (Ind., Mich., N.Y., Ohio, R.I.) and the South and offers numerous examples of inclusion and exclusion of blacks in the South from jury service.

(162) The Supreme Court on Racial Discrimination, ed. Joseph Tussman, New York: Oxford UP, 1963. Chapter 7 (pp. 315-348) deals with discrimination and the jury. The volume only gives excerpts of opinions (Strauder, Smith v. Texas, Patton, Cassell, Avery, Hernandez, Eubanks) without any background information.

(163) Tresolini, Rocco, These Liberties: Case Studies in Civil Rights, Philadelphia: Lipincott, 1968. Quotes from cases on civil rights, placing them into perspective and telling the background of these cases.

(164)   Wilson, Brantner, <u>The Black Codes of the South</u>, Montgomery: U of Alabama P, 1965. The black codes of 1865/66. Wilson sees them as an attempt to exploit blacks while granting them technical freedom. The author claims that neither North nor South realized what the situation of the blacks was: The North was not interested any more, and the South did not want slavery but did not really know "what to do with blacks".

(165)   U.S. Commission on Civil Rights, Report 5: <u>Justice,</u> Washington, GPO, 1961. Chapter 7 deals with jury exclusion. "... the practice of racial exclusion from juries persists today even though it has long stood indicted as a serious violation of the 14th amendment" (p. 103).

## 13. INTERPRETATION

These books on the philosophy and the sociology of the law help the reader see judicial action and reasoning in perspective. They permit an interpretation of the facts gathered in chapter 3 of this dissertation.

(166) Adams, Willi Paul, "Das Gleichheitspostulat in der amerikanischen Revolution", in Historische Zeitschrift, vol. 212 (1971), pp. 59-99. "Equality" was a key symbol and a myth for reformers, and "All men are created equal" became the theoretical starting-point of new liberation movements - quite contrary to the intentions of the founding fathers.

(167) Commager, Henry S., "Constitutional History and the Higher Law", in Pennsylvania Magazine of History and Biography, vol. 62, nr. 1 (Jan., 1938) pp. 20-40. Shows the persistence of the doctrine of a "higher law". By interpreting concepts like "due process" the Supreme Court has been engaged "not only in legislation but in super-legislation" (p. 26). The courts have always protected property first.

(168) Fechner, Erich, "Rechtsphilosophie", in Handwörterbuch der Sozialwissenschaften, vol. 8 (1964) pp. 748-762. About epistemology and the logics of law.

(169) - "Rechtssoziologie", Ibid., vol. 8 (1964), pp. 762-768.

(170) Friedman, Lawrence M., "Some Problems and Possibilities of American Legal History", in The State of American History, ed. Herbert J. Bass, Chicago: Quadrangle, 1970, pp. 3-21. Very little is being done in the field of American legal history; Americans are fascinated by British legal history. The author shows where the problems in this field lie and holds that there is an overemphasis on the Supreme Court.

(171) Frankfurter, Felix, "Supreme Court, United States", in Encyclopedia of the Social Sciences, vol. 14 (1934), pp. 474-482. Until 1875 the Supreme Court was a common law court; after that year there was a shift towards public law. The Supreme Court applies the "Socratic method" (p. 481).

(172) Fuller, Lon L., Legal Fictions, Stanford: Stanford UP, 1967. Originally a series of articles that appeared in the Illinois Law Review (1930/1). Definitions of fiction, legal fiction, and the motives behind them.

(173) Glick, Henry R., Supreme Court in State Politics: An Investigation of the Judicial Role, New York: Basic Books, 1971. The judicial role in state supreme courts (Mass., N.J., Pa., La.). Group interaction, the objects of decision making, the values influencing decisions, and the political environment.

(174) Haines, Charles G., "General Observations on the Effects of Personal, Political, and Economic Influences in the Decisions of Judges", in Illinois Law Review, vol. 17 (1923), pp. 96-116. The classic essay on judicial behavior; debunked the theory of mechanical jurisprudence (Schubert, no. 181).

(175) Hamilton, Walton H., "Judicial Process", in Encyclopedia of the Social Sciences, vol. 8 (1932), pp. 450-457. Essayistic, "common sense" approach

to the "intellectual procedure by which judges decide cases" (p. 450). Good short bibliography of the relevant books and articles that appeared around 1930.

(176) Hart, H. L. A., "Philosophy of Law, Problems of", in The Encyclopedia of Philosophy, ed. Paul Edwards, vol. 6 (1967), especially pp. 268-272 "Problems of Legal Reasoning". See also Ibid., vol. 4 (1967), s. v. "Justice", pp. 298-302.

(177) Horowitz, Morton J., "The Emergence of an Instrumental Conception of American Law, 1780-1820", in Law in American History, edd. Donald Fleming and Bernard Bailyn, Cambridge, Mass.: Charles Warren Center for Studies in American History, 1971 (Vol. 5 of Perspectives in American History), pp. 287-326. The idea of a judge-made law was a fully formulated doctrine by 1820 (at the latest) and thus by no means unknown to 19th century jurists; implied is a departure from English precedents, i.e. a legal breakaway movement analogous to the political movement for independence.

(178) Hurst, James W., "Legal Elements in United States History", in Law in American History, edd. Fleming and Bailyn (no. 177), pp. 3-92. Handling the materials of legal history (pp. 14-67) and The desirable and practicable subject matter of legal history (pp. 67-91).

(179) Miller, Charles A., "Constitutional Law and the Rhetoric of Race", in Law in American History, edd. Fleming and Bailyn (no. 177), pp. 147-200. There are various means by which the courts evade the issue of race (legal fiction, non-racial argumentation, etc).

(180) Rosenblum, Victor G., Law as a Political Instrument, Garden City, N.J.: Doubleday, 1955. On judicial policy making. 1. Interrelations of law and politics. 2. How does law operate as a political instrument in specific cases? 3. Is judicial discretion in respect to policy making limited? 4. Is judicial policy making consistent with democracy? Conclusion: Judicial policy making is "healthy" (p. 82).

(181) Schubert, Glendon, "Judicial Behavior", in International Encyclopedia of the Social Sciences, vol. 8 (1968), pp. 307-315. Good synopsis of research on judicial behavior during the period of 1920 to 1965. Good bibliography of books and articles in the early 1960s.

(182) Smend, Rudolf, Verfassung und Verfassungsrecht, München: Duncker & Humblot, 1928. The individual vs. the institution.

(183) Stevens, Robert, "Two Cheers for 1870: The American Law School", in Law in American History, edd. Fleming and Bailyn (no. 177), pp. 405-548. In the beginning - and late into the 19th century - American law education was more an apprenticeship than a serious academic pursuit. Harvard introduced the study of (appellate) cases. This "Socratic method" became standard until 1920. Only in the second half of the 1880s did a movement begin to make law schools compulsory for future lawyers. Reforms of the law schools were usually patterned on prevailing standards at medical schools. In the 1930s it was the social sciences themselves that made their integration into the legal education impossible, not the law schools: paucity of data. The article describes legal education, 1776-1970.

(184) Vaihinger, Hans, The Philosophy of "As if", London: Kegan Paul 1924.

Original: Die Philosophie des Als Ob, Berlin: Reuther & Reichard, 1911. A very perspicacious analysis of the mechanism of fiction.

FOOTNOTES


Books and articles appearing in the bibliography of this dissertation are cited in the following manner: author or title - (number of item in the bibliography) - page, chapter, etc.

INTRODUCTION

1   "Apologie pour l'histoire ou Métier d'historien", Cahiers des Annales, nr. 3, Paris 1949, p. 4.
2   Miller (179)
3   Op. cit., p. 78
4   Dahl (100), 6-7
5   Below, pp. 129-134
6   Arthur Marwick, The Nature of History, London: Macmillan, 1971, p. 131.

CHAPTER I

1   Lawrence Stone, The Crisis of the Aristocracy 1558-1641, Oxford: Clarendon, 1965, pp. 3-4.
2   Aristotle, Nicomachean Ethics, I, vii, 18
3   Historical Statistics (HS), series A-2
4   HS, series A-99, 106, 113, 120
5   Source: Kuznets (84) vol. 3, pp. 262
6   Source: Ibid., vol. 1, table P-3. Only net migration flows of more than 10'000 persons were taken into account. One dot on the following maps represents 10'000 persons.
7   Sources: HS, series A-2, 59, 65, 134, 137; Kuznets (84) vol. 1, pp. 352, 353, 356, vol. 3 p. 200.
8   See Clark (49), Drake and Cayton (75), Duke (76), Kennedy (83), Urban League (86, 87), Chicago Riots (88), Osofsky (89), Scott (90), Spear (91), Taeuber and Taeuber (92), Slums (94).
9   Regarding the problem of locating the frontier, see Merle E. Curti, The Making of an American Community, Stanford: Stanford UP, 1959, on Trempealeau County, Wisconsin.
10  Heberle (79) 20
11  Morison/Commager, The Growth of the American Republic, 2 vols., New York: Oxford, 1969, vol. 2, p. 31, where the figures below are mentioned.
12  Ibid., p. 44
13  The "Granger Cases" of 1876 (Munn etc.)

| | |
|---|---|
| 14 | Spiller, Literary History of the United States, New York: Macmillan 1949, p. 977 |
| 15 | Ibid., p. 985 |
| 16 | Scott (90) 6, 16. Synonyms: Ark of Safety, House of Refuge. |
| 17 | Travelers Official Railway Guide, June, 1869, New York: National Railway Publication (Pratt), 1868. Only one copy of the original edition exists; it is in the New York Public Library. Reprint by University Microfilms, Ann Arbor (1968); see nrs. 200, 267, 270, 272 in this guide. |
| 18 | Travelers' Official Railway Guide, March, 1891, New York: National Railway Publications, 1891, p. 563. |
| 19 | Travelers' Railway Guide, May, 1905, Chicago: American Railway Guide Company, 1905, p. 31. |
| 20 | Travelers Railway Guide, Eastern Section, New York: Knickerboker, March, 1915, p. 228 |
| 21 | Ibid., p. 228 |
| 22 | The Official Guide of the Railways, New York: National Railway Publications, Sept., 1925, p. 653. Same for Sept., 1935, p. 615, for Sept., 1945, p. 593, and for Sept., 1955, p. 657 |
| 23 | Same for Sept., 1965, p. 429 |
| 24 | HS, series Y-27 to 31, 80 to 128 |
| 25 | See International Encyclopedia of Social Sciences, vol. 12 (1968), s. v. Political Participation for motivation to participate in politics, especially pp. 256-265. |
| 26 | These correlation coefficients were computed on a pdp-8 computer. I am indebted to my brother, prof. W. Schaufelberger, for his assistance in programming and data processing. |
| 27 | Ginzberg and Hiestand in Davis (12) 205 |
| 28 | In Davis (12) 342 |
| 29 | Ginzberg/Hiestand, loc. cit., p. 220 |
| 30 | Scott (90) 50 |
| 31 | C.H. Culver of the Detroit Employer's Association, cit. ibid., p. 130 |
| 32 | This does not say anything about the motivation for migration, of course. |
| 33 | Kuznets (84) vol. 3, pp. 362-365 |
| 34 | Ibid. |
| 35 | Stone, "Sterling's Depressed Communities", in Poverty Amid Affluence, ed. Leo Fishman, New Haven: Yale UP, 1966, p. 75 |
| 36 | Abraham A. Weinberg, Migration and Belonging, The Hague: Nijhoff, 1966, p. 35 |
| 37 | Taeuber/Taeuber (93) 154, cp. (96) 313-321 |
| 38 | (96), p. 315 |
| 39 | Ibid., p. 450 |
| 40 | Weinberg, op. cit., p. 47 |
| 41 | Population Census, vol. I, p. 417 |
| 42 | Chicago Police Department, Annual Report, 1885, p. 21. This figure only includes Americans. |
| 43 | Sources: Censuses of Population, 1890: I, 527, 1900: I, 613, 1910: II, 504, 1920: III, 261, 1930: III, 1/628. Annual Reports, 1890: p. 52, 1900: p. 32, |

1916: p. 25, 1920: p. 34, 1930: p. 22
44 Annual Reports, tables classified by age. 1930: p. 21, 1920: p. 16, 1916: p. 21, 1900: p. 31, 1890: p. 51, 1885: p. 20
45 Kennedy (83). The figures for the population pyramids were taken from the Censuses: 1880: I 548-551, 1920: II 158-9, 211, 1960: I 1-150, II 15-61
46 Census 1880: I-576-577
47 Census 1920: III-248

## CHAPTER II

1     The Maryland "Act for the Liberties of the People" of 1639 contained a restatement of chapter 39 of Magna Carta in the form of a due process clause but it did not mention trial by jury specifically.
2     Schwartz (147) 75
3     Legislature
4     Winthrop's Journal: The History of New England, ed. J.K. Homer, 2 vols., 1908. Vol. I, 151, 157. Holt (129) 46. Schwartz (147) 70, 85. "As a result in the same year grand and petty jury were brought into existence for the first time". Andrews (21) I 455
5     Holt (129) 63
6     Stubbs (137) 126
7     (140) and (142). Literature cited in (140) and in Heller (127) 152, footnote 13
8     Maitland (132) 115-124. Pollock/Maitland (134) I 144. Plucknett (133) 19
9     Capitularies: see Pollock/Maitland (134) I 16
10     MGH, Capitularia II, 188: Introductio
11     DuCange, Glossarium, Niort: Favre,     1885, s.v. inquisitores (vol. 4, 373-376) It is of course the Latin Glossarium.
12     How exactly it reached the Normandy is not quite clear. Cf. Plucknett (133) 110 and Pollock/Maitland (134) I 66 ff.
13     V.H. Galbraith, Regius Professor Emeritus of Modern History at Oxford, in Encyclopedia Britannica (1970), s.v. Domesday Book.
14     Inquisitio Comitatus Cantabrigiensis in Stubbs (137) 101. (Hamilton 1876, 97)
15     Stubbs (137) 170
16     Originally equivalent to the manor.
17     Holdsworth (128) I 310-312. Plucknett (133) 113-115. Pollock/Maitland (134) II 598-600.
18     Plucknett (133) 114
19     F.W. Maitland, Selected Pleas of the Crown, London, Selden: 1888, nr. 116, p. 75
20     Holdsworth (128) I 305-308. Plucknett (133) 115-116. Pollock/Maitland (134) II 634-637
21     3 and 4 William, c. 42
22     Holdsworth (128), 308-310. Plucknett (133) 116-118
23     Rex non pugnat nec alium habet campionem quam patriam (Bracton f. 142 b.) Cit. in Holdsworth (128) 323.
24     Holdsworth (128) 309, Plucknett (133) 117.
25     Ibid., 302-305. Pollock/Maitland (134) II 601, 637
26     Thayer, James B., A Selection of Cases on Evidence at the Common Law, Cambridge, Mass.: Harvard UP, 1925
27     Plucknett (133) 111
28     Ibid., 118
29     Fourth Lateran Council, Canon 18 (U of Pennsylvania Translations and

Reprints from the Original Sources of European History, iv, nr. 4 (16-17)). Plucknett (133) 118-119.
30 The address is lost. Conjecture by C.B. Adams in Malden (131), 41
31 Adams, Ibid., 43
32 Cit in Holt (129) 344. Rot. Litt. Pat., 141
33 Statutes of the Realm (London, 1963 reprint of the 1810 ed.), I, 7
34 Ibid., I, 11
35 Stubbs, Const. Hist. I 578 n. For judicium parium in Europe cf. Plucknett (133) 24, Powicke (136) 96-121
36 Maitland (132), 115 ff.
37 Holt (129) 229. Mc Kechnie (130) 438.
38 McKechnie (130) 439
39 McKechnie pointed out an Act of the Scottish Parliament (I. 318) containing a trial by peers provision with the addition "But no inferior may be judged by a superior". Ibid., 440.
40 McKechnie (130) 438. Pollock/Maitland (134) I, 153.
41 Plucknett (133) 24. Holdsworth (128) I, 59.
42 Powicke (136), 102
43 Pollock/Maitland (134) I, 139 ff. Black's Law Dictionary, s.v. Domesmen.
44 Maitland (132) 169-170
45 Maitland, Selected Pleas of the Crown, London, Selden, 1888, p. 100/101 nr. 157
46 Plucknett (133) 125
47 Plucknett (133) 130, but compare Ibid., pp. 128-129
48 Brunner, "Schwurgericht", in Holtzendorffs Rechtslexikon, 2nd ed., vol. 2 pp. 559-570, p. 565
49 Ibid., 566
50 Plucknett (133) 132.
51 For early English jurisdictions and communities see Pollock/Maitland (143) I, 527-688
52 Coke, Littleton (1 Inst.) 125
53 4 Anne c. 16 § 6, extended to criminal law by 24 Geo II c. 18. See Blackstone, 3 Commentaries 360.
54 See above, p. 44
55 Philip B. Kurland in Samuel E. Thorne, The Great Charter, New York: 1965 (Four essays on Magna Carta and the history of our liberty), p. 52. Andrews (21) I 457. Mass. Col. Records III, 232
56 Holt (129) 6-7
57 Schwartz (147) 17
58 Dunham in Thorne, op. cit., p. 38
59 2 Institutes 48
60 Ibid., 49
61 Ibid., 28/9
62 But cf. Holt (129) 15
63 Handbook of Anglo-American Legal History, St. Paul, Minn.: West, 1936. Cf. Max Radin, "The Myth of Magna Carta", in 60 Harvard Law Review (1947), 1060-1091.

| | |
|---|---|
| 64 | Handbook &c., loc. cit., p. 286 |
| 65 | Cit in Holdsworth (128), V, 430 |
| 66 | Ibid., 456 |
| 67 | Encyclopedia Britannica (1970), s.v. Coke |
| 68 | Holdsworth (128) V, 472-89 |
| 69 | Chapter 23 |
| 70 | Ibid., 350* |
| 71 | Ibid., 355* |
| 72 | Ibid., 379* |
| 73 | London, Mansell, 1969 |
| 74 | Vol. I, p. iii |
| 75 | Vol. I, p. v |
| 76 | Vernon X. Miller, Dean of the Columbus School of Law, Catholic University of Washington, in Encyclopedia Britannica (1970), s.v. Blackstone. |
| 77 | See Stevens (183) |
| 78 | Miller, loc. cit. |
| 79 | Allan Nevins and Henry Steele Commager, A Short History of the United States, New York: The Modern Library. 1956, p. 12. |
| 80 | From the Petition of Rights (1628), Statutes of the Realm, V, 23, Citing 9 Hen. III, Magna Carta c. 29 |
| 81 | Statutes of the Realm VI, 142 |
| 82 | Schwartz (147) 43 |
| 83 | Charter to Sir Walter Raleigh, Poore (135) 1380. |
| 84 | Thorpe, Federal and State Constitutions, colonial Charters, and other organic laws of the States, House Documents, 59th Congress, 2nd session, vols. 87-91, Washington: GPO 1909, 49-53 |
| 85 | Charter to Sir Walter Raleigh, Poore (135) 1381 |
| 86 | First Charter of Virginia, Ibid., 1891-2 |
| 87 | Second Charter of Virginia, Ibid., 1901 |
| 88 | Henry S. Commager, Documents of American History, New York: Appleton, 1968 (8th ed.), p. 48. |
| 89 | The Charter of New England, Poore (135) 925-6 and ibid.: Grant of New Hampshire (1629) 1272, (1635), 1273-4; Grant of the Province of Maine (1639) 778; Patent for Providence Plantation (1643) 1595; Charter of Connecticut (1662) 255; Charter of Rhode Island and Providence Plantations (1663) 1598; Charter of Carolina (1663) 1384-5; Charter of Carolina (1665) 1392; Grant of the Province of Maine (1674), 786; Commission for New Hampshire (1680) 1276; Charter for the Province of Pennsylvania (1681) 1511. |
| 90 | The Charter of New England (1620), Ibid., 925 |
| 91 | The Charter of Massachusetts Bay (1629) 937, 940, 941, The Charter of Maryland (1632) 813, Grant of the Province of Maine (1639) 778, Charter of Rhode Island and Providence Plantations (1663) 1598, Charter of Carolina (1663) 1385, Grant of the Province of Maine (1664) 785, Grant of the Province of Maine (1674) 787, Charter for the Province of Pennsylvania (1681) 1511, The Charter of Massachusetts Bay (1691) 951, Charter of Georgia (1732) 372-3. |

92   Above, p. 44
93   Schwartz (147) 75-80
94   Poore (135) 1400
95   Ibid., 1404
96   Ibid.
97   Ibid., 1408
98   Schwartz (147) 159
99   A. Leaning and J. Spicer, The Grants, Concessions, and Original Constitutions of the Province of New Jersey, 2nd ed. (1881) pp. 393-398. Schwartz (147) 127-129.
100  Thorpe, op. cit. 3052-63. Schwartz (147) 133
101  Schwartz (147) 141
102  Ibid., 165-6
103  Ibid., 197
104  Ibid., 209
105  Journals of the Continental Congress, 1774-1789, ed. Worthington Chauncey Ford, Washington: GPO, 1904, vol. I, pp. 69, 72.
106  Schwartz (147) 222-3
107  Ibid., 235, 244
108  Journal of the Continental Congress, vol. 22, pp. 281-343. All these documents are cited in Schwartz (147), pp. 276-379
108a Schwartz (147) 438
109  Ibid., 446
110  Pamphlets on the Constitution of the United States, 303-370
111  Schwartz (147) 455
112  Pamphlets on the Constitution of the United States, 181-187
113  The Federalist, ed. Jacob E. Cooke, Middletown, Conn.: Wesleyan UP, 1961, p. 558
114  Ibid., p. 562
115  Ibid.
116  Ibid., p. 574
117  John P. Roche, Courts and Rights: The American Judiciary in Action, New York: Random, 1963, p. 51
118  Louis B. Schwartz and Stephen R. Goldstein, Law Enforcement Handbook for Police, St. Paul, Minn.: West, 1970.
119  Magna Carta, c. 38
120  Schwartz and Goldstein, op. cit., pp. 122-3
121  Ibid., p. 5
122  Schwartz / Goldstein, op. cit., pp. 30/1.
123  Black's Law Dictionary (1970), s.v. complaint and affidavit, pp. 356/7, 912.
124  Schwartz / Goldstein, op. cit., p. 8
125  Ibid., p. 12
126  Ibid., pp. 18, 22
127  Osborn v. Bank of the United States, 9 Wheat (22 US) 738 (1824), 866
128  No case is in all respects identical with a precedent, nor can any act of legislation encompass all aspects of a particular case. The judge's job is to ascribe relevant features to a case and compare it to others with similar

relevant features. That this leaves the judge considerable discretion is apparent but the problem goes much deeper and involves a whole system of legal philosophy. For an introduction to the problems touched on here see The Encyclopedia of Philosophy, ed. Paul Edwards, New York: Macmillan, 1967 vol. 4, pp. 298-302 (s. v. Justice).

129 See below, p. 114
130 People v. Lieber, 357 Ill 423 (1934) 427
131 Jurors Act, § 1
132 Ibid., § 29 = § 4 of Jury Commissioners Act, repealed by L. 1931
133 Ibid., § 30 = § 5 of Jury Commissioners Act, repealed by L. 1931
134 Schwartz/Goldstein (152) 13
135 16 Wall (83 US) 36 (1873) 65
136 With respect to the jurisdiction of the Illinois Supreme Court see Constitutions of 1818 (art. iv, sect. 2), 1848 (art. v, sect. 5) and of 1870 (art. vi, sect. 2)
137 Saint Louis and South Eastern RR Co. v. Wheelis, 72 Ill 538 (1874) 539: "The presumption always being in favor of the court below, the party alleging error must show it by the record, which has not been done in this case".

## CHAPTER III

1 Swift v. Tyson, 16 Pet (41 US) 1 (1842) 18
2 Coughlin v. People, 144 Ill 140 (1893) 170
3 Morris's Lessee v. Vanderen, 1 Dall (1US) 64 (1782) 67
4 See above, p. 58, p. 60 (n. 100).
5 Pawlet v. Clark, 9 Cr (13 US)* 292 (1815)* 333
6 Van Ness v. Pacard, 2 Pet (27 US) 137 (1829) 144
7 Missouri v. Lewis, 101 US 22 (1879) 31
8 Wheaton v. Peters, 8 Pet (33 US) 591 (1834), 658
9 Dartmouth v. Woodward, 4 Wheat (17 US)* 518 (1819)* 581
10 Powell v. Alabama, 287 US 45 (1932) 68
11 Maintained on behalf of the plaintiff in Hurtado v. California, 110 US 516 (1884) 521.
12 Bullock v. Geomble, 45 Ill 218 (1867), 222
13 Harris v. People, 128 Ill 585 (1889), 590. Reference to Criminal Code, Division 13, § 8
14 Coughlin v. People, 144 Ill 140 (1893) 165
15 Morris's Lessee v. Vanderen, 1 Dall (1 US) 64 (1782) 67
16 Doe v. Winn, 5 Pet (30 US)* 233 (1831)* 241. 3 Edw. VI, ch. 4, and 13, Elisab. I, ch. 6
17 Respublica v. Mesca, 1 Dall (1 US) 73 (1783)
18 Ibid., 75
19 The whole argumentation reminds one somewhat of the reasoning in England before the general introduction of counsels for defense. Apparently it was argued that defendant could demand no lawyer because this would imply that the judges are not able to arrive at an unbiased judgment themselves. Similarly, a defendant in a trial for high treason could not adduce witnesses for defense because the opposing party was technically the king and nobody could be expected to take the witness stand against the king. See John P. Roche, Courts and Rights: The American Judiciary in Action, New York: Random, 1963, pp. 49-54
20 Blackstone, 4 Comm. 353. Cited as repeated by Justice Story in Lewis v. United States, 146 US 370 (1892) 376.
21 Scott v. Sanford, 60 US 393 (1857) 411
22 Bank of Columbia v. Okely, 4 Wheat (17 US)* 235 (1819)* 244
23 Scott v. Sanford, loc. cit., 407/8
24 See Miller (179) 157n. Books on the case by Vincent C. Hopkins (1951), Stanley I. Kutler (1967) and Charles Warren (1922, vol. 2, pp. 279-319)
25 Hurtado v. California, 110 US 516 (1884) 539/40
26 Historical scholarship was in those days of course less advanced than it is today. But some tools of serious research would have been at the disposition of the learned judges. On the state of history as a discipline at that time see Arthur Marwick, The Nature of History, London: Macmillan, 1970, ch. 2: "The development of Historical Studies to the End of the Nineteenth Century", especially section 4, pp. 43-50: "Anglo-Saxon Attitudes".

27  Cathcart v. Robinson, 5 Pet (30 US)* 264 (1831)* 280
28  Hurtado v. California, 110 US 516 (1884) 543
29  Robert E. Spiller, Literary History of the United States, New York: Macmillan, 1949, pp. 1278-9
30  Parsons v. Bedford, 3 Pet (28 US) 433 (1830) 446
31  Ex parte Milligan, 71 US 2 (1866) 118-121
32  Snyder v. Massachusetts, 291 US 97 (1934) 105
33  Capital Traction Co. v. Hof, 174 US 1 (1899) 13f. Patton v. United States, 281 US 276 (1930), 288. In a five-to-four decision rendered in spring, 1972, the Supreme Court decided that only verdicts leading to death sentences have to be unanimous. At the time of this writing this decision was not yet available to me and could therefore not be considered for this dissertation.
34  Smith v. Texas, 311 US 128 (1940) 130
35  Glasser v. United States, 315 US 60 (1942) 85/6
36  Thiel v. Southern Pacific Co., 328 US 217 (1946) 220
37  People v. Vitale, 364 Ill 589 (1936) 592. Cit. in People v. Drymalsky, 22 Ill 2nd 347 (1961).
38  Hunt v. Rosenbaum Grain Co. 355 Ill. 504 (1934) 511
39  Bullock v. Geomble, 45 Ill. 218 (1867) 222
40  George v. People, 167 Ill 447 (1897) 457
41  Sinopoli v. Chicago RR Co., 316 Ill 609 (1925) 619
42  Constitution of 1870, art. 2, section 5.
43  People v. Kelly, 347 Ill 221 (1932) 227/8
44  Art. 3, section 2
45  7th Amendment
46  Downes v. Bidwell, 182 US 244 (1901), one of the "Insular Cases".
47  Ibid., 282/3, 287
48  Hawaii v. Mankichi, 190 US 197 (1903) 218
49  Ibid., 225/6
50  Palko v. Connecticut, 302 US 319 (1937) 325
51  Ward v. Farwell, 97 Ill 593 (1881)
52  Flaherty v. McCormick, 113 Ill 538 (1885) 544
53  Bank of Columbia v. Okely, 4 Wheat (17 US)* 235 (1819)* 244
54  Schick v. United States, 195 US 65 (1904) 72
55  Patton v. United States, 281 US 276 (1930) 312
56  People v. Scates, 3 Scam* 351 (1842)
57  People v. Fisher, 340 Ill 250 (1930) 258, 261/2, 265
58  Capital Traction Co. v. Hof, 174 US 1 (1899) 13
59  United States v. Perez, 9 Wheat (22 US) 579 (1824) 580
60  Etting v. Bank of the United States, 11 Wheat (24 US) 59 (1826) 75
61  Scott v. Sanford, 60 US 393 (1857) 405, 426. "This unfortunate race" is the black people.
62  Cahill's Statutes 1923, chapter 78, § 1.
63  People v. Barnett, 319 Ill 403 (1926) 410
64  Ibid., 408, referring to Calkins v. Calkins, 216 Ill 458 (1905)
65  Spies v. People, 122 Ill 1 (1887) 266/7
66  People v. Izzo, 14 Ill 2nd 203 (1958)

67  Ibid., 207
68  Myrdal (15) 524
69  Neal v. Delaware, 103 US 370 (1881)
70  Virginia v. Rives, 100 US 313 (1880)
71  Reported in Neal v. Delaware, loc. cit., 393/394
72  Ibid., 397
73  People v. Cohen, 268 Ill 416 (1915) 417
74  Coke, Littleton (1 Inst.) 155 d (1628)
75  Chapter 78 of the Revised Statutes of Illinois, § 2 (Fourth)
76  Ibid., § 14
77  Etting v. Bank of the United States, 11 Wheat (24 US) 59 (1826) 62-65
78  United States v. Quincy, 6 Pet (31 US) 445 (1832) 466
79  The phenomena must be distinct because the judge and the jury do not determine facts and the law together. The judge instructs the jury as to the law, but the jury then arrives at the facts in closed session and has the right to disregard the instructions of the judge.
80  See Harker (143)
81  Where Do We Go From Here?: Chaos or Community, New York: Harper & Row, 1967, p. 158
82  King, above, and justice Henry Billings Brown, below.
83  Plessy v. Ferguson, 163 US 537 (1896) 551
83a Ibid., 561
84  Powell v. Alabama, 287 US 45 (1932) 52
85  Norris v. Alabama, 294 US 587 (1935) 593
86  Cit. in Brownfield v. South Carolina, 189 US 426 (1903) 428
87  Queen v. Hepburn 7 Cr (11 US)* 290 (1813)* 297
88  Ibid., * 297/8
89  Chicago and Western Indiana RR Co. v. Bingenheimer, 116 Ill 226 (1886)
90  Ibid., 232
91  Coughlin v. People, 144 Ill 140 (1893) 171
92  Gates v. People, 14 Ill* 433 (1853)* 435
93  35 Ill 2nd 263 (1966) 272
94  Reviewing Witherspoon v. Illinois, 391 US 510 (1968) 514, People v. Witherspoon 36 Ill 2nd 471 (1967).
95  See quote 134 on page 72, above.
96  United States v. Burr, Fed. Cas. 14692g, 14693 (1807). Circuit Court for the District of Virginia.
97  Joseph P. Brady, The Trial of Aaron Burr, New York: Neale, 1913, pp. 21-4
98  Winnesheik Insurance Co. v. Schueller, 60 Ill 465 (1871)
99  Ibid., 472
100 Borrelli v. People, 164 Ill 549 (1897) 558-9
101 People v. Ortiz, 320 Ill 205 (1926) 209
102 Gray v. People, 26 Ill 344 (1861) 346-7
103 Above, p. 70
104 People v. Berman, 316 Ill. 547 (1925) 549
105 Van Blaricum v. People, 16 Ill* 364 (1855)

| | |
|---|---|
| 106 | Baxter v. People, 3 Gilm* 368 (1846)* 368n. Lycoming Fire Insurance Co. v. Ward, 90 Ill 545 (1878) 547. |
| 107 | Reynolds v. United States, 98 US 145 (1878) 147 |
| 108 | Ibid., 157 |
| 109 | 299 US 123 (1936) 133 |
| 110 | Ibid., 143 |
| 111 | Ibid., 145 |
| 112 | Davison v. People, 90 Ill 221 (1878) 227 |
| 113 | Ibid., 235. Dissent! |
| 114 | Baxter v. People, 3 Gilm* 368 (1846)* 377 |
| 115 | Coughlin v. People, 144 Ill 140 (1893) 181, 184 |
| 116 | Aldridge v. United States, 283 US 308 (1931), 310 |
| 117 | Ibid., 314 |
| 118 | Hayes v. Missouri, 120 US 68 (1887) 71 |
| 119 | Glasser v. United States, 315 US 60 (1942) |
| 120 | Fay v. New York, 332 US 261 (1947) 299/300 |
| 121 | Brown v. Allen, 344 US 443 (1953) 473/4 |
| 122 | Mangum (159) 308 |
| 123 | 43rd Congress, 2nd Session, ch. 114. 18.2 Stat. L. 335 |
| 124 | § 4 |
| 125 | Strauder v. West Virginia, 100 US 303 (1880) reviewing 11 W. Va. 745 (1877) |
| 126 | Guinn v. US 238 US 347 (1915) 357/8 |
| 127 | Ibid., 364 |
| 128 | Ex parte West Virginia, 100 US 339 (1880) 340, 348 |
| 129 | Ibid., 368-370 |
| 130 | Smith v. Texas, 311 US 128 (1940) |
| 131 | Ibid., 130-2 |
| 132 | Whitus v. Georgia, 385 US 545 (1967) 552 |
| 133 | Eubanks v. Louisiana, 356 US 584 (1958) 586 |
| 134 | Norris v. Alabama, 294 US 587 (1935) 598-9 |
| 135 | Hill v. Texas, 316 US 400 (1942) 402 |
| 136 | 69 Ill 523 (1873) 526 |
| 137 | 72 Ill 468 (1874) 472 |
| 138 | People v. Madison County, 125 Ill 334 (1888) 340 |
| 139 | Siebert v. People, 143 Ill 571 (1892) 578 |
| 140 | 5 Ill Law Rev. (Dec., 1910) 283-299 |
| 141 | See above, p. 68 |
| 142 | 357 Ill 423 (1934) 425/6 |
| 143 | People v. Gierens, 400 Ill 347 (1948) 350 |
| 144 | Source: 5 Ill Law Review, pp. 291-2 |
| 145 | Ibid., 295 |
| 146 | Ibid., 299 |
| 147 | People v. Mankus, 292 Ill 435 (1920) 440. Cf. People v. Cochran, 313 Ill 508 (1924) and People v. Fudge, 342 Ill 574 (1931) 582 |
| 148 | People v. Lembke, 320 Ill 553 (1926) 556-7 |
| 149 | People v. Coffman, 338 Ill 367 (1930) 369, 371. Cf. People v. Corder, |

306 Ill 264 (1923) 273-4. People v. Walsh, 322 Ill 195 (1926) 200. People v. Colegrove, 342 Ill. 430 (1931) 436. People v. Schraeberg, 347 Ill 392 (1932).
150  People v. Johnson, 2 Ill 2nd 165 (1954) 168
151  People v. Ford, 19 Ill 2nd 466 (1960)
152  Akins v. Texas, 325 US 398 (1945) 406
153  Ibid., 407
154  Ibid., 410
155  Cassell v. Texas, 339 US 282 (1950) 288n.
156  Lewis v. United States, 146 US 370 (1892) 376
157  1 Inst. 156
158  People v. Stevens, 335 Ill 415 (1929), 422
159  People v. Hotchkiss, 347 Ill 217 (1932) 218/9
160  People v. Stevens, loc. cit.
161  People v. Clampitt, 362 Ill 534 (1936) 537
162  4 Comm. 353. Cited, for example, in Lewis v. United States, loc. cit.
163  United States v. Marchant & Colson, 12 Wheat (25 US) 480 (1827) 481. But compare Stilson v. United States, 250 US 583 (1919).
164  Stilson v. United States, loc. cit. 586. Cf. Swain v. Alabama, 380 US 202 (1965) 242-3 (dissent by Justice Goldberg).
165  Donovan v. People, 139 Ill 412 (1891) 415
166  People v. Harris, 17 Ill 2nd 446 (1959) 450-1
167  Swain v. Alabama, loc. cit., 212, 219, 220, 223
168  Ibid., 224
169  Coke, 1 Inst. 155, 156 b. Coughlin v. People, 144 Ill 140 (1893) 164
170  Above, p. 70
171  Chase v. People, 40 Ill 352 (1866) 358
172  Robinson v. Randall, 82 Ill 521 (1876) 522
173  Hayes v. Missouri, 120 US 68 (1887) 71
174  By 24 Geo II c. 18 the jury became de *corpore comitatus* and not simply *de vicineto*. See above, pp. 46-51
175  7 Cr (11 US)* 290 (1813)
176  Ibid.,* 297
177  Bell v. People, 1 Scam* 397 (1839) 398. It is section 72.
178  People v. Meech, 101 Ill 200 (1882), 205-6. Reference to "An act to amend certain sections of an act to provide for the election and qualifications of justices of the peace, etc". (Laws 1881, p. 103)
179  Maryland v. The Baltimore and Ohio RR Co., 3 How (44 US) 534 (1845) 550
180  Harris v. Board, 105 Ill 445 (1883) 451
181  Buckrice v. People, 110 Ill 29 (1884)
182  183 Ill 423
183  232 Ill 112 (1908) 114
184  People v. Rodenberg, 254 Ill 386 (1912) 393/4
185  People v. Green, 329 Ill 576 (1928)* 579
186  Thomas v. Texas, 212 US 278 (1909) 282/3
187  Price v. People, 131 Ill 223 (1890) 228/9
188  Jamison v. People, 145 Ill 357 (1893) 366-368

| | |
|---|---|
| 189 | Ibid., 369, 374 |
| 190 | People v. Pfanschmidt, 262 Ill 411 (1914), 441 |
| 191 | Above, p. 95. People v. Cohen, 268 Ill 416 (1915) |
| 192 | 314 Ill 296 (1924) 311 |
| 193 | 413 Ill 69 (1952) 74-75 |
| 194 | Ibid., 75 |
| 195 | Hirabayashi v. United States, 320 US 81 (1943) 100 |
| 196 | 332 US 261 (1947) 287 |
| 197 | 347 US 475 (1954), 479/80 |
| 198 | Jamison v. People, 145 Ill. 357 (1893) 374 |
| 199 | Above, p. 108, n. 125 |
| 200 | Neal v. Delaware, 103 US 370 (1881), 407 |
| 201 | Fay v. New York, 332 US 261 (1947) 288/9 |
| 202 | The Federalist, ed. Jacob E. Cooke, Middletown, Conn.: Wesleyan UP, 1961, p. 564. |

## CONCLUSION

| | |
|---|---|
| 1 | Nr. 179 |
| 2 | Ibid., p. 148 |
| 3 | Ibid., p. 162 |
| 4 | Ibid., p. 160 |
| 5 | See Stevens (183) |
| 6 | 110 US 516 (1884) and 339 US 282 (1950) |
| 7 | 339 US 282 (1950) 285 |
| 8 | On statistical proofs in jury discrimination cases see Finkelstein (141) |
| 9 | Above, p. 117, n. 155 |
| 10 | 339 US 282 (1950) 292 |
| 11 | Ibid., 293 |
| 12 | Ibid., 297 |
| 13 | Ibid. |
| 14 | Ibid., 299 |
| 15 | Ibid., 304/5 |